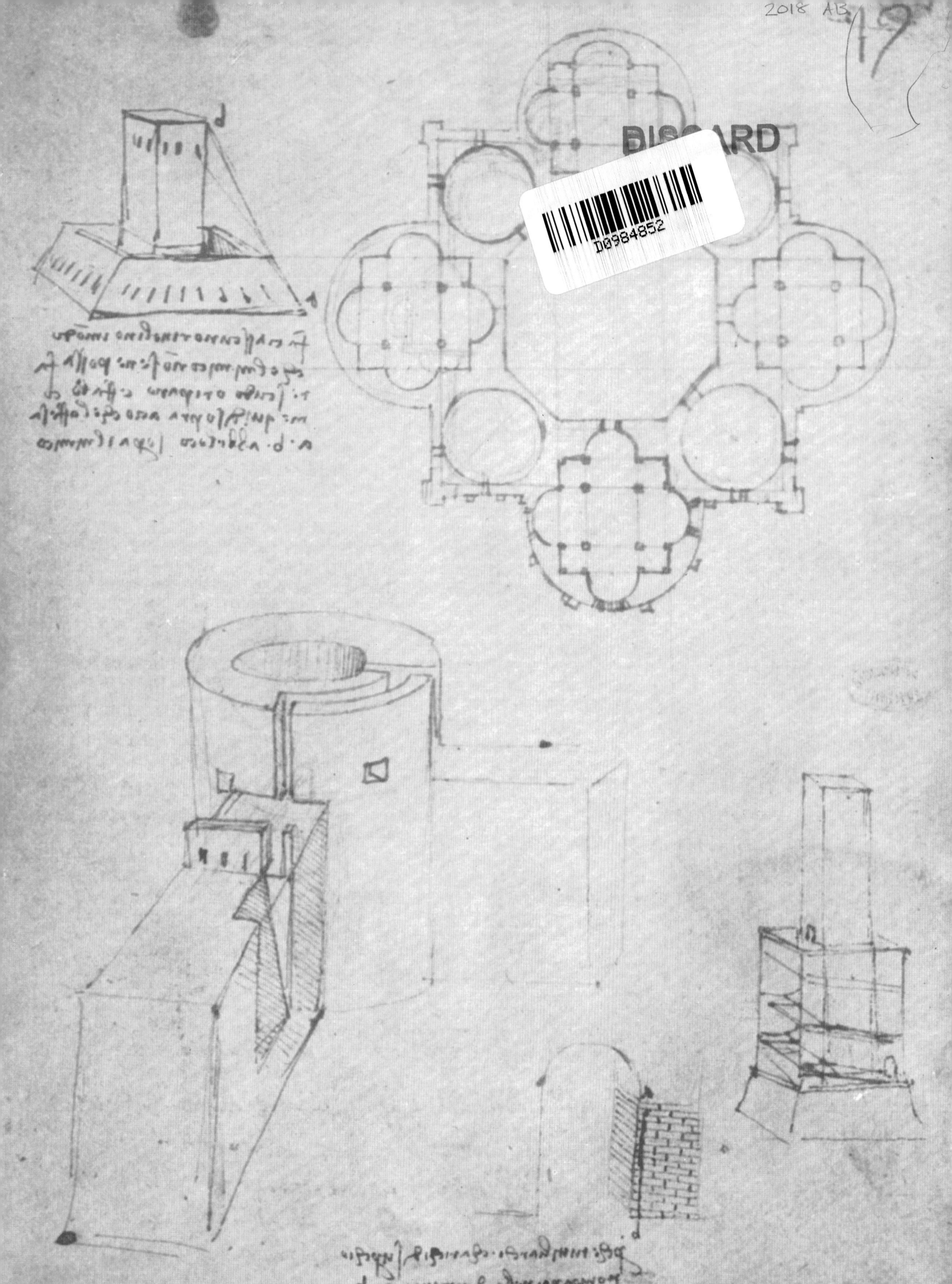

THE SECRET LANGUAGE OF
SACRED SPACES

Decoding Churches, Temples, Mosques and Other Places of Worship Around the World

Jon Cannon

DUNCAN BAIRD PUBLISHERS

LONDON

⬣ FOUNDING FATHERS

*c.*1205–1210, NORTH PORTAL, CHARTRES CATHEDRAL, FRANCE

At the last moment, Abraham was prevented by God from sacrificing his son Isaac, as sculpted on the central portal of the north transept of this great Gothic cathedral. Abraham is viewed as a founding figure by Jews, Christians and Muslims; next to him is Melchizedek (left, wearing a hat), the first priest mentioned in the Hebrew Bible, and for Christians a prefiguration of Jesus Christ.

◀ SHRINES IN A SACRED LANDSCAPE

2004–2007, DRUK WANGYEL *CHORTENS*, DOCHULA PASS, BHUTAN

The *chorten* or *stupa* is the defining architectural form of Buddhism. This cluster of Bhutanese-style wood-and-stone *chorten*s, numbering a highly auspicious 108 in total, have been erected by Queen Ashi Dorji Wangmo Wangchuck at the top of the Dochula Pass in honour of the king. The spot offers a panoramic view of the sacred Himalaya mountains.

OTHER PICTURE CREDITS

TITLE PAGE Infinite and eternal, the geometric patterning of this fritware tile, which once decorated an Islamic *madrasa*, evokes the infinite perfection and complexity of God. *c.*1444, Ghiyathiyya *madrasa*, Khargird, Iran.

PART OPENERS (Pages 12–13) Buddhist prayer flags in Tibet. (Pages 62–63) Santa Maria del Fiore (Florence cathedral), Florence, Italy.

ENDPAPERS (DOUBLE-PAGE) Design for a centralized church building, *c.*1492 (Ms.B f.18v/19r), by Leonardo da Vinci (1452–1519); (SINGLE-PAGE) Japanese landscape with pagoda, ink on silk, by Sobun Morikawa (1847–1902).

The Secret Language of Sacred Spaces
Jon Cannon

First published in the UK and USA in 2013 by
Duncan Baird Publishers, an imprint of
Watkins Publishing Limited
Sixth Floor, 75 Wells Street
London, W1T 3QH

A member of Osprey Group

Osprey Publishing Inc., 43-01 21st Street,
Suite 220B, Long Island City, NY 11101

Managing Editor: Christopher Westhorp
Managing Designer: Allan Sommerville at Blok Graphic
Picture Research: Susannah Stone, Julia Brown and
  Emma Copestake
Production: Uzma Taj
Commissioned artwork: Allan Sommerville

A CIP record for this book is available from the British Library

ISBN: 978-1-84899-111-8

10 9 8 7 6 5 4 3 2 1

Typeset in Adobe Garamond
Colour reproduction by PDQ, UK
Printed in China

Abbreviations used throughout this book:
CE Common Era (the equivalent of AD)
BCE Before the Common Era (the equivalent of BC)

A note about dates:
The dating of ancient buildings can be a complex issue. Records may not exist, or their meaning may be equivocal. Many buildings have been dated using archaeological, stylistic or contextual criteria alone. Scholars may themselves disagree. In this book, every effort has been made to fix each building in time as accurately as possible; the year (or the earliest likely date) at which construction began is given wherever feasible.

CONTENTS

INTRODUCTION

The Taj Mahal, Chartres cathedral, Angkor Wat – such buildings would be close to the top of any list of the greatest in the world. Yet, apart from the burial of the dead, none has a practical, worldly function in the same way that a railway station, an office block or a home does. The colossal effort and expense involved in creating each one were directed entirely at the requirements not of the mundane but of the spiritual. These are sacred places – structures erected for the faithful – and this book is their story.

Most societies since the dawn of humanity have put enormous effort and resources into building such edifices. The aim was a profound one: their creators believed that these places helped to further a relationship between man and the divine, upon which existence itself depended.

The buildings that resulted vary enormously in scale. A small wayside shrine can be considered a religious structure. At the other extreme, the ancient Egyptian temple of Amun-Re at Karnak, Angkor Wat in Cambodia, Hindu temple-cities such as Srirangam in India and Seville cathedral in Spain, although all very different, were until recent times among the largest buildings in the world. Furthermore, with their abundance of sculpture, painting and liturgy, these were also the venues for the richest cultural experience in most people's lives. Religion, for those who live with faith, can extend far beyond the gates of a place of worship: it suffuses life, embracing every aspect of daily existence. Sacredness can be anywhere and everywhere. This means that the scope of this subject is almost infinite. Therefore, the overriding focus of this book is on religious buildings that still stand, are built of permanent materials and are of unusual ambition or are especially significant or influential (and usually at least several centuries old). Covered more briefly are works of sculpture of an architectural scale, and ways in which landscapes as a whole have been sacralized, especially if that has had important architectural implications. Places of burial are included, again only if their scale is exceptional and their function emphatically includes provision for worship. The book does not cover structures that are small-scale or temporary, nor places of worship that have not been designed

as such, unless they are exceptionally significant; converted private houses, holy wells, wayside shrines, and so on, are thus usually excluded. Buildings that have disappeared, or whose religious function is unclear, are covered only if their influence has been remarkable.

These principles have guided the sometimes difficult decisions that have been made about how many pages to give to the buildings of a particular faith. In spite of these restrictions, the book includes many of the greatest works of architectural art to survive from ancient times, and it shows how the form of these buildings reflected the beliefs of those who created them. The result is neither a history of religion nor a history of architecture, although it contains elements of both. It is a history of the places of worship of each faith, emphasizing what they reveal about the belief system itself.

There have been surprisingly few previous attempts to do this, and, given the enormous geographical and historical scope of what will follow, it is worth giving a few words of orientation to provide a framework into which to fit the many extraordinary monuments to come.

A global picture

Geographically, India and the Middle East are the two great fountainheads of religious ideas and religious architecture. The story of the Middle East is one of extraordinary achievement and dramatic disjuncture: this is where the first cut-stone temples were created, but also where the great monotheisms of Judaism, Islam and Christianity rejected the religions of the past, reinventing the architectural traditions they had inherited, while accepting an infusion of architectural ideas from ancient Rome. These younger faiths were

◗ VISIONS OF HEAVEN

1603–1619, SHAIKH LUTFALLAH MOSQUE, ISFAHAN, IRAN

A long, low gloomy passageway leads the devoted, their anticipation heightened, into this glazed and glittering, soaringly high-domed chamber, its tiled surfaces sparkling in the steady sunlight that pours in through the sixteen windows. The experience is a glimpse of heaven, enclosing and uplifting those gathered in prayer beneath.

congregational, and their architecture was designed to host regular gatherings of ordinary people, resulting in buildings whose interior spaces were of particular importance.

In India, the continuities with the past are more marked. Many ideas of truly ancient origin remain alive in Hinduism, Buddhism and the other Indian faiths, helping to shape their art and architecture. Beliefs about the significance of symbolic geometry in religious buildings, ideas that are more hazily glimpsed in the architecture of the monotheistic traditions, are made explicit in this tradition. These include a conviction that the very shape of a building (or a work of art) can enhance the efficacy of the rituals for which it is the venue. As a result, the form of these buildings can be charged with meaning, and they can seem more like great open-air sculptures than vast, roofed environments.

Such ideas were transformed in their encounter with a third area in which major faiths originated: East Asia. There, uniquely among major world cultures, the indigenous traditions of China, Japan and Korea largely resisted the creation of a permanent and distinctive architecture of faith; yet the architecture of these societies strongly reflects shared spiritual assumptions. Regions such as Central and Southeast Asia provide a "clearing house" of ideas from many traditions, resulting in syncretic religious buildings of great originality and importance.

Ancient America developed in relative isolation, providing a fascinating comparison for what we see elsewhere, and also reminding us of the historical uncertainties surrounding a project such as this. Our knowledge of the beliefs of the peoples of the Americas depends greatly on accounts made by potentially biased or partial observers, aided by evidence from archaeology and information left by those cultures that developed a form of writing.

◗ **MEDIEVAL DISPLAY**

967/968, BANTEAY SREI, NEAR ANGKOR, CAMBODIA

The Hindu and Buddhist buildings of the medieval Kham empire are among the most elaborate and exquisitely sculpted in the world. These female divinities (*devas*) and guardian spirits protect the 10m-high (33ft) innermost sanctuary of a small Hindu temple complex dedicated to Shiva and built in distinctive red sandstone by the Brahmin Yajnavaraha, a royal counsellor, and his brother.

Throughout the world, the paucity of records leaves much unknown, of course, including the names of most of the artists and craftsmen who designed and built these structures. Many such creative minds were geniuses, and working for them were untold hordes of labourers: although barely mentioned, they are the true heroes of this book.

The ages of sacred space

Religious art is as old as humankind. The earliest sacred places were often natural features with an architectonic quality, such as caves and mountains. The first sacred buildings emerged as early as 9000BCE. But it was from the late fifth to the late third millennium BCE that the first major monuments in Mesopotamia and the Americas appeared, and in Egypt an audacious leap took place into a true architecture of cut stone. This was a remarkable step, and difficult to achieve technically, but it resulted in buildings of extraordinary permanency. Almost every major culture would develop the ability to do this, but in many places only religious buildings were constructed of such materials.

In terms of religious practice, the next few millennia were dominated by polytheistic faiths, whose deities demanded acts of sacrifice, usually in the form of the killing of an animal, the body of which was offered on an altar to be burned. This was the golden age of the manmade mountain, as witnessed by the pyramids produced by several early cultures worldwide. This period can seem distant and strange, but it lasted until as late as the sixteenth century in the Americas. Today's two most widespread faiths, Christianity and Islam, are young by comparison, and all the most basic elements of religious architecture emerged for the first time during this long "era of origin".

Into this world, in or around the period 800–200BCE, materialized the teachings of the Buddha, Laozi and Confucius (and others, whose roles in the architectural story are comparatively insignificant), characterizing an era of revolutionary change in thinking known as the Axial Age. As far as architectural history is concerned, the most important thing came next: a "millennium of development", from *c.*500–*c.*300BCE to *c.*500–*c.*700CE, in which the architecture of all the surviving great religions was defined.

In the Middle East, the invention of the synagogue (by *c.*200BCE) and the destruction of the Temple of Jerusalem (70CE) created important precedents for churches (from *c.*300CE) and mosques (by 632CE) alike. Christ and Muhammad themselves taught during this era; political leaders, such as the Roman emperor Constantine (reigned 306–337) and the Umayyad caliph al-Malik (reigned 685–705), turned simple templates for the church and the mosque into influential buildings of enormous ambition as part of their efforts to build imperial states defined by monotheistic faiths.

Meanwhile, in the East, the teachings of the new thinkers and the caste-restricted practices of the Brahmins underwent radical change, during which religion in general gradually became more theistic in nature. The Buddhist monastery (*c.*300BCE) and the Hindu temple (*c.*500CE) were invented, and rulers such as Ashoka (reigned 274–236BCE) used architecture to spread Buddhism in the service of forging a state. In China, temples became separate buildings from palaces, and they began to appear in vast numbers. Elsewhere in East Asia, Korea and Japan adopted many aspects of Chinese architecture and religion.

Fundamental questions remain unanswered about this crucial and fascinating time. Perhaps the most important of these relate to the precise way in which synagogues, churches and mosques attained their final appearance, and the nature of the religious buildings that existed in the Indian subcontinent prior to the appearance of permanent stone Buddhist and, later, Hindu temples.

The next phase is over a millennium long, from around the fifth century to around the seventeenth century CE. This period, which can be thought of as the "great age of faith", is when most of the truly astonishing religious buildings of the world were created. Intriguingly, these came in waves: for example, in the fifth to eighth centuries were built the church of Hagia Sophia in Constantinople (Istanbul), the Dome of the Rock in Jerusalem, the great Mayan temples in Mexico, Borobudur in Java, the Kailasa at Ellora in India, and the Todaiji temple in Nara, Japan. Then, in the eleventh to twelfth centuries, the Romanesque and Gothic styles between them created the great cathedrals of Europe; influential new

forms, *madrasa*s and *iwan*-mosques, appeared in Islam; and an extraordinary series of temples were built in Southeast Asia, from Hindu Angkor to Buddhist Pagan. These achievements seem to have been most intense on the fringes, rather than in the ancestral heartlands, of their respective traditions: Iran, western Europe and Southeast Asia.

There was a final peak to this "great age of faith" that occurred between the fifteenth and the seventeenth centuries. In this 200-year period were built a series of great domes, each in different ways outdoing the Roman and Byzantine achievements which had lain fallow for a millennium or more: from west to east, St. Paul's cathedral in London, Santa Maria del Fiore in Florence, St. Peter's in Rome, the Suleymaniye in Istanbul, the Imam and Shaikh Lutfallah mosques in Isfahan, and the Moghul mosques and mausoleums in India, which culminated in the Taj Mahal. Comparable episodes of architectural gigantism occurred in Hinduism (for example, Dravidian temple-cities such as Srirangam). In Tibet and Iran, the ascendancy of new kinds of theocracies had enormous architectural and artistic, not to mention political, consequences. Elsewhere, reactions against over-elaborate religious practices led to the creation (or the bringing to perfection) of the Christian Nonconformist chapel, the Sikh *gurdwara* and the Japanese Zen monastery, each in its distinctive style among the world's more quietly numinous and reflective religious spaces.

The secular challenge

Until this point, in most times and places (ancient Rome and classical China are the most obvious exceptions), religious buildings had dominated the story of architecture itself. But from the eighteenth century this relationship began to change. Europeans began to colonize much of the globe, taking Christian architecture with them – even as humanistic doubt about religion began to emerge and spread. Today, even in major centres of faith, airports, hotels and public buildings are at least as ambitious architecturally as any places of worship.

In the Western world, and in those countries where communism resulted in an official atheism, art galleries, museums and commemorative monuments have taken on many of the functions that were once the preserve of places of worship. The architecture of faith, with notable exceptions, has tended to become rather conservative; traditional skills that might otherwise have disappeared have been preserved, but uninspired or backward-looking architecture has all too often been the result.

Of course, new faiths have arisen too, and among the most architecturally interesting are Baha'i, originating in Iran (but based in Israel); Mormonism, in the United States of America; Caodaism, in Vietnam; and the New Religions (*shinshukyo*) in Japan: none is included here because their role in the grand narrative is not yet clear.

In summary, the great creative achievement of the Middle Eastern tradition has been to create extraordinary interior, or enclosed, spaces in which large groups of people can congregate. This is, ultimately, a result of the disjunctures brought by monotheism and the creativity that accompanied its success. The principal achievement of the Indian tradition has been to preserve an ancient idea that the form of a structure can itself be spiritually efficacious, and that major religious structures need not have interiors. If by "great" one means the transformation of a profound spiritual idea into daring and aesthetically convincing architecture, the Gothic cathedrals are arguably the crowning glory of the first tradition, and the Southeast Asian *mandala*-like temples are the greatest achievement of the second. Meanwhile, the Americas (until the 1520s–1560s) and China (until 1912) both preserved monumental traditions of exceptional antiquity, relating to pyramids and open-air altars, until relatively recent times.

Today, throughout the world, people expect ambitious, impressive buildings of all kinds to display constantly evolving styles, innovative structural engineering, and striking and well-illuminated interiors. Fascinatingly, prior to the modern age these became lasting characteristics of architecture only in one type of building: the churches of Western Christendom, where such ideas defined development continuously from the eleventh century onwards. This innovation is in turn deeply rooted in spiritual ideas about light, and in recurrent and profound themes in Christian spirituality. The modern world owes much more than it realizes to the ancient architecture of faith.

○ VISION OF HEAVEN

*c.*1200–*c.*1300, SÉES CATHEDRAL, NORMANDY, FRANCE

Europe's cathedrals are characterized by their ceaseless spirit of stylistic invention. Gothic architects used flying buttresses and pointed arches to create skeletal structures with vast windows. Such luminous interiors, filled with stained glass (well preserved at Sées in the chapel of St. Latuin), are vivid evocations of the "Heavenly Jerusalem" of Christian thought.

PART ONE

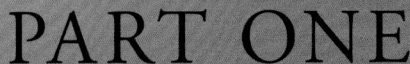

THE THEMES OF THE SACRED

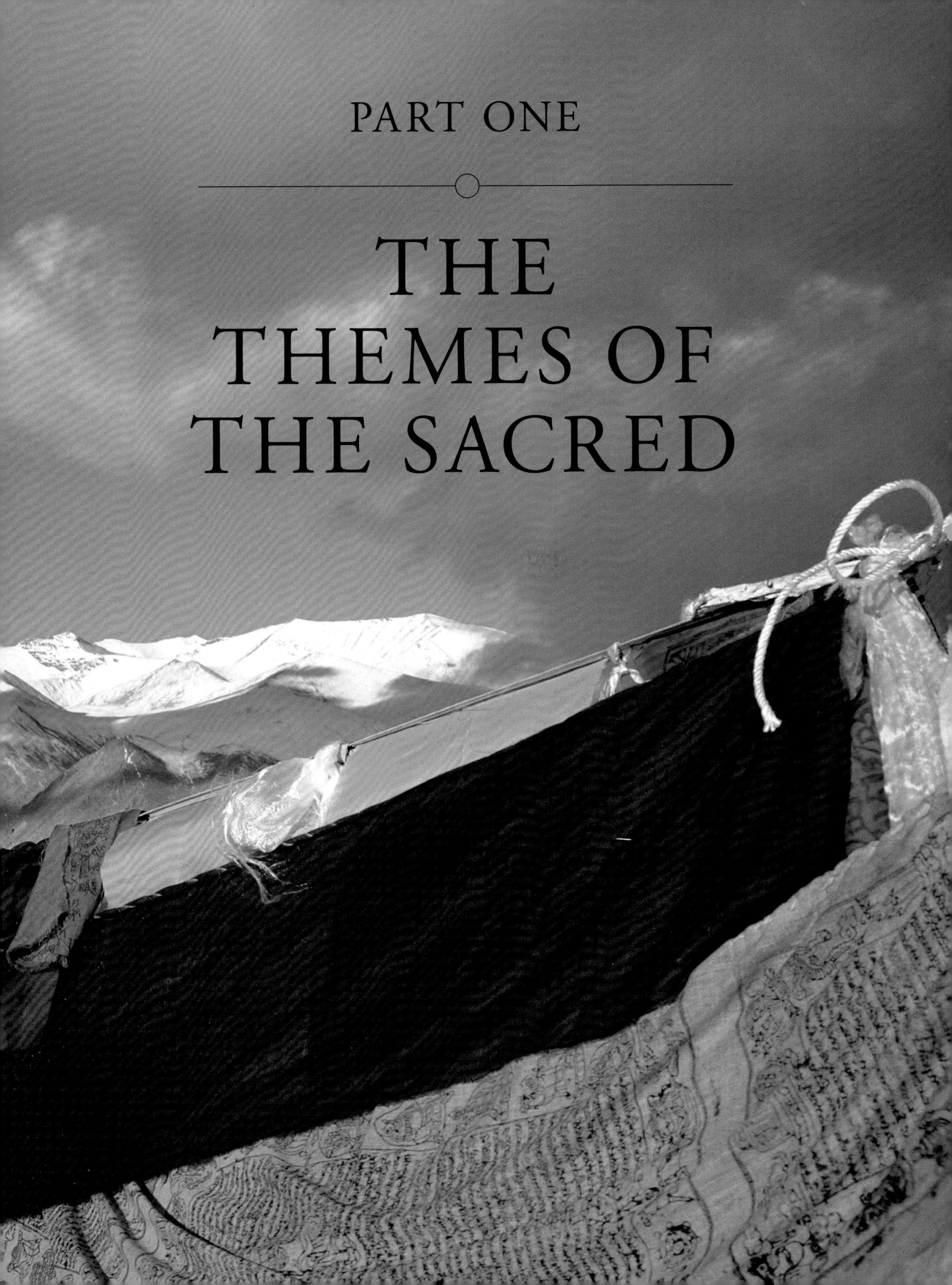

AN ARCHITECTURE OF SACREDNESS

TURNING BELIEFS INTO BUILDINGS

———————————○———————————

For most people throughout history, it was a fact beyond questioning that divine forces of infinite power existed. Religious rituals were of fundamental importance, affecting every aspect of life. These acts could take place in a wide variety of settings, but the creation of special venues for them – places of worship – was an early development in many cultures.

The resulting buildings are, by their very nature, not like others. Their aim is a most profound and challenging one: to create an architecture in which there can be human contact with the divine. Fittingly, the structures for such an awesome and profoundly mysterious experience have often been aesthetically overwhelming.

In attempting to analyze places of worship, two aspects stand out in particular. The first is their form, which means the overall shape of a building. The second is their style: the way in which the form is articulated – from the profile of the roof to the shape of the windows – in order to achieve a certain effect. The result will often embody fundamental aspects of the faith for which the building was created.

◖ **ENCOUNTERING THE SACRED**

*c.*1610, AMER, RAJASTHAN, INDIA

One woman chants and plays music while another makes offerings to Shiva at a *linga* altar in a small Hindu shrine set in the middle of a lake. Religious architecture brings together place, architecture and ritual, providing an appropriate setting for humankind's encounters with the divine.

KEY ELEMENTS OF RELIGIOUS BUILDINGS

On auspicious occasions such as New Year, the people of Tibet take strings of brightly coloured fabrics and wrap them around special places, such as hilltops or groves of trees. These "prayer flags" have a dramatic effect upon the landscape in which they are set. They mark areas out, identifying them as separate. Such sites can elicit powerful emotions, from profound contemplation to awestruck fear.

Although prayer flags are relatively fragile and temporary, the act of enclosure, of setting aside, that they represent lies at the root of sacred architecture. Manipulating the environment in this way imparts a special status to a place.

Architecture is unique among the arts in that it is about the design of things we inhabit and move around in. The environments that architecture creates may be purely functional: a house does not need to be beautiful to fulfil its purpose of providing shelter; it merely needs walls, windows, doors and a roof. Religious buildings are different. Their primary aim belongs, by definition, to the realms of the spiritual and of the cultural, rather than of the practical and the mundane, and they reflect a given civilization's world view and sense of aesthetics. Historically, places of worship have been where architecture's true potential was first explored fully. The first buildings of cut stone were religious, and the demands of faith drove most of architecture's great achievements thereafter.

While sacred structures around the world can seem bewildering in their variety, they share many forms in common: basic elements which have been returned to again and again, providing us with the essential underpinning through which we can understand religious buildings, even when they overlap with and cross-fertilize each other. These forms are specific ways of shaping sacred structures and they are created using a panoply of features, such as windows and walls, which are common to buildings of all kinds.

The enclosure

The open-air enclosure is the simplest of these forms and it is also the most varied. Such enclosures are likely to have been among the earliest of religious monuments, but as these were largely of an impermanent nature (groves and shrines wrapped in prayer flags, for example), few have survived. Those that do, such as the great earthworks surrounding the stone circles at Avebury (*c.*2500BCE; see pages 68–69) in England, still exude a powerful, elemental presence. Even when the enclosure is on this massive scale – as it also is with the stone fences that surround early Buddhist *stupa*s (see pages 168–169) – this basic component of the architecture is often taken for granted. The buildings of a Chinese temple

⦿ **DOME OF THE TREASURY AND COURTYARD**
706–715, UMAYYAD MOSQUE, DAMASCUS, SYRIA

Built in 789, on Roman columns, to house the mosque funds, this treasury stands in the axial courtyard of the earliest surviving mosque. The overall form of the mosque has its origins in the Prophet's house in Medina, but at Damascus it was transformed by the addition of arcades, towers, domes and a sanctuary-like aisle, enriched with mosaic decoration, based on Christian precedents.

⏷ **MOUNTAIN ENCLOSURES**

LATE EIGHTEENTH CENTURY, MOUNT LONGHU, JIANGXI, CHINA

This detailed topographical painting by court artist Guan Huai depicts two Taoist temples at sacred Mount Longhu (Dragon and Tiger Mountain). The Monastery of Orthodox Unity (left) and Supreme Highest Purity Palace (right) are set carefully in the landscape, their walls enclosing several halls arranged along an axis.

and the prayer hall of a mosque abut their high outer walls, which define the edge of the enclosure as a whole.

However, more typically the enclosure consists of a low wall, perhaps entered through a single gate, and it is the buildings within that dominate visually. In the Greek temple, the sacred ground within the surrounding wall was known as the *temenos*. It contained an open-air altar that was overlooked by the temple itself. Comparable principles apply to Christian churches, within their walled-off burial grounds; Hindu temples, on their high platforms; and, in a different way, Mayan temple-pyramid and plaza complexes, marked out from the rest of the city's structures by being whitewashed or, sometimes, painted. In most cultures, everything within the enclosure will have been consecrated in a religious rite and must be kept clean, for to cross the threshold of the enclosure is to prepare oneself for an encounter with the sacred.

Enclosures may even be nested, one within the other, and increasing in significance as the user or visitor moves inwards – this is true both of the concentric sequences of gated walls seen at Hindu temple-cities and the gradual progression from open-air to roofed structures in an ancient Egyptian temple. The creation of an enclosure sets up a hierarchy of spaces: it suggests there is a place of yet greater significance further within, often described as a progression from "holy space" to "sacred space": the sanctuary (see box, page 19).

The manmade mountain

A recurrent feature of many such complexes is the presence of a colossal hill-like structure. These need not have an interior. There are examples in Egypt, Iraq (ziggurats), Peru and England (Silbury Hill and the Marlborough Mound) that were erected during the third millennium BCE. Usually in the form of a pyramid or a hemisphere, the manmade mountain may have stairways or stepped sides. A small sanctuary or open-air altar is often constructed at its highest point, as was the case with ziggurats and many Mayan and Aztec temple-pyramids. The placing of that sanctuary as near to the gods as possible is one potential reason why these vast forms were created; another is burial. Sheer scale is clearly also part of the aim, and many such buildings evoke both natural forms and cosmological ideas. This symbolic dimension perhaps explains the transference of the concept of the manmade mountain into less enormous, but equally significant, structures such as the Hindu *sikhara* spire (see pages 191–192) and the Chinese imperial sacrificial altar (see pages 212–213).

The *sikhara* of the Hindu temple has a highly attenuated outline – as do later Buddhist *stupa*s, which culminate in their East Asian variant, the pagoda. All are part of a common development, in which the manmade mountain transforms into a range of emphatically vertical forms, also massive, such as towers. These share with the manmade mountain an ability to make a religious building more visible – and in the case of minarets and bell-towers, in Islam and Christianity respectively, audible.

It was the ancient Romans, however, who perfected the dome – most influentially in the Pantheon, the temple to all the gods, in Rome itself (*c.*118–*c.*128CE). This incredible feat of engineering turned the manmade mountain into a shell, a building whose interior was as awe-inspiring as its exterior: the dome, in other words, was both externally massive and entirely hollowed internally. In Islamic mosques and, later and perhaps most impressively, in churches built from the Renaissance onwards, the role of the dome in turning the interior into a vivid evocation of heaven is one of their most memorable features.

The hall

Covered spaces (walled and roofed) capable of housing large gatherings of people are the final elemental form of sacred buildings, and probably the last to have been developed. Preceded, logically and to an extent chronologically, by a range of open-air spaces, the first true examples are encountered in the hypostyle halls of Egyptian temples (as in the Djoser complex at Saqarra, *c.*2630–*c.*2611BCE), which share with almost all their later variants a quality that adds greatly to their impact: the subdivision of the internal space by rows of columns, or by arcades.

Generally present for structural reasons, the columns sometimes result in subsidiary spaces, lower or narrower than the central one, and known as aisles, which are found in both Buddhist *chaitya* halls and Christian churches. In other halled buildings the roof is all at one height, creating a unitary interior filled by a forest of columns – a form called hypostyle and seen in mosque prayer halls and Hindu *mandapa*. Where the interior is ringed by columns, the effect is courtyard-like and known as peristyle (a form also seen in early Egyptian temples, such as that at Medinet Habu, *c.*1184–*c.*1153BCE, see page 77), and when these same columns

⊙ ORATORY OF ST. PHILIP NERI
1675–1731, GLOGOWKA, POLAND

The main entrance of this Baroque monastery church is marked by an elaborate façade topped by two short towers. The centralized interior is crowned by a great dome. The monastery was built for a joint community of priests and lay brothers, founded in Rome in the sixteenth century, and the design reflects an Italian influence.

support an upper level that is open to the main space, the upper area is called a gallery (frequently seen in synagogues and larger churches). Synagogues were the first halls whose main function was to host large communal gatherings of ordinary people, rather than to act as the setting for grand ritual: this is one of the turning points in the story of religious architecture (see pages 104–105).

Axial and centralized plans

The interplay of sanctuary (see box, opposite) and hall, often involving intervening spaces of various kinds, is one of the great themes in religious architecture, and its possibilities might seem infinite. However, the plans of religious buildings tend to be symmetrical, derived from simple rectangles, polygons and circles. Many such shapes – for example, in Indian and Chinese culture – had metaphysical significance. One result of this concern with regularity is that complex religious buildings – some of which may contain all the

THE SANCTUARY

The greatest degree of sacredness is usually to be found at the innermost part of the enclosure. At its most simple, this may be an open-air sacrificial altar, in which offerings are made and burned so that their smoke can rise towards heaven. In imperial China this primordial form became a sophisticated kind of architecture (see pages 212–213), but in most other cultures the altar was replaced by, enclosed by or set adjacent to a roofed building that, despite often being small, was of the greatest significance. This structure is the sanctuary.

Sanctuaries may have their primeval origins in caves, which retain powerful religious associations in many cultures. Examples are the *cella* of the Greek temple, the *garbhagriha* of the Hindu temple and the chancel or presbytery of the Christian church. The sanctuary may contain an altar, an image or even nothing at all, because although the space is often the focal point of the building, its precise significance – the level of sacredness accorded to it – varies hugely. The Holy of Holies of the Temple in Jerusalem was held literally to contain the invisible presence of God, and it could be entered only once a year and only by the High Priest; whereas the *Aron Kodesh* or Holy Ark of the Jewish synagogue and the space around it can, in principle, be approached by anyone who is suitably prepared and reverential. In both cases this inner area can be called a sanctuary.

The architectural spaces around the sanctuary can be complex. For example, ambulatory aisles pass behind the sanctuaries of larger Hindu temples and Christian churches. And in churches and Egyptian temples, chapels constitute miniature sanctuaries, which are not necessarily near the complex's main sanctuary. A further layer in the hierarchy of sacredness may be added by having a space preceding or surrounding the sanctuary – as is the case with a courtyard mosque's covered prayer hall, which extends either side of the true sanctuary represented by the *mihrab* niche and the bay around it. These, in turn, relate to the Ka'ba at Mecca much as the Holy Ark does to the Temple in Jerusalem. Such intervening structures can turn the otherwise simple idea of an enclosure and a sanctuary into the complex buildings, and groups of buildings, that characterize the great religious structures of the world.

⊙ A SUMPTUOUS SPACE
1868, SPANISH SYNAGOGUE, PRAGUE, CZECH REPUBLIC

This sanctuary is set aside by low balustrades and an elaborate Moorish-styled tabernacle topped by the Ten Commandments. This is the Holy Ark, which contains the sacred Torah scrolls, inscribed with the words of God. The "eternal light" before it is a reminder of that which burned in the Temple of Jerusalem.

above elements – can, by looking at their plans, be divided into two types, axial or centralized. An axial plan is longer than it is broad and is symmetrical along its longer axis. A rectangle is axial, as is an oval, and in both cases the axis concerned is the longer one. Mesopotamian temples had this form from early on. At its simplest, the result is a rectangle with the sanctuary or focal point in the middle of the far wall, where an arch, a screen or other feature marks it out. Many architectural forms can be added to such a building, as seen in the case of cathedrals, without losing track of its underlying axial plan. In the East Asian and Islamic traditions, spaces are arranged across, rather than parallel to, the axis, but the underlying principle of axiality holds true.

The second form of plan places the sanctuary in the middle, rather than at the end, of the building, resulting in a centralized structure. Such buildings are usually circular, regular polygons (such as squares or octagons), or are cross-shaped. Such plans are typical of many of the earliest sacred structures, such as the round temples at Gobekli Tepe in Anatolia (*c.*9000BCE) and the manmade mountains of the ancient world. Later on, centralized buildings are less common than axial ones, although they continued to dominate Buddhist architecture, in the form of the *stupa*, and Eastern Orthodox Christian architecture, in the form of the domed church with a cruciform plan. The interplay of centralized and axial plans has been a source of much inspiration to designers, not least in Christian buildings (see box, page 114).

Platforms and entrances

Finally, there are a couple of other matters relating to the overall shape of a building, which – although arguably less

◖ AN EXPRESSION OF FAITH

1921, GRUNDTVIG'S CHURCH, COPENHAGEN, DENMARK

The emphatically axial plan of this colossal brick Lutheran church leads the eye unerringly towards the light-filled sanctuary with its altar, while providing space for large congregations. The church, 22m (72ft) high and 76m (249ft) long, was designed by Peder Vilhelm Jensen Klint (1853–1930) and built to commemorate the famous Danish hymn-writer and philosopher N.F.S. Grundtvig (1783–1872). Its bare design draws on aspects of the northern European Gothic, vernacular Danish and twentieth-century Expressionist architectural styles.

fundamental or universal – have had a recurring and defining impact on religious architecture. For example, many such structures are raised high above the ground on a solid platform, which places the sanctuary above the worshipper and intensifies its impact by obliging the devotee to climb towards his or her objective. In some cases the motive is an allusion to the idea of the manmade mountain – as with the emphatic platforms common even in smaller Mesoamerican temples, which are designed to evoke temple-pyramids nearby. It also helps to set the building apart, as with Hindu temples, or to ensure its visibility above enclosing walls, as in ancient Mesopotamian temples. In Western Christianity, a vaulted crypt may raise the sanctuary above the rest of the church: here, the platform has an interior which is often a secondary sanctuary in itself.

The entrance is the final key building block of sacred form. Entrances often reflect important aspects of how a building was used. For example, in many Christian churches certain doors were reserved for priests or kings (see page 48). The pylons of ancient Egypt constitute a major architectural focus of the exterior. In some mosques, the gateway is often the only elaborate feature to punctuate the enclosing walls. The entrances to the long barrows of northwest Europe, from the period *c.*3800–*c.*3500BCE, are set in walls formed by arrangements of colossal stones: the results are the earliest façades, a now well-established practice in which the principal elevation (usually) of a building is made particularly impressive. For centuries, the entire entrance walls of many Christian cathedrals served as major, often richly decorated, stone tableaux – liturgical stage-sets that could be understood by the illiterate masses.

From enclosures to entrances, these elements were common to the form of sacred buildings of all kinds and were combined and re-combined over many millennia. However, irrespective even of such factors as exceptional size and height, the power of religious architecture resides just as much in how the multitude of resulting forms are detailed and decorated. It is in this manner that they can be imbued with meaning, and made to express aesthetic effects and moods, and communicate important ideas. This is the province of sacred style.

SACRED STYLE

Architectural style consists of the way in which various details, many of them decorative, combine to create a consistent overall aesthetic effect. The quality of their impact can vary enormously: architecture, just like poetry or music, can have a wide range of expression, from the brutally powerful to the delicately elegant. Certain aspects of style are seen repeatedly in sacred architecture; indeed, particular combinations of form, when united with specific stylistic qualities, can eloquently represent important aspects of a faith.

The language of ornamentation

In many religions the architectural adornment of the building – meaning its carved details, and the way individual elements are shaped, or articulated, so as to have a specific aesthetic effect – follows a defined vocabulary, specific to a given culture and period, which is followed consistently. This ornamental language governs exactly how foliage must be carved or what form parts of the building such as capitals and columns will have. The conventions for such motifs may have been transmitted orally, or they may be recorded in some detail in prescriptive texts, such as those known from ancient China and India. For example, in Japan only Shinto temples are permitted the distinctive details encoded in the *yuiitsu shinmei-zukuri* ("only divine style"). In the Western world there were bodies of writing about architecture, present in the classical world and reborn in the fifteenth century, which, while not regarded as rule books, also greatly influenced the design of religious buildings.

Generally, sacred architecture tends to be richly decorated, but there are instances – as in Japanese Zen temples, some mosques, and early Renaissance churches – when it is not, and then it is the careful use of well-judged details that achieves spiritually uplifting effects. The role proportion plays in the overall effect becomes particularly important in this situation, and proportions were often generated with simple geometrical procedures, or by using a module, such as a particular part of the human body (see page 163). The mathematical harmonies that arose as a result were assumed to reflect the divinely ordered nature of the universe.

The power of many

Ordered repetition, of decorative patterns and structural elements alike, is common in religious buildings. The fractal power of this repetition – which is sometimes deepened by the symbolism and meaning of specific forms, such as spiral columns (see box, page 24) – is illustrated by, for example, the impact on the senses of the tiled walls of some mosques in the Persian tradition (see pages 142–143), or by the much simpler and more emphatic repetition of arches in an arcade.

◖ A MORAL ARCHITECTURE
1841–1846, ST. GILES, CHEADLE, STAFFORDSHIRE, ENGLAND

The various fittings that enrich the sanctuary of this church are ornamented with architectural forms, such as repeated Gothic tracery patterns and niches. It was the conviction of the architect A.W.N. Pugin (1812–1852), who had studied the medieval Gothic in great depth, that Gothic was an inherently moral style.

Often, this impressive effect includes micro-architecture – smaller features fashioned like buildings, as seen in Christian tombs, tabernacles and other complex fittings of the Gothic period, or the *sikhara* spires of Hindu temples, which are frequently covered with flattened, miniature sculpted *sikhara*s. In both these traditions, sacred images are carved standing within a little aedicule, tabernacle or niche: a tiny sculpted home, quoting full-scale buildings so as to evoke the idea of a throne or a sanctuary. Usually brightly painted, such images would have been more important to viewers than the buildings in which they stood.

Beauty and structure

However a religious building is ornamented, certain structural elements are crucial to its appearance. Lintels, arches, columns and so on will be used as supports, or to cover openings such as windows and doors; ceilings and roofs seal the interior from the elements; and the storeys into which a building is divided may be marked by horizontal features such as entablatures, corbel tables or string courses. The overall aesthetic effect of the building is particularly concentrated in such details, which help to organize and control its decoration. For example, horizontal corbel tables known as *talud-tablero*s are a defining feature of Mesoamerican stepped pyramids, while the semi-circular arch immediately distinguishes Roman temples from Greek ones, which use lintels to cover openings.

Indeed, lintels have been the most common way of covering windows and doors, and of forming roofs, and they are used in Mesopotamian, Egyptian, Greek, Hindu and East Asian temples alike. These buildings are thus divided up by orthogonal, or right-angled, forms, which help to shape the clear geometrical rhythm of their architecture.

In such a structure, a curved opening stands out immediately. This delightful effect can be achieved simply by carving a piece of stone into an arched form, and placing it in a lintel-topped opening, as is often done in Hindu temples. These are not true arches, because they do little to bear the weight of the structure above them, work which is still done chiefly by the lintel. The true arch spans the opening itself and is made up of wedge-shaped stones called voussoirs,

⬥ PERSIAN-INSPIRED PARADISE
1480, HAZRAT ALI MOSQUE, MAZAR-I SHARIF, AFGHANISTAN

Clear horizontal divisions give structure to the intensely coloured geometric and vegetal patterns, and passages of sacred text, which enrich this Timurid shrine; combined with pointed arches, they comprise a distinctive version of Islamic style, originating in Persia.

sealed at the top by a keystone. An arch has exceptional rigidity and strength, and was known in many cultures, but it was the Romans who first exploited its full potential. Arches then became defining features of both Christian and Islamic architecture.

Islamic masons explored a wide range of types of arch. The pointed or equilateral arch was one of the most attractive, and it diversified, perhaps with Indian influence, into the sensuous ogee and other variations. European Gothic architecture created buildings that can seem to consist of nothing but a skeleton of such openings.

Roman engineers developed further arch-based techniques, such as the roof-vault and the dome, to cover structures – techniques that were again inherited and further developed within both Christian and Islamic architecture. They enabled the builders of churches and mosques to cover enormous spaces without their being interrupted by columns, and allowed those spaces to fill with natural light, creating spiritually uplifting settings – like evocations of heaven itself – for the worshippers within. Windows, the main source of illumination in most religious buildings, were often small prior to these developments, resulting in shadowy interiors pierced by the occasional shaft of light. However, from the Gothic era onwards, and thanks to further advances in glazing techniques, Christian churches made the window into a major element of architectural style.

Columns, or thicker structures known as piers, mainly provided the vertical supports for roofs, windows and other openings. The articulation of such supports is a major aspect of sacred style; a capital, which stands at the top of a column, performs a practical role while at the same time helping the eye to bring order to a building. This effect is found far and wide: even architectures that developed in relative isolation, such as in East Asia, give a comparable role to the bracket set or *dougong*. The design of capitals is often a diagnostic marker of an architectural style, as with the capitals of the three ancient Greek orders: Doric, Ionic and Corinthian.

Each of these details, such as the form of a column or capital, can be articulated in myriad ways. In combination with the building's underlying form, the overall effect is unmistakable. The way in which rows of pointed arches surround the worshipper in the dome-dominated courtyard of a mosque is as unerringly Islamic as the thickly sculpted surfaces of a *sikhara* spire are Hindu. Indeed, such buildings often provide the means to decode an entire world view.

MEANING IS IN THE DETAIL

Architectural details in religious buildings often have specific, if ever-shifting, significance. For example, by the fifth century CE the shrine of St. Peter in Rome was surrounded by six ancient columns, famous for their spiral form. Many people believed these were from the Jewish Temple in Jerusalem. At various times and in many places, this twisted-shaft shape, known as the "Solomonic column", has been deliberately used to evoke sacredness, highlight shrines or act as an emblem of the authority of Rome – for example, in Durham cathedral in England (from 1093), where six huge columns with spirals carved into them marked the eastern half of the building, which held the shrine of St. Cuthbert. The motif then became popular in English architecture, but also began to lose its specific associations. Spiral columns were quoted in arguably their most eye-catching form in the 1620s, when the architect Bernini used versions of them to support the *baldacchino* canopy over the high altar in St. Peter's itself. Known as "barley sugar" columns, they became part of the stock-in-trade of Baroque architecture.

◯ CLOISTERED COLUMNS

1205–1241, SAN PAOLO FUORI LE MURA, ROME, ITALY

The cloister of this Christian monastery, which holds the tomb of St. Paul, is enriched with multicoloured spiral columns, giving the courtyard shrine-like associations and reminding the monks of biblical descriptions of heaven.

⬢ CAVE 19 AT AJANTA

LATE FIFTH CENTURY CE, MAHARASHTRA, INDIA

Chaitya halls are places of worship – normally Buddhist but sometimes Jain – that have been carved into natural cliff-faces, and they are found throughout India from as early as the third century BCE. Their design appears to copy that of existing structures made of reeds, earth and timber, transferring the motifs found in them into permanent materials – a process that explains many details of architectural style, in ancient Greece and Egypt as well as in India. This *chaitya* hall is 14m (46ft) long and 7.3m (24ft) wide. It has an axial plan, with a sanctuary at one end (above) containing a miniature *stupa*. Massive columns run along each side, and behind them aisles form a narrow corridor along which worshippers could circumambulate the *stupa*. Each column has a base, shaft and capital in the bulbous style typical of early Indian architecture; above them are carvings of *buddha*s, elephants and flying *apsara*s (cloud and water spirits), positioned on carved imitations of timber features, such as beam-ends. The vaulted roof has ribs, reminiscent of timber or bamboo. Cave 19 is part of a series of twenty-four Buddhist monasteries and five *chaitya* halls at Ajanta, carved into a bluff overlooking the Waghora River and originating in the second or first century BCE. It may have been funded by a minister to the monarch Harishena (reigned *c.*475–*c.*500) of the local Vidarbha kingdom, or by King Upendragupta in the sixth century CE. Buddhism had disappeared from India by the twelfth century when the monasteries were abandoned.

روجاوزبنضاع اليله قبض يدوب علينة رفع ايلر ۞ وكافرلوك جانارين صول اليله قبض يدوب بجنينه انصال ايلر ۞ ودخاانس ابن مالك صلى

عنهماسند صحيح ايله رسول حضرت عليه السلام مذ روايتايدوب ايدى كم ادم عليه الصلوة والسلام اشبوازلكى كوكذ رئ ودخينارفم انبوكوكذ

اقوا اااعلا زكىانك كفاك ۷۰۰ زفانالحكاحكها اهار ازشهان ازع ات اكماشم ازلكقات كوك فاكاف ۱۱۸ازلكافقم

A HOLY
UNIVERSE

EMBODYING DIVINE ORDER

———————○———————

Religious buildings are filled with meaning. The architecture might be intended to replicate the features of the sacred landscape in which it is set, or to represent a culture's deepest ideas about the ordered nature of the cosmos and humankind's place within it, from earthly life to the ultimate mystery of what lies beyond mortal death. From miniature re-creations of ideal cities to visions of a blissful afterlife, it is part of the function of these buildings to embody and address cosmological and spiritual ideas, not only in their structure and style but also in the blessed images and sacred texts that frequently feature in their decoration. The role of these was often to instruct as well as to uplift, to reinforce an ethical message and to remind viewers of sacred stories. Text, image and building worked together, evoking the ways in which human beings could perfect themselves for this world and achieve salvation.

◀ **COSMIC PLAN**

1583, ARABIC MANUSCRIPT OF *THE TALES OF LUQMAN*

Many cultures have imagined the cosmos as a nested series of layers. For Jews, Christians and Muslims, the divine realms were at the edge of the universe, and in the middle was the Earth with, for many, Jerusalem or Mecca – sacred places with their own equivalent in heaven – at its cosmic centre.

LANDSCAPE & THE COSMOS

To early man, the landscape seemed to contain divine forces: mountains appeared to control the movement of clouds and therefore precipitation; caves provided natural shelter, but suggested the existence of an underworld; and springs and rivers were the source of life-giving water. Meanwhile, heaven and Earth alike moved in accordance with patterns and rhythms – such as the turning of the seasons and the cycles of the heavenly bodies – that suggested that the cosmos was an ordered place. Such ideas were expressed in sacred architecture in many different ways.

The cave and the mountain

Of all natural forms, caves and mountains have had perhaps the most powerful influence on architecture. The two

⊙ A HOUSE FOR THE DEAD

c.3600–c.3200BCE, POULNABRONE DOLMEN, CLARE, IRELAND

Originally covered by a high mound of stones, the 1.8m-high (6ft), cave-like burial chamber or dolmen within this long mound might have been conceived as a palatial home for the dead. Between sixteen and twenty-two adults and six children were buried in it.

are often linked, in nature and architecture alike, and the enormous pyramidal mounds and small dark sanctuaries of antiquity provided a template for many later monuments. Caves and mountains remain venerated features of the landscape in many parts of the world, from Thailand to Mexico.

Caves were the setting for some of the earliest known sacred spaces, such as those at Lascaux in France (c.23,000–c.8000BCE). From the Christians of Cappadocia in Anatolia to the Buddhists of China, later peoples created places of worship by reshaping caves or by carving churches and temples into the rock.

Likewise, many of the earliest religious structures seem to evoke or replicate sacred peaks: the ziggurats of Mesopotamia and the pyramids of the Americas (both from c.3000BCE) are two of the best-attested examples, but such connections recur at many more recent sites, such as Borobudur in Indonesia (c.780–c.850, see pages 178–179).

The long barrows of Neolithic Europe (c.3800–c.3500BCE) can seem to unite the cave with the mountain, for they are very like hills that contain artificial caves, which serve as a

resting place for the spirits of the dead. Such metaphorical thinking often underlies the mythological and cultural associations of religious sites: mountains provide access to heaven, or are the abode of the gods; and caves lead to the underworld, or are associated with birth and regeneration, like wombs within Mother Earth.

The interconnection of mountain and cave has survived into the present in the Indian tradition. The spire of a Hindu temple, covered in small sculptures of gods, is a *sikhara*, or "mountain peak", reflecting the belief that the gods inhabit Mount Meru. A small, dark sanctuary lies directly beneath this *sikhara*, and the name of this space – *garbhagriha* – means "womb-house", while its form and location evoke a cave. Burmese *stupas*, which like all such buildings are also emblems of Meru, have *sikhara* spires on the Hindu model and are hollowed to form chapels known as *ge*, or caves. Such connections are less explicit in the great monotheistic faiths, but it is striking that some of the most sacred buildings and sites of Jerusalem are associated with hilltops – the Dome of the Rock, the Jewish Temple, the Holy Sepulchre church, Temple Mount and Golgotha – and they contain caves (Bir el-Arwah, or the "Well of Souls", and Christ's tomb).

Some religious buildings recreate entire mythological landscapes. When the Egyptian pharaoh Sety I (reigned *c.*1294–*c.*1279BCE) built the Osireion in his temple at Abydos, he created what looked like a hill, possibly even planted with trees. In fact, it was a subterranean tomb-like building, its interior a hall supported by columns: a cave beneath a mountain. The interior was filled with water from a natural spring, leaving a dry, island-like area in the middle. The ancient Egyptians believed that creation had begun with the appearance of a hill in the middle of a swamp. This addition of water to architectural representations of the cave and the mountain clearly emulates the natural world, and is also seen in Mesoamerica and at Angkor, Cambodia, where the great temples are images of Meru, surrounded by manmade stretches of irrigating water, called *barays*.

Energies of the Earth

Many cultures have regarded the whole world as sacred, and the landscape as alive with specific deities and sacred forces,

⏺ **MEDITATIVE RETREAT**
SIXTH CENTURY, KHAO LUANG CAVE, PHETCHABURI, THAILAND

Thailand has at least 120 sacred Buddhist caves, some in use since the sixth century. Khao Luang contains more than 180 statues.

present in individual rocks, springs, trees and stones. The scale and setting of Shinto temples are carefully judged, so as to work with and complement the numinous power of natural phenomena. Even the mightiest religious monuments might be deliberate attempts to enhance the sacredness already inherent in the surrounding landscape. The grand mountain-and-cave pyramids, temples and temple-plazas of Mesoamerica and the Andes were nodal points in tracts of land that were believed to be filled with subtle sacred energies. It is often argued that the designs on the desert floor at Nazca in Peru are attempts to monumentalize such complex, subtle sacred energies and the myths and

◀ NATURAL ARCHITECTURE

*c.*150CE, TEMPLE OF QUETZALCÓATL,
TEOTIHUACÁN, MEXICO

The feathered serpent god adorns
the sloping face of this volcanic-
stone temple façade, set in the city's
ciudadela, with the Pyramid of the
Moon framed by the mountains
in the distance.

rituals associated with them, as are the complexes of stone settings in Neolithic Europe. A comparable experience can be had in a modern context; for example, in both Greece and Tibet, major temples, churches and monasteries stand in landscapes richly set with wayside chapels and shrines, many of which have abundant, if strictly local, mythological and religious associations. Some indigenous societies have maintained such beliefs without monumentalizing them. For the Anangu Aborigine people of Australia, Uluru (Ayers Rock) is a sacred presence, as impressive as any cathedral, in a landscape filled with associations of the Dreamtime.

The integration of sacred architecture and natural sacred landscape is seen on a grand scale at Teotihuacán in what is now Mexico, where the Pyramid of the Moon echoes the nearby mountain of Cerro Gordo and the Pyramid of the Sun is connected to a lava tube beneath. Perhaps this natural feature was once a kind of *axis mundi* ("cosmic axis") at the sacred heart of the entire empire, an entrance to the underworld and the fountainhead of creation. Specially constructed stone drains provided channels to bring water here for some ritual purpose, echoing the thinking of Sety I in ancient Egypt (see page 29). Sacred architecture that recreates natural landscapes often also reflects a culture's cosmology – its beliefs about the origin and shape of the universe.

Man and the universe

Cosmology systematizes and orders the universe, emphasizing not merely its outward form but also its apparently regular underlying geometry. Its roots lie ultimately in observations of the natural world: that the year has a predictable shape to it, which is marked out in the movements of the heavenly bodies, especially the solstices and equinoxes and the phases of the moon; that the environment has cardinal directions, implying an orthogonal underlying order; and that the skyline or horizon appears to be a perfect circle. Religious buildings are often designed to make this divine order more visible, both to people and to the gods.

This may be one of the reasons for the universal use of regular geometrical shapes in religious architecture. Circles and squares, symbolizing heaven and Earth respectively, were used in ancient Chinese open-air altars, and these shapes play a key role in structures such as the Temple of Heaven in

Beijing (see pages 212–213). All Hindu temple architecture is derived from the grid-like *vastupurushamandala* representing the "cosmic man" (see page 163), an idea earlier evoked in the forms of Vedic altars.

Many cultures created elaborate geometrical diagrams to express their cosmological ideas. The *mandalas* of Tantric Hinduism and Vajrayana Buddhism (see below and page 182) are at one and the same time diagrams of sacred universes, images of imagined buildings and aids to spiritual progress. They influenced architecture in a variety of ways and places, from the monastic plans of Sri Lanka to the designs of the *stupa* at Borobudur in Java (see pages 178–179).

Orientations

The vast majority of sacred buildings, like the *mandalas*, are aligned with the cardinal directions, with their walls facing north, east, south and west. Most have their sanctuaries facing either east, the rising point of the sun, or west, its setting point. Indeed, the overwhelming majority face east, the exceptions being temples in the Americas, which generally face west. In ancient Egypt, temple orientation varied between east and west, depending on which bank of the Nile a building stands. China favours a different orientation, north–south; but this is the exception that proves the rule, because to the Chinese the south was the direction of warmth and the season summer, and hence, once again, the association is with the sun.

Not every culture measured orientation precisely; for example, in ancient Greece about 80 percent of temples face roughly east–west, of which 72 percent face east. However, in other places the orientation is highly specific: circular Stonehenge in England and the complex of Chavín de Huántar (*c*.1000–*c*.200BCE) in Peru are structures that are aligned with the sunrise at the midwinter solstice and summer solstice, respectively. Calculated alignment means that the light of the sun can also be used to theatrical effect, reaching the innermost sanctuary of Newgrange burial mound in Ireland (3100–2900BCE) and the top of Ramesses II's temple of Abu Simbel (1285–1255BCE), at significant moments of the year (see also page 91).

Although sun worship in particular had pagan associations, a mysticism of light survived into both Christianity

◖ AXIS OF FAITH

1772, CLOISONNÉ *MANDALA*, CHINA

Mount Meru, a colossal mountain that forms the axis of the universe, plays a key role in Hindu, Jain and Buddhist cosmology, profoundly influencing the architecture of these faiths. For Buddhists it is Sumeru ("wonderful Meru"), and in the esoteric traditions of Buddhism it became metaphorically a palace and a model for spiritual transformation. Its image was used in the sacred diagrams known as *mandalas* ("circle/enclosure") and was evoked in temple art (see page 182), actual buildings (see pages 56–57 and 178–179) and exquisite liturgical and devotional objects such as this one, 56cm (22in) high, from imperial China's Qing dynasty. Here, the mountain is decorated with coral, jade and silver, and topped by a *stupa* **A**, a Buddhist shrine, acting as the axis of the cosmos, with a sun and moon at its peak. This sits atop a sanctuary **B** with four prominent gates, empty apart from a lotus to symbolize the state of *buddha*hood. The roofs of these structures have bells and auspicious or honorific victory banners and parasols, much as actual temples and *stupas* would. The steep lower section, with its pyramid-like steps **C**, is a particularly direct evocation of a mountain; it stands on a circular base **D**, which is at once a protective enclosure and the cosmic oceans and mountains that surround the world.

and Islam. Christian theology concerning light is said to have fuelled the birth of Gothic architecture, with its enormous windows and multicoloured stained glass, while in Islam the Quran's *sura* 24 ("The Light") is the most frequently seen of all the inscriptions which decorate the *mihrab*s and portals of mosques: "God is the light of the heavens and of the Earth. His light may be compared to a niche that enshrines a lamp, the lamp within a crystal of star-like brilliance."

However, neither mosques nor synagogues are oriented with the sun, but with a holy city (Mecca and Jerusalem, respectively), towards which Muslims and Jews turn when they pray. The altars of Christian churches are theoretically aligned with Jerusalem, but in reality they face east – often a rather approximate east – a tradition that is possibly a result of the strong association between Christ and the sun seen in the early centuries of Roman-influenced church architecture.

Cities of the gods

A city might seem a very different thing from a sacred landscape, but many religions have settlements – such as Jerusalem, Thebes, Varanasi, Mecca, Gaya or Beijing – that

are of cosmic significance. Religious buildings and cities are closely linked; in Mesopotamia it seems that the creation of temples was itself a cause of early urbanization, while in medieval Europe, as in the Khmer empire of Southeast Asia, large religious institutions dominated and defined urban settlements. In early Islam, the caliphs permitted only one congregational mosque or *jami masjid* in every town, and the possession of such a building became a badge of urban identity much as, in Europe today, the presence of a cathedral is a marker of a city.

Religious buildings can be images of cities in themselves: for example, every church evokes the idea of the Heavenly Jerusalem (see illustration, below). In China, the layout of the imperial capital was itself a kind of religious architecture – the axial south–north road and the central palace and suburban temple complexes were all elements in a sacred pattern that was intended to ensure that the emperor at its heart maintained the harmony between heaven and humanity (see page 200). In spite of decades of modern city development, such an arrangement is preserved in the layout of the last imperial capital, Beijing, to this day.

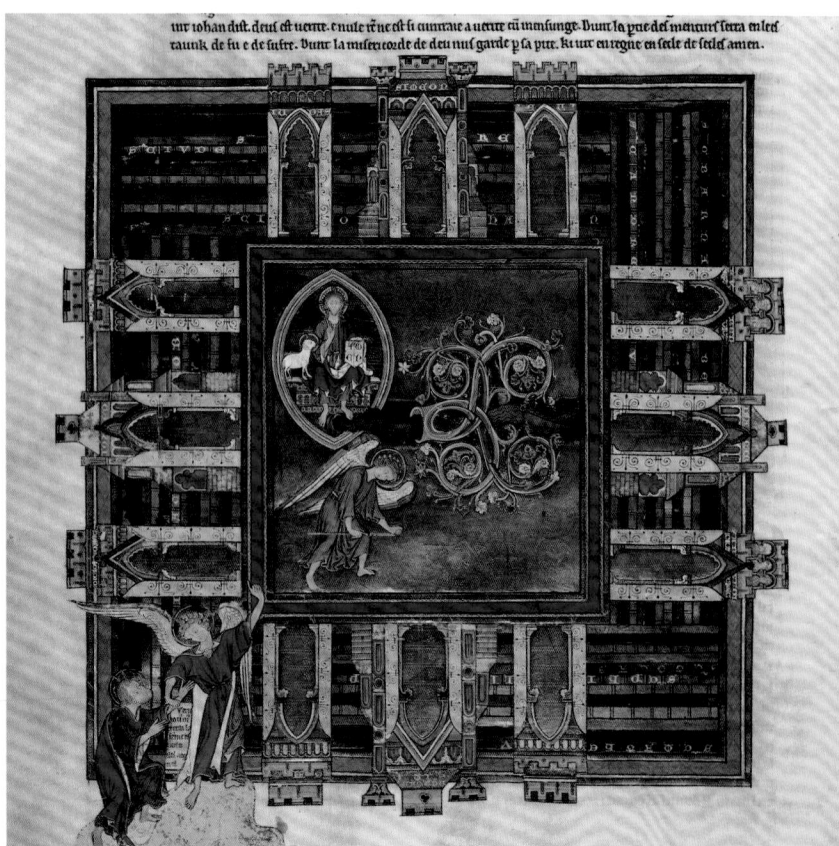

◖ THE HEAVENLY JERUSALEM

*c.*1250, *TRINITY COLLEGE APOCALYPSE*, CAMBRIDGE, ENGLAND

For medieval Christians, descriptions of a divine equivalent to the city in which Christ died and was resurrected (Jerusalem) provided a vision of heaven itself – massive, regular and apparently made of precious stones – which had an enormous influence on church design. Jews, Christians and Muslims alike believed the apocalypse, the Last Judgment, which would precede the end of time itself, would begin at the real Jerusalem.

◗ ZIGGURAT OF ISLAM

848–852, SAMARRA, IRAQ

The Great, or Mutawakkil, Mosque at Samarra was once the largest in the world, and its enormous minaret, originally 53m (174ft) high, has a distinctive spiral form which seems to be modelled on that of Mesopotamian ziggurats, already ancient features of the local landscape. These evoke in turn the mountains which fringe the basin of the Tigris and Euphrates rivers.

HEAVEN & THE AFTERLIFE

While bereavement is traumatic for most human beings, belief in the finality of death was rare before the modern era. Most religions have sought to equip people for some form of an afterlife, and religious architecture has often served both to commemorate those who have been lost to this earthly world and to express ideas about where their souls have gone.

For many cultures, the dead were present everywhere. At the village of Çatalhoyuk, which dates to the eighth millennium BCE in what is now Turkey, the deceased were simply buried beneath the floor of what was, no doubt for important reasons, effectively an ancestral tomb-home. Chinese temples may have originated as places where the ancestors could be honoured and invoked, a practice that continues in the Confucian tradition to this day. In several places, such as ancient Egypt and the Americas, temples were partly designed as palaces, to be inhabited by the dead after their demise. The centre of the ruined city of Chan Chan (founded between 800 and 1100 CE in Peru) contains ten such palaces, called *ciudadelas* ("citadels") by the Spanish, each built by successive kings of the Chimú. It appears that these men were believed to continue inhabiting their palace after death, necessitating the construction of a replacement by their successor.

Mausoleums and the ways to heaven

Such temple-tombs express their creators' beliefs about the afterlife. The Chimú structures are thus partly mausoleums, a type of building also richly associated with Christianity and Islam, two faiths with strong beliefs in an afterlife, a heavenly world of bliss, into which only the righteous will be admitted. Historically, bodily burial was essential among Christians and Muslims to ensure a proper resurrection at the end of time. By contrast, Hindus and Buddhists believe in reincarnation, and tend to prefer cremation to burial; mausoleums are rare, although Buddhist *stupas* can have a marked commemorative function.

Christian churches have highly visible burials, which fill the area within the enclosure, and grander Christian and Islamic mausoleums often have a distinctive centralized design, with a tomb in the centre and a domical roof. This form originated in Roman mausoleums, especially those of

◖ VISION OF HEAVEN
1631–1647, TAJ MAHAL, AGRA, INDIA

This mausoleum is an image of the paradise that its builder, Shah Jahan (reigned 1627–1658), hoped was awaiting his favourite wife, Mumtaz Mahal (died 1631), who is buried there. It sits at one end of a Persian-styled garden (right), quartered by watercourses, which evoke Quranic descriptions of paradise as containing four gardens "watered by running streams" (Quran 47:12). The white marble building, 74m (243ft) high, is adorned with the most complete programme of Quranic inscriptions in Islamic architecture, all on themes of divine mercy, the Day of Judgment, and paradise.

emperors. The impressive scale of such buildings is especially intriguing in Islam, for Muhammad specifically counselled against lavish burial practices, which might be why many tombs exist as more public-spirited complexes alongside a mosque, a hospital or a *madrasa* (college of religious law).

Churches and mosques aim to offer their faithful an experience of heaven. It is surely no coincidence that the dome and the vault, two powerful evocations of this heavenly realm, are so fully explored in these buildings. In both faiths, the afterlife is often imagined as a garden-like place, filled with delightful buildings, an image that profoundly affected the decoration of Islamic mosques. Over time, and especially under Persian influence, actual planted gardens that evoked heaven became an element in the design of mosques and mausoleums – for example, at the Taj Mahal in India. Similar visions are articulated in Pure Land Buddhism, which very often depicts a delightful garden filled with beautiful buildings from which souls might more easily attain enlightenment. Such paradisiacal imagery had a wide influence in East Asian religious architecture (see page 181).

In Hinduism, the temples, with their *sikhara* spires inhabited by many statues of gods, act as architectural images of Mount Meru, although it is not implied that the ordinary human devotee might inhabit such a zone. Nevertheless, Hindu temples reflect some ideas about the fate of the soul that bear similarities with the beliefs of Christians and Muslims. Those Hindus who founded temples often did so to acquire *punya* ("merit"), which would lead to a better rebirth in a future life. The building itself may not be a mausoleum or represent the attainable afterlife, but certain beliefs about death provided the motivation for its creation. Similarly, the Buddhist doctrine of *parinamana* tells us that merit acquired can be transferred to others, alive or dead. This belief, again, encouraged the endowment of monasteries and temples as part of one's earthly legacy. In medieval European Christianity, the doctrine of purgatory – a place in which human souls awaited the purification necessary for a place in heaven, and where their fate could still be affected by good deeds done in their name by the living – resulted in the foundation of many of the most magnificent religious institutions. In addition to its impact on churches of

⚫ **A PURE LAND**

*c.*1700, DISTEMPER WITH GOLD PAINTED ON CLOTH, TIBET, CHINA

Mahayana and Vajrayana Buddhists believe that there are various cosmic realms or Pure Lands, each overseen by a specific *buddha*. Sukhavati Western Paradise is ruled over by Amitabha. From this blissful place enlightenment is easily attained. It is imagined as a garden-like place scattered with temples and delightful buildings.

all kinds, the doctrine resulted in the creation of a specific building type called the chantry chapel, a small structure within a church that contained a tomb and an altar where a dedicated priest might say masses for the soul of a specific individual – one of the most vivid conflations of the place of worship and the burial site.

DEPICTIONS OF THE DIVINE

The idea that a deity might seek to inhabit a representation of itself is one of the defining features of early temples. In Mesopotamia, Egypt and Greece, the ultimate purpose of the building was to act as an image-house, a suitable setting for such a holy likeness; this tradition is still alive in Hinduism, where the statue enshrined in a temple may, if treated appropriately, be inhabited by the deity it represents.

Holiness of imagery

In such cultures, no matter how much we may admire the design of a building, it is the statues – for which the architecture is merely the setting – that matters most. This can be true even when the image itself is not divine; the prominence given to images of the saints and *bodhisattva*s, who are holy to Christians and Buddhists respectively, can mean that they dominate some churches and temples, although the images are not holy in themselves. The significance of such beings within their religions is reflected in the dedication of many buildings: either to a particular saint, such as St. Andrew at

Wells cathedral (see pages 48–49), or to a particular concept, such as the "residence of the Dharma" that is Beopju temple in South Korea (see page 202).

The creation of such images could itself be a ritual act. In Indian and Chinese religious sculpture, the completion of a statue is marked by the painting-in of the statue's eyes, a moment marked by rites, which help to establish that the statue is not only complete as a work of art but potentially efficacious as an object of devotion. Sometimes a detailed canon of rules also guides the creation of images – in ancient Egypt, and still in Hinduism, the precise proportions of individual figures are specified. To depict a god incorrectly was to make the image itself less effective.

Iconography of the deities

In many religions, the gods and goddesses themselves needed to be able to recognize such images, especially where a being had many aspects, only one of which was being invoked. The Egyptian god Osiris may have green or black skin, symbolizing his regenerative potential, but his *ba* – his essence or soul, represented by the ram hieroglyph – was sometimes worshipped separately as the ram-headed god Banebdjed. Hindu Vishnu may appear as a blue-skinned person with four arms, or as one of his ten principal avatars, such as the boar Varaha. Monstrous or many-armed depictions aimed to convey the enormous power of the deity. None of these distinctive physical characteristics was necessarily believed to be the actual appearance of a given being – rather, this was a way of signifying their qualities and powers.

◖ TRANSFIGURING IMAGE

*c.*1450, VIRGIN HODEGETRIA, ICON OF SMOLENSK, RUSSIA

The Virgin Mary points at her son, Jesus Christ, indicating that he is the way to salvation (Hodegetria: "She who shows the Way"). One such image was believed to have been painted in the presence of Mary by St. Luke, and it was highly venerated at Smolensk in Russia, where many copies of it, such as this one, were made. Icons are painted according to strict rules: no light and shade is shown, because the image itself provides spiritual illumination; the emphasis is on the eternal. They are images of divine realities, and the very act of painting them helps artist and viewer alike to draw closer to God.

More practically, rules of depiction helped ordinary mortals to interpret religious images. Those who have attained *buddha*hood are recognizable by, among other things, their *ushnisha* (a top-knot or cranial protuberance). The Buddha, Shakyamuni, also had distended earlobes, a vestige from the years he spent wearing earrings as a prince. Christian saints can often be identified by the attributes they carry – for example, Catherine of Alexandria with the wheel on which she was martyred or Andrew with his diagonal cross (see page 49).

Such statues and pictures are designed partly to provide a focus for devotion, but they are also used to reinforce doctrine and to instruct. It is possible that clerics were on hand to explain to viewers the abstruse sculpted schemes of European cathedral portals, such as those at Chartres in France, or the reliefs on the gallery walls of the Buddhist temple at Borobudur in Java (see pages 178–179).

A sublime aesthetic

Religious art is rarely naturalistic. More often it idealizes human form, as with the ancient Greeks and Hindus, or is highly stylized, with bodies and clothes arranged into striking graphic forms and standardized facial types indicating if a being is good or bad, a king or a peasant.

Colours, too, emphasize pattern, and sometimes meaning: in Vajrayana Buddhism, blue, yellow, red and green are repeatedly used, each apportioned to a different cardinal direction, element, *buddha*, part of the body, meritorious quality (such as healing) and *mantra*. In general, colour schemes are intense and rich, with golds, blues and greens placed close together. The resulting flattened, patterned effect, designed in conformity to a canon of rules, has been called "iconic" art, after the Greek Christian sacred images, and its colours, graphic patterns and intensely stylized imagery can have a particularly powerful effect on the viewer, which may be why this aesthetic is prevalent in religious art.

The striking visual impact of such images does not depend only on the figures and scenes they represent. There is something about the complex and harmonious abstract form of a *mandala* or a rose window, with their geometrical patterns and powerful colour combinations, that can deeply move even those who have no idea of the specific meaning of

◐ ANOINTING THE LIBERATED ONE
*c.*900, SHRAVANA BELAGOLA, KARNATAKA, INDIA

At the Mahamastakabhisheka festival, held every twelve years, this giant 18m (58ft) monolith of Bahubali (Gommatesvara), the Jain *arihant* (a highly realized and powerful soul), is anointed with milk. Bahubali, son of the first *tirthankara*, was said to have stood in a forest in meditation until creepers grew around him. He thus attained liberation (*moksha*): his devotees hope to do likewise.

the scenes depicted. This may help to explain why most of the buildings in this book were originally brightly painted. Original colour schemes survive only in exceptional cases – for example, where the colour is to some extent integrated with the structure of the building. This is true of the tilework of later mosques in the Persian tradition, and of East Asian architecture in general, which is often thickly painted to help protect from decay the timbers from which it is constructed. Here we can glimpse often dazzling sensual effects, which have been lost in thousands of religious buildings across the world.

SACRED WORDS

The banning of idolatry in the form of "an image … of anything in heaven above or on the Earth beneath or in the waters below" (Exodus 20:4) and a prohibition on worshipping such creations is one of the Ten Commandments, texts of foundational importance to Judaism and Christianity alike. Idolatry is banned in the Quran too, and many other religious traditions have also reacted against the use of rich imagery. Although the strength of their attitudes to this injunction has varied historically, Judaism, Christianity and Islam all assert an immanent universal God who can be worshipped liturgically and reached through prayer, but who does not inhabit images.

Divine scripture

Instead, the major monotheistic faiths have attached deep importance to the revealed *word* of God. Jews, Muslims and many Christian denominations have created an architecture focused on the sacred word. Nonconformist Christian chapels and meeting houses are often internally bare buildings, sometimes enriched with edifying painted quotations and dominated by prominent pulpits, from which sermons are preached – the altars become comparatively insignificant. Such buildings thus have much in common with synagogues, with their Hebrew inscriptions, the *bimah* from which prayer is led and Torah scrolls; and with mosques, with their Quranic inscriptions and the *minbar* for Friday sermons (see pages 142–143). Torah scrolls, Bibles, Qurans and other sacred books are often the centrepieces of such places of worship. Rich and partly symbolic patterning has often replaced imagery in the decorative arts of such religious traditions.

Islam in particular has built an entire body of art around devotion to the revealed word of the Quran. Judaism, earlier, did something equally reverential: the sacred word as revealed to Moses by God, and written by divine power on

For Jews, the ineffable four-letter name of God (YHWH), the Tetragrammaton, is too sacred to be uttered, and the Ten Commandments clearly proscribe images of the deity. As a result, the written word of the Hebrew Bible has taken on enormous significance, and Torah scrolls are the most important objects in a synagogue. Edging this page are quotes from the books of Jeremiah and Psalms which proclaim God's omnipotence.

tablets of stone, was the main object in the Holy of Holies of the Temple in Jerusalem, and Torah scrolls remain the sole truly sacred object in synagogues. Often, in such cases, the inscribed word has become a form of art, attracting the kind of intensity of response that other faiths reserve for images of gods and goddesses. Many of the Muslims who would have viewed the stylized inscriptions in the great mosques will not have been highly literate; the viewing of beautifully rendered Quranic quotations could be just as much a mystical encounter with what was believed to be a beneficial and talismanic divine text as it was a reading of a specific and comprehensible message.

There is no necessary contradiction between an art of the word and an art of the image. In many traditions the two coexist. Chinese culture, like that of Islam, has made calligraphy into one of the most significant of art forms. Inscriptions are commonplace in Chinese temples, and are seen in sacred parts of the landscape, such as on Mount Tai in Shandong, where emperors left epigraphs as part of sacrificial rituals. "Spirit tablets", on which the names of a god or an ancestor are written, are often placed on Chinese altars – for example, in the Confucian tradition at the Temple of Heaven in Beijing and the ancestral temples which dotted the Chinese countryside – and people prostrate themselves before them and provide libations, just as they would to statues in other traditions. Some Buddhist texts when chanted,

● MESSAGES TO HEAVEN

1302–c.1644, TEMPLE OF CONFUCIUS, BEIJING, CHINA

These prayer tablets are inscribed with requests for simple, beneficent interventions such as good health and career success. Calligraphy has often been used in Chinese culture to evoke or communicate with deities, spirits and ancestors.

such as the influential Lotus Sutra, are believed to have the power to progress practitioners towards *buddha*hood, and belief in their efficacy is such that they may also be used as sacred deposits in *stupa*s or placed on the altars of Buddhist temples, such as those of the Nichiren school in Japan. In ancient Egypt, hieroglyphics were phonetic signs and ideographs, and this form of writing was literally a codified art; the Egyptians called it "divine word" because they believed this magical knowledge had been given to them by the god of wisdom, Thoth. Such was its power that it could reach the spirits of dead ancestors and gods alike, and it could even animate items presented as funerary offerings.

Just as a certain abstract power – deriving from their graphic intensity, their complex patterning and their colour schemes – is present in religious images and the geometrical forms seen on and in religious buildings, it can also be present in holy texts, ranging from Christianity's illuminated gospels and Islam's Quranic calligraphy to chanted Buddhist *sutra*s. In Hinduism, the emphasis has been on the spoken word, with certain phrases and individual sounds (*mantra*s) believed to be potent carriers of divine energy. The "seed *mantra*", *om*, is the most sacred of all, the sound of the absolute.

SANCTIFICATION THROUGH BLOODSHED

*c.*725CE, LINTEL 24, STRUCTURE 23, YAXCHILÁN, CHIAPAS, MEXICO

The city-state of Yaxchilán was a significant Maya centre located on the south bank of the Usumacinta River, in what is now Chiapas, southern Mexico. It largely dates to the Classic period (*c.*250–*c.*900CE) and many of the buildings in the city's central plaza are still standing. This limestone lintel, widely recognized as a masterpiece of Mayan art, comes from "structure 23", a temple set on a low mound, which is believed to have been built for King Itzamnaaj Balam II (Shield Jaguar II, reigned 681–742) after a series of military conquests. The position of the load-bearing lintel, above a doorway, made it popular with the Maya as a location to display decorative carving.

The temple was dedicated to Lady K'ab'al Xook (Xok or Xoc), one of the king's wives, during the forty-fifth year of his reign. She is depicted here undergoing a bloodletting ritual, which took place on the Long Count date of 9.13.17.15.12 (the Gregorian calendar's Thursday 28 October 709). The rite may be associated with the anniversary of her husband's accession. As the wives and mothers of rulers, women held positions of power and prestige at court.

Auto-sacrifice – not fatal to those who practised it – was an important part of the duties of the élite in the stratified Mayan society, performed both in private (which may be what is depicted here) and in public, on platforms in an open plaza. Just as the gods had shed their blood – the sacred liquid of life – in order to create the first humans, so it was believed that reciprocal sacrificial acts by Mayan royalty would not only return life to the gods but also help to win their favour, thereby perpetuating life and maintaining order in the cosmos.

❶ King Shield Jaguar II stands over his consort, illuminating her activity by holding a flaming torch. His hair is prepared in a top-piece in the manner of a penitent, which, along with the rope-collar, indicates that he will draw his own blood when his wife has finished. He wears a beaded necklace and a sun god pectoral, wristlets and knee bands, a nosepiece, an elaborate loincloth belt with a quatrefoil representing birth, water and the underworld, and possibly a jaguar pelt and jaguar pelt sandals. She wears a woven pleated cape and jewellery of jade and shell.

❷ The king wears the shrunken head of a sacrificial victim, probably a prisoner of war, which reminds us of his high status as well as his ritual and martial prowess. The taking of captives in war for sacrifice was done partly to provide sustenance to the gods.

▶ LADY XOOK DRAWS HER OWN BLOOD

*c.*725CE, LINTEL 24 FROM THE DOOR OF STRUCTURE 23, YAXCHILÁN, CHIAPAS, MEXICO

With its flattened, stylized depiction of a ritual event, combined with a bold use of inscriptions and bearing traces of the red and blue pigments that once coloured it, this lintel is a fine example of the religious art of the Maya. Some 10cm (4in) thick and measuring 110cm (43in) by 80cm (32in), the work is now in the British Museum, London. Even today, Yaxchilán remains isolated, although it is still visited for religious purposes by local Maya. Lintel 24 is part of a set (with lintels 25 and 26), from above the structure's southeastern, central and western doorways, depicting a series of rituals performed by King Shield Jaguar II and his wife.

❸ Lady Xook kneels before her husband, pulling a thorn-lined rope cord through a hole in her tongue, pierced by using an awl or "perforator". These ropes were also studded with obsidian flakes. Her blood drips into a basket beneath. Men and women auto-sacrificed differently; men pierced their genitals, while women drew blood from their earlobes or tongue.

❹ Lady Xook's headdress is of a type related to war, sacrifice and the high nobility of Teotihuacán. The headpiece was also worn by wrathful Tlaloc, god of war, storms, lightning and fertility, whose image adorns it on the top. Tlaloc was known to the Maya as the rain god Chac. It may be that an act of sacrifice by a royal woman dressed in this way both reaffirmed her dynasty and renewed the ties with a war god who would destroy her husband's enemies.

❺ The basket into which the rope falls contains blood-soaked bark paper and the stingray spine used as an awl to open the wound. For the gods to be able to consume the blood it had to be burned to create smoke.

❻ The first three glyphs of the inscription indicate the date ("5 Eb 15 Mak") and the nature of the event: "it is his image in penance with the fiery spear", which identifies the king as the one holding the torch and tells us that he is also about to let blood.

PEOPLE & SACRED SPACE

A WINDOW ON HISTORY

───────○───────

Religious buildings document history: they stand witness to the beliefs and personalities of the past. From simple, sometimes intimate, halls in which to pray, to grand forums for a richly theatrical liturgy, their designs reveal not only the tenets of a given faith but also its internal hierarchies and ideas about authority.

The most ambitious buildings were often paid for by royal patrons or other wealthy individuals; sometimes, too, entire communities came together to construct a place of worship. The motivation for such generosity can be as much political as pious. Their designers were often anonymous, the chief monument to their genius being the building itself. The armies of artisans who made these ideas into reality often did so in the knowledge that such massive buildings might not be completed in their lifetime. Repeated interventions by different patrons over the decades and centuries mean that religious buildings may be replaced or extended many times, resulting in structures of great complexity which provide us with a window into the history of changing patterns of religious belief.

◀ **A ROYAL TOUR**

1563, *THE TOWER OF BABEL*, PIETER BREUGHEL THE ELDER

The Tower of Babel was a Mesopotamian ziggurat, but Breughel has reimagined it as a sixteenth-century building site. The king tours his works (their design partly modelled on Roman ruins) accompanied by his court and a master mason; all around can be seen the vast labour force required for such vainglorious projects.

RITUAL & PERFORMANCE

It is the prime function of most religious buildings to provide a venue for acts of worship. Indeed, their very construction has a ritual element, for in many faiths the selection of the site, the laying of the foundation stone or the consecration upon completion were liturgical events. Yet religious rituals in general can differ enormously, from the very simple to the very elaborate.

Sacred theatricality

Worship in a mosque is marked by the coordinated rise and fall of a large congregation, led by an *imam*, praying in unison, five times a day, with a sermon on Fridays. The architecture creates a large space in which worshippers can gather as well as ensuring that the *imam* is visible from most parts of the building. By contrast, the Catholic Church historically had a full liturgy that took up eight or nine hours a day, was especially rich on Sundays and other holy days, and took place whether or not any lay devotees were present. The Eucharist had to be performed at the high altar and also at any side chapels – of which there might be a dozen or more – and each such service involved a sensory assault of sounds, sights, scents and actions.

The complex arrangement of spaces in the east end of many larger Christian churches was therefore designed to enhance their role as the setting for a particularly theatrical liturgy. Historically, in many Catholic cathedrals and monastic churches this space was subdivided, so that the choir, where up to sixty monks might have chanted or sung, precedes the presbytery or sanctuary, where the high altar stood. Both spaces were screened off from the side aisles and from the western part of the building.

This general arrangement is comparable to that seen in another faith with an elaborate liturgy – that of ancient Egypt, where the hypostyle hall, the largest roofed space in a temple, was used primarily for rituals and as a processional route for the priests as they approached the sanctuary.

In churches and Egyptian temples alike, the sanctuary, and the image or altar associated with it, was the main focus of liturgical activity. What that area, which is often small, actually contains may vary greatly: in Islam, the *mihrab* is simply an empty niche that acts as a focus for prayer. Here, few other fittings are necessary, though an elaborate *minbar*, or pulpit, and *maqsura*, or royal pew, may stand nearby. The elaborate liturgies of the Christian church, by contrast, filled the sanctuary with a constantly developing range of fittings: elaborate screens such as the Greek Orthodox *iconostasis* might render activities at the altar almost invisible; special seats were used by those officiating at the mass, such as the stone sedilia seen in many churches in England. The consecrated bread and wine used for the Eucharist were especially sacred and were set aside or "reserved" in a special structure often called a tabernacle, after the tent of early Judaism where the presence of God himself resided. In the Greek Orthodox tradition these are often small metal models of a church; in medieval, Catholic, Germany they became magnificent stone fittings, like small spires, known as *sakramentshäuser*.

◑ DAWN PRAYERS AT NEW YEAR
SERTANG MONASTERY, SICHUAN/GANSU, CHINA

Tibetans gather to watch monks of the Gelugpa order unfurl a giant image of the Buddha during the Monlam prayer festival, enacting a spatial distinction betwen congregants and celebrants.

◐ FROM DARKNESS INTO LIGHT

FROM 1220, SALISBURY CATHEDRAL, WILTSHIRE, ENGLAND

For Christians, Christmas and Easter are the two most sacred festivals of the year. The season begins at least a month before Christmas itself, a period known as Advent (or the Nativity Fast in the Orthodox Church). Here, at Salisbury cathedral, to mark the start of 2001's season of preparation and anticipation, 1,300 candles were carried in a grand procession which moved around the entire church, watched by a large congregation.

Such fittings were part of a rich array of ways in which the events in a sanctuary were given special intensity: it is impossible to fully appreciate the architecture of most such spaces without factoring in the wearing of special clothes by the celebrants, the use of elaborate liturgical implements, the chanting or singing of sacred compositions, the lighting and scents that created a distinctive atmosphere and enriched the performance further, and the elaborately prescribed movements of the rituals themselves. One particularly widespread practice – procession – had a marked effect on architecture.

Procession

Sacred journeys, or pilgrimages, are major features of many faiths, from the Muslim *hajj* to Buddhist and Hindu journeys to such holy mountains as Mount Kailash (Kailas or Kailasa) in Tibet. Although places of worship may be located along such routes, and be clustered around the ultimate destination, the form of these buildings is not usually in itself very different from that of other such buildings. Exceptions include the Ka'ba at Mecca (see page 144), a unique structure that is the central focal point of all Islamic worship.

The more organized liturgical practice of procession is effectively a subset of such pilgrimages. It is found in many traditions, and the requirement to make space for it and to aggrandize or sacralize its paths has had a major impact on sacred architecture. Procession was often a way in which ordinary people could participate in intensely communal religious experiences. This is especially true of those processions that were held outdoors. Holy imagery is carried through the streets in Hindu, Shinto and Christian festival processions. Permanent way stations for the idols, such as the barque chapels of ancient Egypt or freestanding Hindu *mandapa*,

may be positioned along the route. Ancient Egyptian processions, like those of ancient China and Buddhist Cambodia, were more exclusive affairs, although some were witnessed by large crowds. In these places the processional route was sometimes flanked by avenues of stone creatures – an idea echoed in the uncarved standing stones which line the approach to the great monuments of Neolithic Europe, and the *sacbe* ("white ways") that led to temples in Mayan cities. The events which passed along such routes could be dramatic: when 100 sheep and cows were driven by Athenians down the Via Sacra of the city and onto their acropolis for the New Year Panathenaia (see pages 88–89), it must have been quite a spectacle. Such routes played a fundamental role in the layout of cities: in ancient Babylon and China, the most important road in the capital city appears to have been designed at least partly as the setting for an annual procession by the emperor, an event of the highest significance (see box, page 73).

Even more structured and exclusive liturgical processions might take place within places of worship, marking out an exclusive kind of route inside and around the architecture

⬥ CHARIOTS OF THE GODS

MEENAKSHI AMMAN TEMPLE, MADURAI, TAMIL NADU, INDIA

Elaborate models of places of worship often house sacred images taken on outdoor processions. One such tops the chariot (*ratha*) carrying Meenakshi (Parvati) and Sunderaswarar (Shiva) during the month-long celebration of their marriage at Madurai temple-city.

itself, and explaining much about the design of Egyptian hypostyle halls and church naves, façades, cloisters and ambulatory aisles. The latter, for example, ensured churchmen in solemn liturgical procession could pass behind the high altar and sprinkle holy water on the side altars of the building; they also often allowed lay pilgrims to reach the church's shrine. Naves are today largely associated with lay activity, but they were once used, and sometimes still are, for formal processions. In the early Christian era, only the aisles that run alongside these naves were generally open to congregants. Some medieval church naves had the starting positions of the procession itself marked into their floor.

Circumambulation, or ritualized meditative walking, is a related activity, if rather less formalized than procession itself. In Hinduism it is called Parikrama, or Pradakshina, and is one of the reasons Hindu temples, like Christian churches, often have ambulatory aisles running behind the sanctuary or *garbhagriha*, as at the Kandariya Mahadeo in Khajuraho (early eleventh century). Circumambulation has had a profound influence on Buddhist sacred buildings. Often accompanied by ritual chanting, this technique helps to assist the soul in its progress towards enlightenment. The ambulatory aisle of the early Buddhist *chaitya* hall, and the fences and platforms that surrounded *stupa*s such as Sanchi, are used in this way (see pages 168–169), as are the routes that climb Borobudur in Java and pagodas such as Foguangsi in Shanxi, China. Circumambulation blurs the boundaries between its participants: all Islam is united by the *hajj* pilgrimage, of which circumambulation of the Ka'ba is a chief goal. However, other ways in which devotional behaviour shaped architecture served to enhance the separation of sacred areas from other parts of the building, while at the same time making special provision for large gatherings of lay devotees – something that particularly affected the architecture of those faiths that demanded acts of congregation.

Congregation

Many of the religious buildings featured in this book combine a small and select sanctuary, the focus of liturgical activities, with a larger associated space where ordinary people can witness these events. Only occasionally, however, does the presence of a group of such lay people play an essential role in the rites themselves. A large number of spaces, from the areas around the pylons of Egyptian temples (and possibly the courtyards beyond) to the plazas of the ancient Americas, appear to have been designed at least partly with the presence of large crowds in mind, but the rites would presumably have continued whether or not anyone came to see them. In Hinduism, those services that offer *darsana* or a devotional view of and interaction with the deity in the *garbhagriha* are popular with lay devotees, and the *mandapa*, like a church nave, is there for them to occupy, but the rites will still take place whether they are present or not. In this respect, the theatres built for the Dionysiac rituals of ancient Greece are something new: early drama would have been pointless, and the theatres functionless, without an audience. Much later, and less focused on a specific ritual, large and freestanding "hundred-pillared" *mandapa* were built in some Indian temples, in which religious dance and drama might be performed before a large crowd.

However, Judaism, Christianity and Islam are the faiths in which regular acts of congregation are considered obligatory – effectively, on the Sabbath day, an extension of the liturgy. Congregants themselves are expected to chant or sing, to pray, stand, sit or genuflect at specified moments. These faiths have made the creation of large spaces for mass gatherings a defining feature of their places of worship.

Originating with the synagogue (although the approximately contemporary Buddhist *chaitya* hall is also a kind of congregational space, probably focused more on monks than on the lay community), the idea of people gathering was to define much about the appearance of both churches and mosques, leading to the creation of massive and enveloping internal spaces that are among the most impressive achievements of religious architecture. Such spaces might be further demarcated, although practice here varied greatly. In several religions, men and women sat apart – this was the function of special galleries in some synagogues and mosques, or it was achieved simply by positioning the two genders on opposite sides of the main space, as in some synagogues and early churches. Separation and hierarchy, in many traditions, go hand in hand.

A SERMON IN STONE

c.1220–c.1240, WELLS CATHEDRAL, SOMERSET, ENGLAND

The west front of Wells cathedral was completed in the early thirteenth century, perhaps to a design by a stonemason called Adam Lock (who died in 1229), and it holds the biggest display of medieval statuary in Europe: 127 out of an original 176 figures survive, many larger than life-size. Most were once brightly painted, with even the patterns on their clothing picked out. The vividness of this gathering must have been an extraordinary sight.

This stone screen dominates the approach to the cathedral, but its form bears little relation to that of the church behind, and it may not have been designed for the towers (added in *c.*1392 and *c.*1425–1436). Although some statues were destroyed in iconoclasms of the 1540s and 1650s, most remain in place.

When Christ's triumphal entry into Jerusalem is celebrated on Palm Sunday (see below), the façade represents the walls of the city. The statues lay out the biblical story, from the creation to the Last Judgment, and provide a vision of eternity. Their magnificent architectural setting ensures that the church appears like the biblical "new Jerusalem, coming down out of heaven from God, prepared as a bride beautifully dressed for her husband" (Revelation 21:2).

▼ WEST FRONT

c.1220–c.1240, WELLS CATHEDRAL, SOMERSET, ENGLAND

The colourful sculpture on the 30m-high (99ft) west front turned the church into an earthly embodiment of the Heavenly Jerusalem. The façade consists of a series of zones: a lower horizontal register containing **Ⓐ** the quatrefoils of the Old Testament and **Ⓑ** the quatrefoils of the New Testament; a central horizontal register **Ⓒ** that was a grand gathering of sacred and royal figures, including many who were either nationally important or particularly relevant to Wells, which brought the story up to the present and made it local; and an upper area **Ⓓ** where the end of time, the Last Judgment and the general resurrection are topped by a Christ in Majesty. Beginning beneath, and rising vertically through the centre, is a zone **Ⓔ** that marks Christ's role, and that of his mother, Mary, in uniting humanity with the divine and history with eternity.

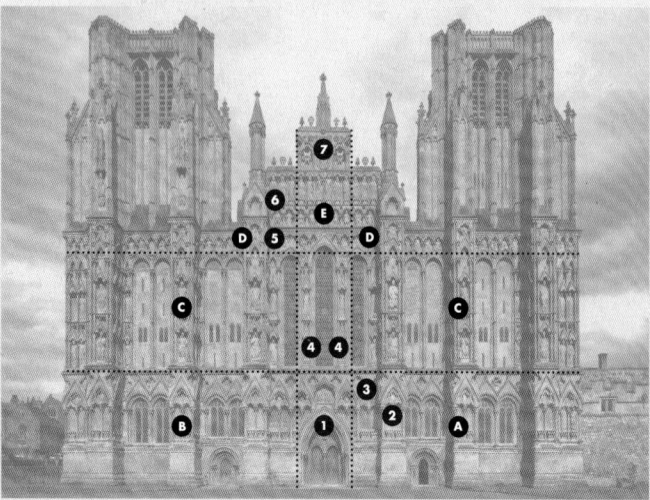

❶ The central door of the west front was only opened for major events, including visits by the bishop or the king and the Palm Sunday ritual. On this day a procession of churchmen formed up in the graveyard outside the front and then approached the door carrying a consecrated Eucharistic host, symbolizing Christ. Upon reaching the door, they requested entry to the church. Above the door is a (once brightly painted) statue of the Virgin Mary holding Christ; gilt-bronze stars, now lost, were set into the stonework. Directly above this is a statue of the Virgin Mary being crowned Queen of Heaven by Christ; originally both figures had glistening metal halos above their heads and suns and moons were positioned around them.

❷ A row of angels stretches along the lowest level of the west front. Hidden behind many of them are porthole-like openings, which can be accessed through a passage in the interior. When the procession of churchmen requested entry, a concealed choir would have replied with the hymn "Gloria, laus et honor", making the angels seem to come to life: "The company of Angels are praising Thee on high...."

❸ Above the angels is a series of scenes depicting the key events from the beginning of the world – such as God's creation of Adam, the first man – to the resurrection and the ascension of Christ into heaven.

4 The central area is flanked by Solomon and the Queen of Sheba. The Old Testament couple became emblematic of the union of Christ and his Church – an anointed one and those who submit to the Messiah. Her visit foreshadows the Adoration of the Magi.

5 The upper register in the centre depicts the resurrection of the dead, which will take place at the end of time, when Christ will return. Medieval observers would have noticed that immediately in front of the façade was an area set aside as a graveyard.

6 The figures in the gable depict the eternal heaven. The apostles are depicted there. Andrew, to whom Wells is dedicated, holds the saltire cross on which he was martyred. Beneath are angels and portholes for trumpet blasts. The gable's proportions are a scaled-down version of the front as a whole.

7 At the top is a robed Christ in Majesty, with angels known as Seraphim on either side. (The traditional hierarchy of angels consists of three groups of three; the Seraphim are among those particularly close to God.) In 1985 a new image of Christ was sculpted by David Wynne to replace the damaged original.

ACCESS & HIERARCHY

Hierarchies within religious buildings are often expressed by the nesting of spaces within, from holy areas with wide public access to parts that are sacred, which few may approach. Who those few people are varies from one faith to another. In many societies, priestly authority and political power went hand in hand because both were seen as divinely ordained. As a result there are many links between sacred spaces and spaces associated with kingship.

Religion and hierarchy

Few religions have created architecture without implied hierarchical relationships. Buddhist temples, which can seem to host an undifferentiated flow of worshippers, often set aside some halls for monastic activity, at least for periods of the day, while esoteric Vajrayana Buddhism has some highly exclusive temple spaces. Even Nonconformist Christian groups such as the Quakers, who reject religious hierarchies, sometimes have an elders' bench set aside in their simple meeting houses. The egalitarian nature of Sunni Islam is expressed by the *hajj*, the great pilgrimage to Mecca, in which the entire global community of the faithful is united in an experience that emphasizes its unity before God. Nevertheless, mosque design has been hugely influenced by the authority accorded to caliphs and *imam*s.

Nested spaces

The main requirement of those who approach the place of worship is usually that they are ritually clean. Washing facilities may lie just outside or inside the enclosure, as with the elaborate water tanks of Hindu temples or the sacred lakes in ancient Egypt. Holy water stoups, in which one dips one's fingers and makes the sign of the cross, stand in or near the porch of Catholic churches. Ritual ablutions are a vital part of preparation for Islamic prayer, and the mosque courtyard often contains a washing place or fountain-house.

In churches, priests or monks and lay people often had separate entrances, and some portals were used only by kings, bishops or abbots, or for key liturgical events. The nave beyond was open to anyone, but the visual focus on the screened-off sanctuary to the east was unmistakable. The *mandapa* of a Hindu temple likewise exists primarily for lay devotees to partake in *puja*, and is visually dominated by the sanctuary beyond.

Priesthood and power

The extent of the exclusiveness accorded the sanctuary generally reflects a faith's ideas about religious authority. In many cultures the priesthood is an élite, set apart from others: Catholic priests are celibate; Hindu Brahmins belong to a special caste. The architecture tends to separate the sanctuary from the rest of the building through the use of screens, doors or subsidiary spaces.

Islam's *imam*s and Judaism's rabbis are more like respected members of the community than a class apart. Spatial

◖ KINGS AND SAINTS
FROM *c*.1246, WESTMINSTER ABBEY, LONDON, ENGLAND

Westminster Abbey was built to be the place of coronation and burial of the English kings, and its most sacred area was the feretory, where the royal tombs clustered around that of their saintly predecessor, Edward the Confessor, in an enclosure behind the high altar.

◖ POWER OF THE WORD

1609–1616, SULTAN AHMED I MOSQUE, ISTANBUL, TURKEY

The prominence given to the *minbar*, from which prayers are led and Friday sermons preached, positioned adjacent to the *mihrab*, the focus for prayer, is a reflection of the significance in Islam of the Quranic word. It also reflects the fact that the early *imam*s were often caliphs, holders of political as well as religious power.

hierarchies – the demarcation of the *bimah* and Holy Ark from the rest of a synagogue, or the *minbar* and *mihrab* bay from the mosque prayer hall – arguably tend to emphasize visibility and access over occlusion and exclusion.

The underlying idea of hierarchy is intimately linked to that of authority. The axial plan, so common an arrangement in sacred buildings, might even be said to be inherently hierarchical, for it encourages gatherings of people to look towards one end of a building, where they are faced with a visual focus – usually an image or a ritual – and a smaller, more select group of people.

Divine kings

This association of axial buildings with power is sometimes implicitly political. This is particularly obvious in the adoption of the basilica – a secular building type deeply associated with imperial power – for the first Christian churches, from about 312CE. The first *imam*s were also political rulers, or caliphs, which helps to explain the long association between the *mihrab* bay and its *maqsura* royal pew. In many traditions, kingship was seen as a kind of priesthood or even as a deified

role in itself. A city's royal palace and major place of worship are often adjacent to one another, as in Mesopotamia at Eshnunna (Tell Asmar in Iraq), at Abbasid-era Baghdad, and in the Christian tradition at (to take just two examples) Hagia Sophia (see pages 60–61) and Charlemagne's Aachen. In some cases, as in the Escorial in Spain (1563) and the Potala Palace (from 1645) in Tibet, it is hard to distinguish palace from monastery; and palaces such as the Forbidden City in Beijing (1420) were centres of sacral as well as political power. Beliefs about royal power explain the very existence of some places of worship, from ancient Egypt to medieval Europe, where Reims cathedral and Westminster Abbey were purpose-built as coronation venues. In imperial China the open-air altar was constructed specifically for the conduct of ceremonies in which the emperor was the fulcrum between humanity and the divine; ordinary people were not permitted access.

When many of these rulers – from Egypt to Angkor – built temples, they were not simply displaying their earthly power and wealth: such men were living gods, performing their sacred obligations.

PATRONS, POWER & PIETY

The grandest buildings were usually paid for by the rich and powerful, from monarchs to wealthy religious institutions. Their motives often seem to have been as much political as spiritual. Emperors such as Constantine (reigned 306–337) in Rome or Shomu (reigned 724–756) in Nara, Japan, used religion as a branch of state-building, and they created colossal structures as symbolic or actual headquarters for their chosen faiths, including the old St. Peter's Basilica (from 324) and the Todaiji Buddhist temple in Nara (745–749).

Institutional inspiration

Both Buddhism and Christianity developed wealthy independent institutions, such as the monasteries, the leaders of which proved to be more than capable of carrying out their own ambitious architectural plans. Such an institution was often endowed with land, enabling it to draw a perpetual income from its holdings. Once set up it was effectively independent. The temples at Angkor owned 3,140 villages and supported 2,740 officials, 2,002 assistants and 615 dancing girls, which suggests they could also fund the maintenance

of buildings. The building of many European cathedrals was largely funded by the bishop and his senior priests living on site, who in the case of the construction of Exeter's cathedral all agreed to donate half of their incomes to the project.

In faiths that lacked a strong internal institutional structure, such as Hinduism and Islam, the finances to build a temple or mosque usually came directly from a pious local ruler or a wealthy and devout layperson, whether male or female. The act of doing so was a way of acquiring religious merit. However, the funds themselves often came in the form of an endowment that created a permanent source of income to the temple or mosque concerned. In Islam, these were controlled by a legal practice known as *waqf*: in some areas, such as the Maghreb, the predominant legal schools specified that, in general, only rulers could make *waqf* endowments. *Waqf* had a direct impact on architecture: for example, a *waqf* designated as a family trust was able to supply an income to one's descendants in addition to that invested in the new mosque, *madrasa*, Sufi convent or other charitable foundation. The result was that each succeeding generation had a strong motive to create new *waqf*s, as much a way of leaving a legacy to their descendants as anything else. The density of religious foundations in Cairo during the Mamluk era (1250–1517) is partly explained by this.

Lay piety and building

The historical contribution made by ordinary devotees to the funding of grand religious architectural projects can be harder to assess. This is partly because, except on rare occasions, we lack information. It certainly occurred. The names of countless merchants are inscribed on the walls of early Buddhist *stupa*s, and medieval French chronicles suggest

◖ THE PATRON GIVES A CHURCH
1303, ARENA CHAPEL, PADUA, ITALY

The banker Enrico Scrovegni built, next to his palace, a chapel decorated by the painter Giotto (*c.*1270–1337). In a mural inside this chapel Scrovegni (left) is depicted, as was typical of medieval patrons, presenting the chapel to its dedicatees (probably John the Evangelist, the Virgin Mary and Mary Magdalene).

that an early Gothic cathedral such as Chartres was partly funded by local donations of labour, goods or cash – for example, from craft guilds. These buildings were extraordinarily expensive. King Henry III of England spent about £42,000 on building Westminster Abbey between about 1246 and 1272, when his annual income had been around £35,000. Therefore, it may have been only on exceptional occasions that the funds gathered from lay donations were significant enough to have a real impact on the budget for a major building.

When this did happen it may have been because a deep-seated religious revival or local cult had flourished: offerings to the tomb of King Edward II of England, popularly acclaimed as a saint, are said to have helped fund the rebuilding of the east end of Gloucester cathedral. Alternatively, a fund may accrue incrementally over a very long period of time, reflecting the deep sanctity accorded a specific place. Many centuries of small endowments have turned southern

◐ PIOUS FOUNDATIONS

1356 ONWARDS, MOSQUES AND A *MADRASA*, CAIRO, EGYPT

For Muslims, the giving of alms is a religious obligation. In Cairo the result over time has been a plethora of patrons and magnificent structures whose domes and minarets fill the city's skyline. Shown here are (foreground) Qanibay Amir Akhur *madrasa* (1503–1504), (background, right) al-Rifa'i mosque (1869–1912) and (background, left) the Sultan Hassan mosque-mausoleum (1356–1362).

Indian temple-cities such as Tirumala Venkateswara, Andhra Pradesh, into institutions of enormous wealth. In all these cases, the donors may have affected the decoration of a building – the guilds of medieval Chartres feature in a series of stained-glass windows at the cathedral there – but they are unlikely to have been able to influence the architecture.

Civic pride and public subscription

Communal piety becomes civic pride when an urban corporation is able to fund building works. The cathedral at

◀ **MODEL FOR PILGRIMS**
PROBABLY SIXTH/SEVENTH
CENTURY ONWARDS,
MAHABODHI TEMPLE,
BODH GAYA, BIHAR, INDIA

The Mahabodhi temple, marking
the spot where the Buddha
attained enlightenment, is the
most sacred place in Buddhism.
Rebuilt and refurbished many
times thanks to centuries of
donations, its form – in which
four smaller *sikhara* spires cluster
around a larger one, in imitation
of Mount Meru (Sumeru) – was
copied in many parts of Asia
by pilgrims after they had
returned home.

Florence was funded by the *opera* ("works"). The emergence of such organizations, whose members were wealthy merchants and bankers rather than lords and princes, enabled a new class of people to be directly engaged in the design of major works of religious architecture. Their willingness to fund the innovative work of Brunelleschi, who effectively invented Italian Renaissance architecture single-handed, suggests considerable self-confidence, as well as a desire to ensure that their city kept pace with the achievements of rival city-states nearby, such as that of Siena.

Groups of relatively low-status individuals were more likely to fund smaller-scale architecture. We know from the inscriptions on the mosaic floors of early synagogues that they were paid for by the community and the rabbi together (see pages 106–107). Many Shinto temples, like Chinese Taoist temples, are run by organizations of local people and priests; while imperial or civic permission might have been required to build, it would not be difficult for such groups to initiate or fund construction.

Even so, the lion's share of grand architectural initiatives was almost certainly taken by those who were both rich and powerful. Although the social and political effects of religion have often been to legitimate and promote the status quo, it does not necessarily follow that such patrons were cynical or calculating in their motivations. Many were genuinely pious individuals, who really believed that their fate, and often also that of their people, depended on their being personally in favour with the gods, and that architecture was one of the best ways of securing that divine beneficence. This sense of sacred obligation, a desire to act to glorify God, is arguably the deepest motivating force in the story of religious architecture, touching pharaoh and pilgrim alike.

ARTISTS & CRAFTSMEN

The construction of a great building was an extraordinary project. A site had to be levelled, stone quarried, transported and carved, and the building erected. The craft skills were of the highest order, and the labour involved was immense. All this was done with little mechanical help: astonishingly, the architecture of the pre-Columbian Americas was created without the use of metal tools, with which to cut stone, or wheeled transport.

The craftsmen involved were rarely accorded much status and their names are seldom known. In India, knowledge and skills were handed on from father to son. In ancient Egypt, craftsmen were closely tied to the temple that employed them. A town of such men was established at Deir el-Medina near the Valley of the Kings at Thebes, and its remains have provided an insight into their lives.

Certain skills might be valued more highly: the names of calligraphers are often recorded on mosque walls. Sculptors during India's Gupta era (*c.*320–*c.*550) seem to have been highly respected. Although the building's designer might be seen as little more than a particularly skilled craftsman, as was the case in ancient China, generally such men were accorded more status. Brahmin priests designed Hindu temples, even if the construction was carried out by men of many castes. It is not until the fourteenth century that we have anything more than a few names for the master masons who created the great cathedrals of Europe, but we know such men had considerable status. Nevertheless, it is only with the Renaissance

that the standing of the architect began to approach its modern level. Before that point, the whole idea of who "created" a particular work might be different from that which we are familiar with today.

Across cultures, surviving records usually tell us that a king or other patron "built" a given work, while the designer is anonymous. This is partly a reflection of the nature of the creative process. The patron might shape the underlying concept for a building. It has been argued that the use of light at St. Denis abbey (from 1140), in Paris, was inspired by the theological ideas of the abbot, Suger, while Borobudur (*c.*780–*c.*850; see pages 178–179) could not have been designed without the input of someone with a deep understanding of Buddhist cosmological and philosophical ideas.

The designer's talent lay partly in his ability to translate such thinking into architecture. Occasionally such men were themselves high-status individuals: like the scientist-mathematicians Anthemius of Tralles and Isodorus of Miletus, designers of Hagia Sophia, or the pharaonic official Imhotep of Egypt (*c.*2600BCE), the first named architect in history. More commonly, a patron might favour a particular designer: the Timurid empress Gawhar Shad employed Qavam al-Din Shirazi to design mosques in Mashhad, Iran (see pages 142–143), and Herat, Afghanistan.

Today these incredible buildings, and the many lifetimes over which they were constructed, stand as eternal monuments to societies in which religion played a central role.

◐ AZTEC CHRISTIAN ART

*c.*1753, SAN FRANCISCO JAVIER CHURCH, TEPOTZOTLÁN, MEXICO

Much religious imagery in the post-conquest Americas was created by indigenous craftsmen, whose faith contained significant traces of the pre-Christian past. The resulting art is aesthetically, and sometimes iconographically, distinctive. This angel, within the Loreto chapel of the Jesuit church of San Francisco Javier (1670–1682), is surrounded by cherubs as well as the sun, moon and stars, celestial objects of especial interest to local indigenous peoples. Elsewhere in the world, craftsmen went where the work took them, and some Christian craftsmen almost certainly helped to build the great mosques of the Umayyad Middle East, just as Hindu builders in India wrote *shastras* (treatises) on mosque design.

CHURNING THE OCEAN OF MILK

AFTER 1113, ANGKOR WAT, CAMBODIA

Angkor was the capital of the Khmer empire and from the ninth century onwards vast temple complexes were built there by a series of rulers who probably regarded themselves as semi-divine. The largest is Angkor Wat (the "capital which is a temple"). It was commissioned by the Hindu Suryavarman II (reigned 1113–c.1150), who was unusual among Khmer kings for being a devotee of Vishnu rather than Shiva.

The main, eastern entrance of the temple proper is set within a wall 202m by 114m (663ft by 374ft) long known as the third enclosure, the galleries of which contain 700m (2,300ft) of bas-reliefs 2m (7ft) high. The main themes are the struggle between good and evil, and the military and heroic deeds of Vishnu. One 90m (295ft) relief shows Suryavarman II as a divine king, surrounded by his court. It is possible that the temple was seen as a palatial residence for both Vishnu and the spirit of the dead king (Paramavishnuloka, or "the dweller in the house of Vishnu", as he was to be called in the afterlife). The reliefs were designed to be circumambulated anti-clockwise and may have been used in funeral rituals.

⬤ ANGKOR WAT COMPLEX

AFTER 1113, ANGKOR, CAMBODIA

An enormous rectilinear moat – 1,500m by 1,300m (4,922ft by 4,265ft) – enclosing the Angkor structure may symbolize the cosmic waters that surrounded the world. Set on a 1.4m (5ft) platform, the three nested enclosures of the temple climb to where the five *sikhara* spires stand – as peaks of Mount Meru. The highest, which probably contained a 4m-tall (13ft) statue of Vishnu, is 58m (190ft) above ground level. A well directly beneath, plunging 23m (75ft) underground, contained a sacred foundation deposit of gold, pure white sand and sapphire.

❶ This is an act of creation, carried out by forces of good and evil. Vishnu persuades the multi-headed chief *asura* demon and his followers to work with benign *deva*s to create *amrita*, the elixir of immortality. He then goes on (not shown) to upend Mount Mandara and use it to churn the cosmic sea.

❷ Vasuki, the world snake, lies beneath the waters. He is about to agree to be used as a rope, which will be wrapped around the divine mountain. There are versions of this story in both the great Hindu epics, the *Ramayana* and the *Mahabharata*, as well as in the Puranas ("stories of the ancient past").

❸ Vasuki is now being gripped and pulled in turn by the *asura*s and *deva*s. He expects to receive some of the *amrita* as a reward.

❹ As the cosmic ocean of milk churns, a crowd of ravishing heavenly beings known as *apsara*s is created and they soar upwards to the sky as they dance for the entertainment of the gods. The churning would also create Lakshmi, the female counterpart, or *shakti*, of Vishnu.

5 The ninety-two lesser *asura*s have demonic faces, matched at the other end of the 47m-long (154ft) relief by the angelic faces of the *deva*s (not visible here). This story is carved at least three times, albeit on a smaller scale, elsewhere at Angkor Wat, partly reflecting the primordial significance of the snake in Khmer culture. The relief faces east and the sunrise, source of life.

6 Fish and strange animals are squashed together as the ocean churns; they are being thrown about ever more violently as the story moves right, towards the upended mountain.

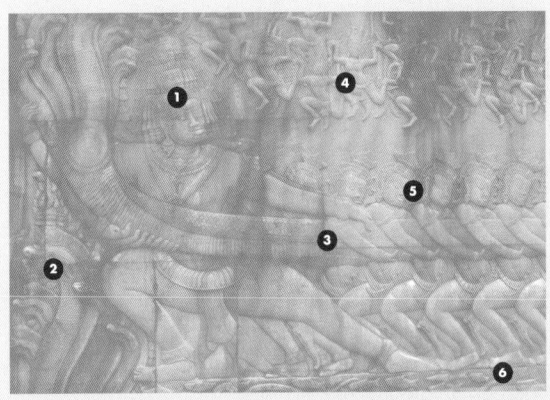

CHANGE OVER TIME

Great places of worship can be complex structures, enlarged and rebuilt many times over a long period. The Mayan and Aztec temple-pyramids were often enlarged by successive rulers simply adding an extra layer to the building, leaving the earlier structure nested inside. In 1978, archaeologists in Mexico City investigating the Great Temple at Tenochtitlán discovered seven older temples, stretching back to the early 1300s, within its structure. By contrast, the Khmer kings did not merely build themselves grand mortuary temples, they rebuilt their entire city at the same time. Angkor is thus only the most recent of three successive capitals on approximately the same site. While their temples stand to this day, the rest of the city is largely discernible only by archaeology.

These patterns of change are sometimes almost invisible. Because architectural style there has changed little and the buildings themselves are of wood, a temple in East Asia can be extended in a manner that is almost seamless. At the other extreme, the rapid stylistic evolution seen in the churches of western Europe from the eleventh century onwards has resulted in the survival of many churches that are visibly the work of different eras. Often, areas such as crypts – as with the ninth- and eleventh-century example beneath Chartres cathedral (from 1194) – are particularly ancient. Some mosques, such as the Friday mosque at Isfahan, Iran, also have this multiphase character.

Careful study of such building patterns can reveal much about the history of a religion itself. At Karnak, the temple built by the reforming pharaoh Akhenaten (reigned 1353–1337BCE), who attempted to introduce a kind of monotheism, was taken down by his successors. His work is a missing link in the complex story of the Great Temple (see pages 79–81), which is otherwise the cumulative result of centuries, even millennia, of addition and expansion by a series of pharaohs.

Sometimes a deliberate attempt is made to indicate continuity with the sacred spaces of the past, as in the large, closely fitted, "Cyclopean" stone blocks of the Mycenaean (c.1500–c.1200BCE) walls, which were kept, highly visible, among the buildings of the sixth century BCE at Delphi and the Athenian Acropolis. In other circumstances, the places of worship of a rival faith are deliberately destroyed: the churches of the conquistadors often sit on the foundations of pre-Columbian temples, and Sultan Mahmud of the Ghaznavid empire is said in 1024 to have had a broken *linga* altar from a Hindu temple transported to Arabia so that its stones could flag the roads to Mecca and Medina, and be trodden underfoot by pilgrims. However, even Christianity

▼ RITUAL REBUILDING

1929, SHIKINEN SENGU CEREMONY, ISE NAIKU, MIE, JAPAN

The artist Wakanari Takatori (1867–1935) painted twelve scrolls depicting the fifty-eighth rebuilding ritual (*sengu*) at Ise. In this image, the sacred symbol of the goddess Amaterasu is transferred to the new temple. For the previous twenty years, its site has been an enclosure containing only an expanse of white gravel and a pole of white cypress, the "sacred central post", kept in a small hut (*oi-ya*).

⏺ LAYERS OF HOLINESS

AFTER 1391BCE, TEMPLE OF AMUN, LUXOR, EGYPT

Major changes were made to the Temple of Amun under Amenhotep III (reigned 1391–1353BCE), Ramesses II (reigned 1279–1213BCE), and even Alexander the Great (ruled 332–323BCE). From the fourth century CE it was reused as a Roman military camp; from the sixth century, several churches were built within its walls. Finally in the thirteenth century the mosque of Abu el-Haggag was constructed, and it still functions today.

and Islam often seem to incorporate the power of pagan holy places. Pope Gregory I (590–604) famously instructed the missionaries he had sent to England under Augustine to re-dedicate rather than destroy the pagan holy places they found there. The Ka'ba at Mecca was for many centuries partly a pagan place of worship. Such situations can be complex: when the entrances to the Neolithic long barrow at West Kennet in England were sealed up with massive stones and the great stone circles constructed nearby (see pages 68–69), the effect might have been as much to increase the sacredness of the barrow as to close it forever. Such acts, even when they were intended to mark a radical change in religious practice, can deepen the continuity of sanctity accorded a particular sanctuary, and enrich the holiness of a particular spot on the Earth's surface.

In some cases, the very process of building and expansion may have been a kind of rite. The Naiku, or Inner Shrine, at Ise in Japan has been re-created almost every twenty years since 685, to preserve its sacral cleanliness. The construction process has become a ritual called the *sengu*, with specific instructions for each stage, and the craftsmen effectively make up a carpenter-priesthood clad in white: even their hammering is a kind of ritual. The result is the existence side by side of two sites at once: the temple itself, and the empty site – the *kodenchi* – that hosted the previous shrine and will house its successor. At Ise, processes of destruction and renewal, often a side-effect of the creation of religious buildings, have themselves become a sacred act.

THE "GREAT CHURCH"

532–537 AND LATER, HAGIA SOPHIA, CONSTANTINOPLE (ISTANBUL), TURKEY

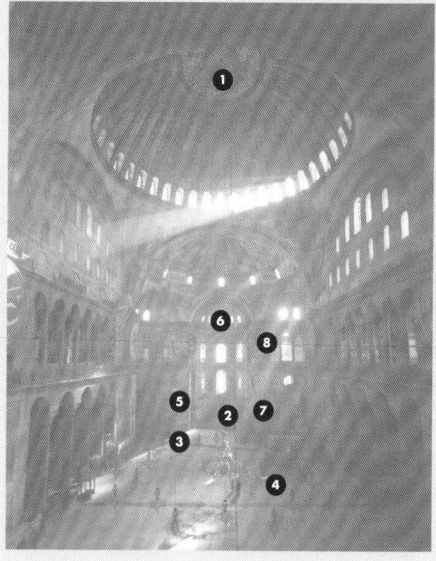

In 360 a cathedral in Constantinople was dedicated to Hagia Sophia, or Holy Wisdom, a metaphor for the Virgin Mary. The Eastern Church's liturgy promoted the emperor and patriarch as "two halves of God". When the building was destroyed by rioters in 532, Emperor Justinian replaced it with a domed building of a scale hitherto unmatched in Christendom. This defining achievement of Byzantine architecture was known for centuries as the "Great Church". When the city fell to Mehmed II in 1453, the sultan made the church into a Friday mosque, Ayasofya. With the Ottoman emperors claiming religious authority throughout Islam, many of the building's imperial and religious associations remained intact, and its significance was enriched by the presence of precious relics of Muhammad.

Hagia Sophia's rich furnishings were swept away, to be replaced with the plainer Islamic *mihrab* and *minbar*, but the Christian mosaics were only gradually replaced with whitewashed walls and Islamic quotations. The mausoleum of Selim II (reigned 1566–1574) was added to the complex, as were four minarets, in stages.

▼ HAGIA SOPHIA

532–537 AND LATER, CONSTANTINOPLE (ISTANBUL), TURKEY

Hagia Sophia is approached through a grand narthex or entrance corridor **A**. Inside, the vast nave **B**, which had primarily been the setting for ritual, from 1453 became a giant prayer hall. The main dome is supported by half-domes **C**, giving the church an axial plan. Smaller apses or *exedrae* **D** open from each half-dome, adding a subtle complexity to the interior. The main apse **E** contained the sanctuary. The huge, shadowy aisles and galleries **F** provided extra space for congregants, probably enabling male to be separated from female worshippers in both church and mosque.

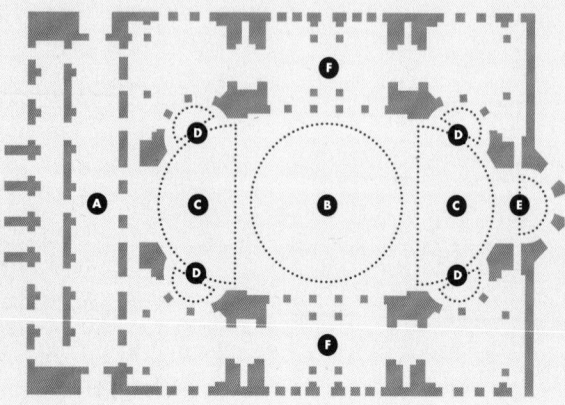

❶ The dome is 31m (102ft) in diameter and had a mosaic of Christ Pantocrator ("Ruler of All"). Probably only in the eighteenth century was this replaced with Quranic inscriptions. The current painting, with its central sunburst, from the mid-nineteenth century, has calligraphy that quotes from the Quran's *sura* 24 ("The Light").

❷ At the start of each church service, clergy would have crossed the nave to the eastern apse, Hagia Sophia's sanctuary, to occupy silver seats by the wall. In the middle of this space stood the high altar, beneath a vaulted canopy. After 1453, Mehmed II had a *mihrab* installed, denoting a *qibla* wall.

❸ A marble line in the floor emphasizes where the *qibla* lies, suggesting that worshippers prayed in rows at a slight angle to the main axis. This marked out the area around the *mihrab* and it left the interior undivided. The line replaced the Byzantine *iconostasis*, which hid the "Great Mystery" (the Eucharistic rites at the high altar).

❹ The emperor's position in the building was crucial. He was originally seated in a screened-off enclosure. An open area (now behind a rail) was later marked with marble as being for his use. He left this spot only at climactic liturgical moments, such as when he exchanged a kiss of peace with the Patriarch at the sanctuary gate.

❺ When Hagia Sophia became a mosque, an imperial presence remained important. An Ottoman royal enclosure, or *maqsura*, had been erected by 1607, and the current, Italian-designed royal pew was installed in 1848 as part of an overhaul of the interior, which included the conservation of its Byzantine mosaics.

6 From about 867, the interior was covered in mosaics. Only from the early seventeenth century were many covered, though the ninth-century image of the Virgin in the main apse seems to have been left untouched. The Seraphim beneath the main dome are among a number of others surviving from the Christian era.

7 The *minbar* was installed in about 1453, and a marble platform for Quranic recitation was erected nearby. Worship in the church was led from the *ambo*, a stepped platform in a screened-off enclosure in the nave. Within that large area a choir stood near the *ambo* and added grandeur to services.

8 Eight wooden roundels were hung over the prayer hall in 1847–1849. They bear the names of Allah (above) and of Muhammad, the first four "rightly guided" caliphs who succeeded him, and the Shi'a *imam*s Hassan and Hussein.

PART TWO

ARCHITECTURE & THE AGES OF FAITH

FOUNDATIONS

THE ANCIENT WORLD

———————○———————

For early man, what we think of as "faith" was simply a perception of reality. Mountains, winds, rivers and the rhythms of nature appeared to be particularly powerful, and in polytheistic religions each of these forces acquired a name and a personality. Although the divinities often had links with specific localities, they could be in many places at the same time. Men tried to embody them through shamanic rituals or attract them into their presence by offering sacrifices. The first temples were often venues for such manifestations.

Many early civilizations created richly poetic mythologies, made subtle philosophical speculations and developed complex urban environments. They built temples and manmade mountains for their gods, inventing architecture in the process. However, the religious multiplicity of Mesopotamia, Egypt, Greece, Rome and, much later, the Americas, was to be supplanted in the Common Era by monotheism, mainly through Christianity and Islam.

◖ **ASSYRIAN RELIEF OF ASHURNASIRPAL II**
883–859BCE, KALHU (NIMRUD), IRAQ

Places of worship needed to be sealed from malevolent spirits by guardian beings. This alabaster relief from Kalhu, the capital of the Mesopotamian kingdom of Assyria, depicts a winged figure – probably an *apkallu*, one of a seven-strong, semi-divine sage priesthood that had helped to bring civilization to humanity.

THE BIRTH OF FAITH

On the hilltop of Gobekli Tepe, in what is today southeastern Turkey, twenty or so roughly circular buildings have been found, 10–30m (33–98ft) in diameter and containing large, T-shaped monoliths carved with what appear to be totem figures. These buildings were almost certainly the site for gatherings in which ritual activity, perhaps sacrificial or shamanic in nature, played an important role. Dated to around 9000BCE, they are the oldest permanent buildings of any kind on Earth. They predate both cities and agriculture. It is possible, then, that monumental architecture was born out of a human need to create a venue for religious activity.

Four millennia later an independent development took place on Europe's Atlantic fringe. People started placing their dead, often in groups, beneath enormous burial mounds. Although the raising of a significant mound over a corpse is a proto-architecture common to many cultures, these tombs are both early and exceptionally ambitious.

By about 3800–3500BCE the greatest of these monuments – variously called long barrows, long mounds and passage graves – had grand entranceways, which provided a visual focus, or façade. Behind this there was usually a stone-lined passage, often carefully oriented – for example, to the direction of the midwinter solstice sunrise. Off this passage led a series of rooms in which human remains were placed. Sometimes the large stones, or megaliths, are carved with patterns. The mounds themselves may be monumental in size – up to 100m (330ft) long and 10m (33ft) high.

These monuments seem to evoke both hills and caves. Hundreds of them survive. Among the more famous are Newgrange in County Meath, Ireland; the Cairn of Barnenez in Brittany, France; and Maes Howe in Orkney, Scotland. Their design implies that ritual was as much a part of their function as was burial.

These mausoleums often occur in clusters (at least thirty are known in the vicinity of Avebury, England), and are sometimes associated with other structures, such as earthen hilltop enclosures like Windmill Hill, also near Avebury, where feasting took place. These are the first permanent architectural interventions known in this part of the world, marking out sacred places in the landscape.

Spiritual landscapes

In spite of their impressiveness, these passage graves are dwarfed by what happened afterwards. By about 2500BCE the emphasis was on open-air monuments: from the stone rows of Carnac in Brittany to the stone circles and earthen banks at Avebury (see pages 68–69) and Stonehenge in southern England, which include standing stones up to 7.5m (25ft) high. Each is only a small remnant of what was once an even larger complex, in which other structures – of wood, earth and stone, some of them also enormous – came and went over several centuries.

◖ SILBURY HILL

*c.*2400BCE, WILTSHIRE, ENGLAND

This flat-topped, manmade mound is the tallest of its kind in Europe, with a height of about 30m (98ft). Although its precise function is unknown, the hill is part of an extensive area around Avebury that is filled with monumental ritual structures. It is possible that a spiral processional path originally wound its way around the slope.

It is clear that these complexes are capable of holding or being viewed by large numbers of people, but we do not know if this happened. That such sites have been the focus for renewed spiritual activity over the last two centuries or so might be because they present the imagination with a blank screen upon which to project one's own beliefs (perhaps at the same time seeking authority for them in the distant past), but it could also be because the places possess certain inherent qualities. For example, most of these northern European sites are linked with their environment. The monuments sacralize the landscape in which they are set. Perhaps it was significant long before structures were placed within it.

It is notable that the dates of origin for these monuments coincide with pivotal moments in the human story: the shift from nomadism to farming, and the introduction of metalworking technologies – neither of which occurred first in Europe. It seems that these were invented nearer to Gobekli Tepe, in the Near and Middle East – a broad area that contains, most famously of all, the once-fertile plain of the Tigris and Euphrates rivers in the region known as Mesopotamia.

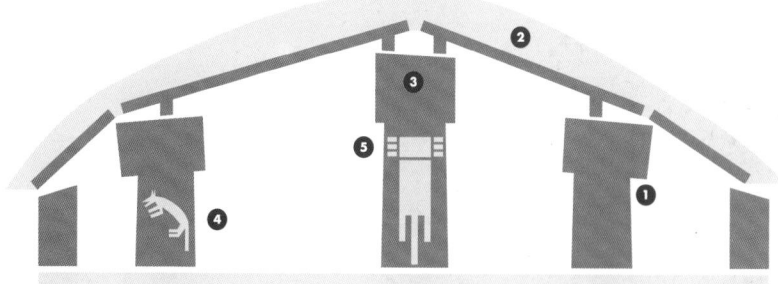

⬖ CIRCULAR TEMPLE OF GOBEKLI TEPE
*c.*9000BCE, TURKEY

Discovered in 1995, these ancient temples consist of rings of T-shaped pillars ❶ of limestone. It is not known if they were roofed ❷, as shown here, or open to the sky. The largest column, up to 5.5m (18ft) high ❸, is in the middle. Some of the columns are carved with an animal emblem ❹, such as a lion, bear or fox. Others have human arms, as if the stones were people. One seems to wear a loincloth belt ❺ (see photograph), perhaps to represent a ritual dancer at a sacred gathering. It is possible that such elaborate temples were used by people to identify themselves with wild animals, either to ward off danger or to equip themselves for the hunt.

THE SACRED LANDSCAPE

*c.*2500BCE, AVEBURY, WILTSHIRE, ENGLAND

A dramatic series of prehistoric sites are scattered across an area of several square miles near the village of Avebury, in the English county of Wiltshire. All are part of a ritual landscape, long predating the village, that was built in the third millennium BCE on a colossal scale, perhaps in many separate stages.

The precise function of these monuments is unknown, but they were built by people of the late Stone Age and early Bronze Age, whose society may have been in the process of a transition from nomadism to sedentary agriculture, and the motivation seems likely to have been religious. Many new discoveries have been made at Avebury in recent years, and by studying these, making comparisons with other monuments of the same era, and looking at the beliefs of similar societies from the more recent past, archaeologists have made informed guesses about its meaning.

▶ AVEBURY HENGE

*c.*2500BCE, AVEBURY, WILTSHIRE, ENGLAND

Archaeological studies suggest that the main "henge" (right) consisted of the earthen bank, enclosing one large circle with 100 stones **Ⓐ**, which in turn enclosed two smaller circles **Ⓑ** with approximately thirty stones each. These contained sanctuary-like arrangements of large stones, known as the Cove and the Obelisk.

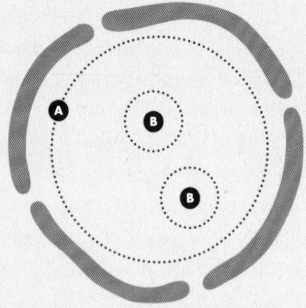

❶ The Kennet River runs through a shallow valley carved into the chalk downlands on which Avebury is set. Among the local peoples, rivers may have been associated with the dead and the journey to the afterlife – and symbolic or actual journeys along the river may have been an important element in the mythology that helped to shape the site.

❷ The West Kennet Long Barrow, a communal burial mound containing a series of stone-lined chambers, was constructed around 3650BCE on a hill overlooking the river. Like other Stone Age sites in the area, it was already ancient when the larger monuments in the landscape were created, at which point its entrance was sealed with a row of enormous stones. This may have marked a change in belief systems, or a desire to simultaneously contain and glorify the power of the ancestors.

❸ The centrepiece of the Avebury complex is an enormous, roughly circular, bank of earth, about 420m (1,380ft) in diameter, within which is a ditch that was originally 10–14m (33–46ft) deep. This arrangement of bank and ditch is called a "henge". Originally, its sides were almost vertical, and made of gleaming white chalk. The bank ensured that the circle's interior was invisible until one entered it.

❹ Modern roads now pass through the gaps in the henge, and ancient routes probably did so too. The form of bank, ditch and entrances – like a circle of hills pierced by four gates – may have had cosmological significance.

❺ At the bottom of the ditch, archaeologists have found up to 500 human bones, perhaps brought from older burial places elsewhere in the landscape. Fires were occasionally lit there too, and tools such as antlers (which were used as pickaxes) carefully deposited. The base of the ditch may have been felt to be particularly close to primal or ancestral forces.

❻ The interior of the henge appears to have been used only on special occasions, and may have been a profoundly significant place. It remains hugely impressive visually. A hundred enormous stones, transported from the surrounding landscape, stood in a great circle around the edge of the ditch. Several of those that remain are more than 4m (13ft) high. Within this circle were further such arrangements of stones, some of which were up to 6m (20ft) tall. These sanctuaries may have been stages for ritual events.

❼ Two great avenues of paired standing stones stretched for up to 2.5km (1½ miles) across the Avebury landscape, each leading from one of the gaps in the henge and ending in an enclosure of stone or timber. These avenues may have been used for grand ceremonial processions, perhaps leading to or from the river.

❽ Silbury Hill, about 160m (525ft) in diameter and 37m (121ft) high, is the largest prehistoric manmade mound in western Europe. It stands on the floodplain of the Kennet River, and the ditches around it flood regularly. The hill took its current form in about 2400BCE, but conceals up to twenty smaller mounds. It may be that the very process of creating the monument was itself a religious act, in which large numbers of people came together.

❾ Near Silbury Hill stood two enormous enclosures made of wooden palisades – some 40,000m (131,000ft) of mature timber may have gone into their construction. Nothing is left above ground today. These enclosures appear to have been the venue for ritual feasting, and may also have been deliberately burned down and re-erected on several occasions, perhaps during rituals of cleansing and renewal.

❿ Swallowhead Spring, a natural source of fresh water not far from Silbury Hill, may once have been a sacred place in itself. In recent years it has become so once again, as have other sites in the Avebury area.

MESOPOTAMIA

At the site of ancient Eridu (modern Abu Shahrein, Iraq) archaeologists have found a temple which, by about 4000BCE, was 17m (56ft) long and raised on a platform. The exterior of the mud-brick building was reinforced by close-set buttresses, forming a tight geometrical rhythm along all four façades. Inside, a series of small rooms surrounded a long, rectilinear central cell, with an altar at one end and an offertory table towards the opposite end. This, then, represents something of a step-change: religious architecture in a form that will be broadly familiar in many cultures, and which survives to this day. The temple's builders lived in towns, one of which surrounded the building, and had invented farming.

Mesopotamia developed a complex civilization, in which a central role was played by temples that maintained the basic architectural characteristics of the Eridu template. In the centuries before 3000BCE, this society invented writing, and thus it became one of the first whose rituals and myths are to some extent known. The earliest cities, such as Ur, Nineveh and Babylon, developed here too. Empires – Sumerian, Babylonian, Assyrian – rose and fell, each with a distinctive culture. Yet the architectural continuities are remarkable.

Mesopotamian temples became massive, complex in plan and richly decorated inside, and they were usually set aside in a walled-off enclosure. The temple itself was axial, with sacred images at one end, accompanied by an altar and an offertory table. These were exclusive spaces, probably used mostly by priests and kings. Indeed, the gods themselves were believed to inhabit the images, and the temple is thus a house or palace of a god.

Although there could also be smaller temples and house-shrines, such a monumental building stood at the centre of every city, next to the royal palace and an enormous stepped mound known as a ziggurat, which had a smaller temple at its peak and dominated the flat landscape for miles around.

Temple-mountains

Mountains were central to Mesopotamian religion, because they fringed the known world and appeared to control the rise and fall of the Tigris and Euphrates, the two rivers on

which civilization depended. Even small temples were raised on a platform. The association of palace, temple and ziggurat is a reflection of the symbiotic relationship between a city, its gods and its earthly rulers.

Each city's temple was a wealthy institution, governed by priests who administered the flow of goods to the deities who lived there. These gods varied in character – indeed, a vast and shifting pantheon of beings was believed to inhabit every

animate being and inanimate object – and their happiness was vital to prevent the world returning to its original chaos. This was secured in part by making offerings and libations to them.

The first cities appear to have developed around such temples and to have evolved into small independent states ruled by a god, which meant that to some extent every human being, including the priests, was in a form of servitude to that divinity. By about 2340BCE, the gods of certain cities

◑ NEO-SUMERIAN ZIGGURAT

*c.*2112–*c.*2095BCE, UR, IRAQ

Ur-Nammu built this ziggurat at his capital, Ur, next to the temple of the city's sponsor, the moon god Nanna. The lowest level of this mighty structure – 61m (200ft) on its longest side – survives. This ziggurat, extended by later rulers, probably once had an additional two levels, with the monumental stairway continuing to a tiny shrine at the top. The platforms may originally have been planted with trees.

▼ VICTORY STELE OF NARAM-SIN

*c.*2250BCE, SIPPAR, IRAQ

This pink limestone stele was carved to celebrate the defeat of Satuni, ruler of the Lullubi people, by King Naram-Sin of Akkadia (reigned 2254–2218BCE). All eyes are drawn to the dominant figure of the triumphant sovereign. Solar disks bestow their favour upon him as he approaches a mountain. At his feet Satuni clutches at a fatal throat wound. Naram-Sin wears a helmet with horns (detail, right), a symbol of the gods. The image served as an emblem of the divine nature of royal authority and the king's close connection to the sacred powers, embodied in the mountains and the heavens.

became more dominant as those cities subsumed others into a wider empire, and at about the same time more and more power was invested in kings, who were regarded as mediators between Earth and the realm of the gods.

By the seventh century BCE, Mesopotamia was not the world's only complex civilization, although Babylon may well have been its largest settlement, with 100,000 people and, according to Herodotus, some 1,179 temples. Above the city rose the ziggurat known in the Bible as the Tower of Babel. Nearby stood at least two magnificent temples and a royal palace, all linked by a processional way that led to the Euphrates. The faith traditions of ancient Mesopotamia died only gradually, by which time they had cross-fertilized with other cultures in the region, such as those of the Phoenicians. Eventually, conquest by the Persians (in 539BCE) and then the Macedonian Greeks (331BCE) meant this was no longer a world set apart. The last inscription in cuneiform, the Mesopotamian writing system, dates to 74–75CE. By the third century CE the area was largely Christian.

These early examples of religious architecture evoke the grandest natural forms while imposing upon nature a regularity that it does not possess. And the Mesopotamian temples in particular, with their axial inner sanctuary in which an altar and an image are the focus, are the first ambitious examples of an arrangement that recurs in many places thereafter. Most of all, given that these were societies where survival must often have been the dominant concern of most people, they suggest a human desire to organize and cooperate on a massive scale in the pursuit of something that would appear not to be essential in terms of practical, day-to-day subsistence: belief, art, ritual, culture – qualities that make us human.

CELEBRATING MARDUK'S MASTERY

The festival for the New Year was the central ritual in the Babylon of King Nebuchadnezzar II (reigned 604–562BCE). It marked the victory of the supreme god, Marduk, over the forces of chaos and evil. For Babylonians, creation itself was only a provisional achievement – order was the result of a struggle between the gods and chaos that was repeated every year at spring. It was humanity's duty to help to ensure that the gods won, and the king was the embodiment of this responsibility.

The focus of the twelve-day festival was the temple of Marduk, which was believed to have been founded to thank the other gods after such a victory. The temple's walls were enriched with alabaster and lapis lazuli, and it contained a 3-ton gold statue of Marduk. Here the king surrendered his sceptre and mace to the god. Later, representations of many major deities from all over Mesopotamia were brought to the temple, where Marduk's sovereignty over them was confirmed, before the king led a great procession of images of deities on a grand journey along the wide processional way that bisected Babylon.

The walls of this street had brilliantly coloured glazed bricks, with relief figures in white, black, blue, red and yellow. Crowds of people knelt as the images passed, accompanied by incense, songs and music. The city had eight fortified gates and the processional route went through the Ishtar Gate, its bright glaze studded with 575 images of sacred bulls and dragons – symbols of Marduk and Adad, the weather god – in yellow, blue and white. Finally it reached the Euphrates to be transported by boat to the Bit Akitu, or "House of the New Year's Festival".

Sadly, we do not know the role that the ziggurat, with its seven storeys rising in different colours to an uppermost level in blue, played in this ritual; nor the significance of reports by the Greek historian Herodotus that the little shrine at the top of it contained a golden table, a large bed and a "native woman chosen from all women", visited occasionally by Marduk himself.

⬦ PROCESSIONAL WAY LION PANEL
*c.*575BCE, BABYLON, IRAQ

The processional way was Babylon's most important street, linking the inner city, via the Ishtar Gate, to the Euphrates. North of the gate the roadway was lined with glazed relief figures of striding lions. Associated with Ishtar, goddess of love and war, this animal protected the street.

ANCIENT EGYPT

A period at most a few decades long, around the year 2630BCE, marks a revolutionary moment in architecture. A burial place and temple for King Djoser (reigned *c*.2630–*c*.2611BCE) of Egypt took shape at Saqarra, an important necropolis not far from Memphis, the first capital, some 40km (25 miles) south of where Cairo is today.

This complex, built for the king by his vizier Imhotep, was 544m (1,785ft) long and contained a prototype pyramid. Unlike any previous building we know of in the world, the entire complex was built of cut stone. Equally significant was the quality of the design: the structure has a consistent architectural language, using specific and refined forms to a clear aesthetic end – defining qualities of true architecture.

"Lord of the Two Lands"

This is a building that is suffused with meaning. Egypt was a country of two parts, or "two lands": the long, narrow Nile Valley in the south (Upper Egypt) and the broad wetlands of the Nile Delta in the north (Lower Egypt). Each had a major shrine in it – at what was later called Hierakonpolis (Kom el-Ahmar) and at Buto (Tell el-Fara'in), respectively – and copies of these, in effect petrified versions of them, were part of the complex at Saqarra. Known as the "Houses of the

North and South", these are dummy or symbolic buildings, not intended to be used by mortals.

Such ideas were part of a complex cosmology, rooted in the fact that Egypt was a land of stark contrasts. The course of the Nile is roughly from south to north. Egypt's fertility depended utterly on the annual inundation of the river, the result of seasonal rainfall in mountains far to the south. This life-giving waterway was also a place of peril, inhabited by murderous hippopotamuses and crocodiles. Equally significant, and at once both glorious and traumatic, was the daily cycle of light and dark, in which the sun emerged in the east to govern the world and then disappeared in the west.

As a result, for ancient Egyptians geography and time fused; history and place were interlocking entities, marked by daily and annual cycles. Sacred buildings like Djoser's tomb-temple were designed partly to help ensure that this rhythm continued to be repeated. It stands on the west bank of the Nile, because it was in this direction that the sun set, when the sun god Re disappeared for a nightly journey through the underworld. Most of the great pyramids, necropolises and mortuary temples stood on the west bank; the main settlements and cult temples were usually on the east, the land of the living. Usually, these buildings lay on an east–west axis, their entrances facing the river (in other words, cult temples faced west and tomb-temples faced east).

Egypt's cosmology, and its resulting images – of the sun, of the river, of cycles of birth and death, which are aligned east to west, and of the land divided into north and south – are uniting themes in Egyptian temple architecture. Even the tomb of a mid-ranking official like Nebamun, whose vivid tomb paintings survive in the British Museum (see pages 82–83), was full of such allusions: to the river and its perils,

◖ DJOSER'S TOMB-TEMPLE COMPLEX
c.2630–*c*.2611BCE, SAQARRA, EGYPT

The mortuary complex of King Djoser consists of a step pyramid and the "Houses of the North and South". Built into the Houses' design are the motifs of the papyrus and the lotus – plants that symbolized Lower and Upper Egypt, respectively. In this manner, Djoser's shrines are an early explicit reference to the king's status as "Lord of the Two Lands".

and the unruly forces of nature they represented; and to the sun god and his daily journey into the underworld and back.

Connecting man and the cosmos

Egypt was a land of cults, which shifted and coalesced, faded and came back into prominence, over the great periods of time during which the civilization thrived. For example, Amun, initially a local god in Thebes, rose to become the major deity, fused with the sun god Re. One feature was constant: the significance of the king, who connected man to the cosmos. Djoser's tomb-temple includes a courtyard with a stone throne-platform at its centre. This was the venue for the *heb-sed* ritual, celebrated on the jubilee of a king's coming to power, in which he symbolically died, was reborn and re-enthroned, before a gathering of all Egypt's gods. He then ran around another courtyard, as if it symbolized his territory, perhaps to demonstrate his fitness to rule.

Kingship provided the glue between the people of Egypt and the gods. Beyond the courtyard, the complex was not for use in this life; it was designed to ensure that the king could continue to perform the *heb-sed* after his death. Beneath

⬤ PYRAMIDS OF GIZA

*c.*2549–*c.*2460BCE, GIZA, EGYPT

Each of the three pyramids – for Khufu, Khafre and Menkaure – at the Giza necropolis had a mortuary temple at its base, and was reached by a long processional way from a lower temple adjacent to the high water mark of the Nile. That of Khufu (reigned 2549– 2526BCE) is the largest and oldest of the three. Indeed it is so large that it is said several of the greatest buildings of the world could comfortably fit inside it, including the Duomo of Florence, St. Paul's cathedral in London and St. Peter's Basilica in Rome.

Djoser's complex – as if on doors to the underworld – is a series of reliefs in which a finely detailed King Djoser strides energetically across a flat surface of stone. Some parts of the site even appear to have been buried in sand on completion. No mortal was expected to read such details, which provide a kind of magical code or instruction book for the afterlife.

Saqarra was dominated by Djoser's 60m-high (197ft) pyramid, an innovation with precursors in the mud-brick temple-tombs, or *mastaba*s, built for earlier kings. Those high-status houses for the dead and Djoser's tomb-complex were ritual palaces, designed to assist with the passage to the afterlife, and then to be used during it.

From Djoser's stepped structure, the familiar, straight-sided pyramid was developed. The result was a century or so in which some of the largest buildings ever constructed were erected, each associated with a smaller mortuary temple: the biggest, the Great Pyramid of Khufu, is 146m (479ft) high. After this burst of activity, pyramids became smaller – and their temples proportionately larger – but for many more centuries the pyramid form remained in use exclusively for Egyptian royal burials.

Their monumental size, unique form and the fact that all are built in combination with a temple makes it clear that Egyptian tombs are not so much places of burial as magical venues for a sacred rebirth; they are, in fact, "tomb-temples".

This desire to endure is probably why Djoser made a structure entirely of stone: the material's imperishability reflected the building's purpose. The only buildings in ancient Egypt to be made of stone thereafter were tombs and temples.

Although the ancient Egyptians had several writing systems, only hieroglyphs – pictures or symbols representing sounds, concepts or objects – were allowed in tombs and temples. Such forms were believed to have magical potential, and their efficacy and permanency were priorities. Ancient Egyptians believed that if images or objects – such as hieroglyphic writing or sculpted figures – were correctly designed and created they would be understood or could be animated by the spirits they evoked. In a similar way, a mummified corpse ought to be suitably prepared to enable its owner's spirit to be reanimated in the afterlife.

Three kingdoms

Ancient Egyptian civilization existed unbroken for well over 3,000 years. Dozens of major religious buildings, and hundreds of smaller ones, still exist – as well as many archaeological sites, which continue to yield new information.

◄ MORTUARY TEMPLE OF RAMESSES III

*c.*1184–*c.*1153BCE, MEDINET HABU, WESTERN THEBES, EGYPT

These vividly painted "papyrus columns", decorated with images of the pharaoh interacting with the gods (see artworks, below), are a reminder of how colourful many – now bare – stone surfaces once appeared. The columns, and the sheer walls adjacent to them, constitute what the massive mortuary temple complex's own inscriptions describe as "a mansion like heaven". Here, at the farthest end of the second of two great courtyards, stands a portico after which there begins the roofed inner area of the temple proper, known as the hypostyle hall. The temple was built in a place that was sacred to Egypt's primeval deity, Ogdoad. In this courtyard great festivals were celebrated, such as those of the fertility god Min. The rites performed in the hall beyond, which led through a series of smaller hypostyle spaces to the inner sanctuary itself, were probably more exclusive and more solemn. In most of the scenes in the portico, the pharaoh faces inwards, towards the door of the hypostyle hall.

In a series of groups wound around the nearest column, he presents milk to Horus, in the presence of the powerful goddesses Isis ❶, Horus's mother, and Hathor, the divine mother of the pharaoh. The two are almost identically depicted, with a distinctive cap containing a cow's horns and sundisk. On the adjacent wall Ramesses III himself sits ❷ in a palatial setting, being confirmed in his kingship by the god Atum, and bearing in his hands the *heqa* or shepherd's crook and flail, while wearing the double crown or *pschent* which combined the thin, straight red crown of Lower Egypt and the bulbous white one of Upper Egypt. Below, a procession of princes ❸ makes its way towards the hypostyle hall. Each prince is adoring a cartouche containing the name of the king himself. Many of these carvings were whitewashed over in the Christian era, when the courtyard was converted to a Coptic church, and the effect of this was to preserve the paintwork beneath.

❶

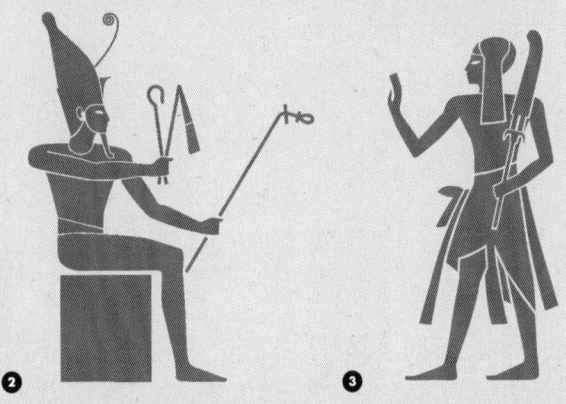

❷   ❸

⬥ DJER DJESURU ("SUBLIME OF SUBLIMES")
c.1460BCE, DEIR EL BAHARI, WESTERN THEBES, EGYPT

The mortuary temple complex built for Queen Hatshepsut near Thebes is a remarkable building, with a stepped terrace of colonnades running up to the foot of a pyramid-shaped sacred mountain, within which lies the queen's burial place and sanctuary. It quotes from the adjacent tomb of Mentuhotep II, an innovator in the design of the rock-cut tomb, which had largely replaced the pyramids by 1800BCE.

Ancient Egypt's history is divided into three broad phases of national unity, each about half a millennium long and separated by an intermediate period of disintegration. These are bookended by the lengthy Predynastic and Early Dynastic periods, and the much briefer Late and Ptolemaic periods. It was during the Predynastic period that hieroglyphs were invented, in about 3200BCE, though what they tell us is limited in the extreme for a thousand years or so.

Djoser lived early in the first of these three great periods, the Old Kingdom (2647–2124BCE). This was also the great age of the pyramids, when monuments of such lasting significance as those at Giza were built. Important cults related to kingship also developed, their focal points being the major gods Re, or Ra, and Horus.

The second great phase was the Middle Kingdom (2040–1648BCE), during which there began to appear royal burial places in the form of tomb-temples cut into rock. Thebes in the south emerged as a spiritual (and sometimes political) capital rivalling the administrative might of northern Memphis. The Valley of the Kings, the most famous of the Theban royal necropolises, was also developed during this period. The cults of Osiris, the god who conquered death, and Amun, a supreme deity, came into prominence too.

Most of the religious buildings that survive from this time are either tombs or the temples associated with them. But temples also existed independently of the tomb-temple complexes. Richly endowed with lands by their pharaonic founders, such independent temples became wealthy institutions (for example, the Great Temple of Amun-Re at Karnak owned 2,400 hectares/5,930 acres). Often the latest examples in a long story of rebuilding and expansion, most of these great stone temples (as they have come down to us) date from the New Kingdom (1540–1069BCE).

The glory of the New Kingdom

This era was a high point of ancient Egypt's power and prestige, when it dominated much of Palestine, Syria and Nubia (northern Sudan). The long, stable reigns of kings such as Amenhotep III (reigned 1391–1353BCE) and Ramesses II (reigned 1279–1213BCE) saw temples constructed throughout Egypt, even in once-distant regions close to the Sudan border (for example, Amenhotep III's temple of Amun-Re at Soleb, or the Great Temple cut into the rock for Ramesses II at Abu Simbel). Such kings built funerary temples of unprecedented ambition on the west bank of the Nile near Thebes, not far from their tombs in the Valley of the Kings. Architectural reliefs and colossal statues at such royal projects promoted the king both as the guarantor of stability and as a victorious warrior – at Ramesses II's funerary temple, the Ramesseum, the seated statue of him was about 22m (72ft) tall. People left votive offerings at these mighty images of divine authority.

Some of these rulers created innovative monuments. The funerary temple of Queen Hatshepsut (reigned 1479–1457BCE), one of the era's great builders, is set into a dramatic cliff on the west bank of the Nile at Thebes. The elegance

of its tiered colonnades would not be matched until Greek temple architecture reached its maturity a millennium later. Amenhotep IV (reigned 1353–1337BCE) renamed himself Akhenaten and with his principal wife, Nefertiti, attempted to institute a radical kind of monotheism, based around the god Aten. This extraordinary experiment, which resulted in major new temples at Thebes as well as the construction of an entirely new capital hundreds of miles away at Akhetaten (Tell el-Amarna), briefly transformed art and architecture alike. Traces of the old gods were expunged – even the relatively obscure official Nebamun (see pages 82–83) had the hieroglyph "Amun" scratched out of his name wherever it appeared in his tomb-chapel – and a new kind of temple was created, centred on a courtyard open to the sun rather than a shadowy inner sanctum. Art briefly became suffused with an expressive, almost caricatured, realism. All this was in turn destroyed under Amenhotep's successors.

By the end of the New Kingdom, the spiritual capital at Thebes contained one of the greatest concentrations of religious buildings that would ever be constructed. They exemplify the Egyptian temple in its mature form, with processional ways, obelisks, pylons, courtyards and pillared halls leading to an inner sanctum housing a sacred image.

The west bank of the Nile here was lined by thirty-six temples, most of them funerary temples to kings. On the east bank was the Temple of Amun at Luxor, dedicated to a manifestation of the god that focused on his fertilizing and regenerative role. At Karnak stood the interconnected temple precincts of Montu (a local god whose cult was displaced by Amun), Mut (Amun's consort) and the Great Temple of Amun-Re itself – a 100-hectare (250-acre) complex known to Egyptians as *Ipet-isut* ("The most select of places").

Karnak and the festival cycle

The Great Temple of Amun-Re at Karnak grew throughout this period, reaching its final form around 1000BCE. It remains one of the largest religious buildings in the world. Most of the pharaohs who enriched and enlarged it left prominent inscriptions, ensuring their good works were known to all, not least the gods whose support they sought, and whom they represented on Earth.

The main axis, roughly 330m (1,080ft) long, started to the west, where the river lay. From here an avenue of stone ram-headed sphinxes formed a processional route, which led up to a great wall-like structure known as a pylon. This was the gateway into the walled-off temple precinct, where, outside

⏶ THE GOD LEAVES HIS TEMPLE

c.1460BCE, RED CHAPEL OF HATSHEPSUT, KARNAK, EGYPT

During the 18th dynasty, under such pharaohs as Queen Hatshepsut, the Great Temple at Karnak (see page 78) and the status of its god Amun-Re were enhanced. Hatshepsut's additions included a structure near the inner sanctuary, where a barque was kept for the god's idol. Built largely of red quartzite, it is known as the Red Chapel. Thutmose III dismantled it, but in 1999–2000 it was painstakingly reconstructed and now stands in the Open Air Museum at Luxor.

This decorative relief depicts a scene from a festival of the dead called the Beautiful Feast of the Valley. A chapel-shaped tabernacle (left), containing the image of Amun-Re, has been taken from its sanctuary and placed on board the barque.

The barque was purified with incense prior to its embarkation. Figures carry fans next to the tabernacle to signify the presence of a deity. Among those crowded into the prow are the gods Maat and Hathor.

A group of priests carry the barque to the Nile for this festival. The destination is Hatshepsut's mortuary temple (see page 78), where Amun-Re would spend the night with the underworld goddess Hathor.

the temple proper, the public could view the spectacular processions. During events such as the annual Beautiful Feast of Opet, the images of the gods Amun, Mut and Montu were transported by land and river just over a mile, riding in a beautifully decorated wooden barque, to the Temple of Amun at Luxor. This noisy and popular outpouring of religious activity, typical of the grander temple rituals, was believed to regenerate the powers of gods and king alike.

Pylons are in effect massive freestanding façades. The outer pylon at Karnak was the largest ever created, at 40m (131ft) high and 15m (49ft) thick, and five further examples lay along the 230m-long (755ft) axial route that ran south-eastwards to the temple's inner sanctuary. Around such pylons stood lesser structures, such as barque shrines, where the processional boats were stored, and pairs of obelisks, associated with the power of the sun god Re.

Karnak's main interior space stood about halfway from the outermost pylon to its inner sanctuary. This was the hypostyle hall, containing a forest of close-set columns arranged on a grid. The main processional axis of the temple ran down the middle of this hall, which symbolized the primeval swamp in which creation began. The hall contained 134 columns, the highest 21m (69ft) tall, carved like closed and open papyrus flowers and dimly lit through a distant clerestory. Walls and columns were carved and painted, and the spaces between the columns were packed with statues of gods and kings.

The axis continued through further pylons and smaller hypostyle spaces until it reached the "central court", which formed the heart of the temple. Within, the axis ended atop a mound, where stood the room-like inner sanctuary within which the sacred image of Amun-Re lived. Tended in this exclusive space, it was visited only by pharaohs and one or two head priests. The mound symbolized that on which, according to Egyptian creation stories, life had begun.

The sacred shrine was small, containing a statue perhaps only 30cm (a foot) or so high. Every day, as the sun rose, the shrine was unlocked and the statue was brought out with great ceremony and ritually libated, clothed and fed. It was believed the deity would be beneficent after having been awoken and encouraged to reinhabit the statue. Shorter, comparable rituals took place in the afternoon and evening.

Such activities were typical of Egyptian temples large and small, although most temples comprised little more than a pylon, a courtyard, a hypostyle hall and a sanctuary enclosure. The enclosure at Karnak contained an artificial sacred lake (both a source of water and the site of ritual ablutions) and a range of stores, kitchens and houses. Karnak also included structures unique to the Great Temple, such as the Akhmenu, a royal temple built by Thutmose III (reigned 1479–1425BCE), and the Wadjet Hall, where for several centuries new kings were consecrated in a rite that was eventually relocated to the hypostyle hall. In addition, a second major axis – with its own sequence of four pylons, followed by a sphinx-lined road – connected the Great Temple with the Precinct of Mut and the Temple of Amun at Luxor. This arm of the temple alone, also used at the Beautiful Feast of Opet, was more than 270m (885ft) long.

None of this disappeared when the New Kingdom came to an end and Egyptian civilization entered its closing phase, from 715BCE to 395CE (the Late and Ptolemaic periods), when successive Sudanese, Persian, Macedonian Greek and Roman dynasties were interspersed with briefer periods of rule by indigenous pharaohs. Some of the most impressive surviving temples – including much of the temple of Isis at Behbeit el-Hagar in the Nile Delta – were constructed well into the Common Era under the Ptolemys, the Macedonian Greek founders of Alexandria. Popular participation in religion widened, and there was a flowering of the cults of Osiris and Isis, deities particularly associated with the afterlife. The cult of Isis became popular throughout the Roman empire, and she even had a major temple in Rome.

The Greeks and Romans saw Egypt as a land of unique achievement and profound esoteric knowledge. Christianity took hold there early and by the end of the fourth century CE the Egyptian Coptic church had largely replaced the traditional religion, whose last temple closed in the 530s. The Copts, in turn, are now a minority in a Muslim country.

KV16 BURIAL CHAMBER
*c.*1295BCE, VALLEY OF THE KINGS, THEBES, EGYPT

This painted relief decoration is from the burial chamber of the tomb (KV16) of Ramesses I (reigned 1295–1294BCE) in the Valley of Kings. It depicts the deceased king hand in hand with the falcon-headed god Horus (left), who is wearing the double crown of Upper and Lower Egypt, and the jackal-headed god Anubis (right), who presided over mummification and assisted Osiris in the underworld.

ASPIRATIONS FOR THE AFTERLIFE

*c.*1350BCE, TOMB-CHAPEL OF NEBAMUN, THEBES, EGYPT

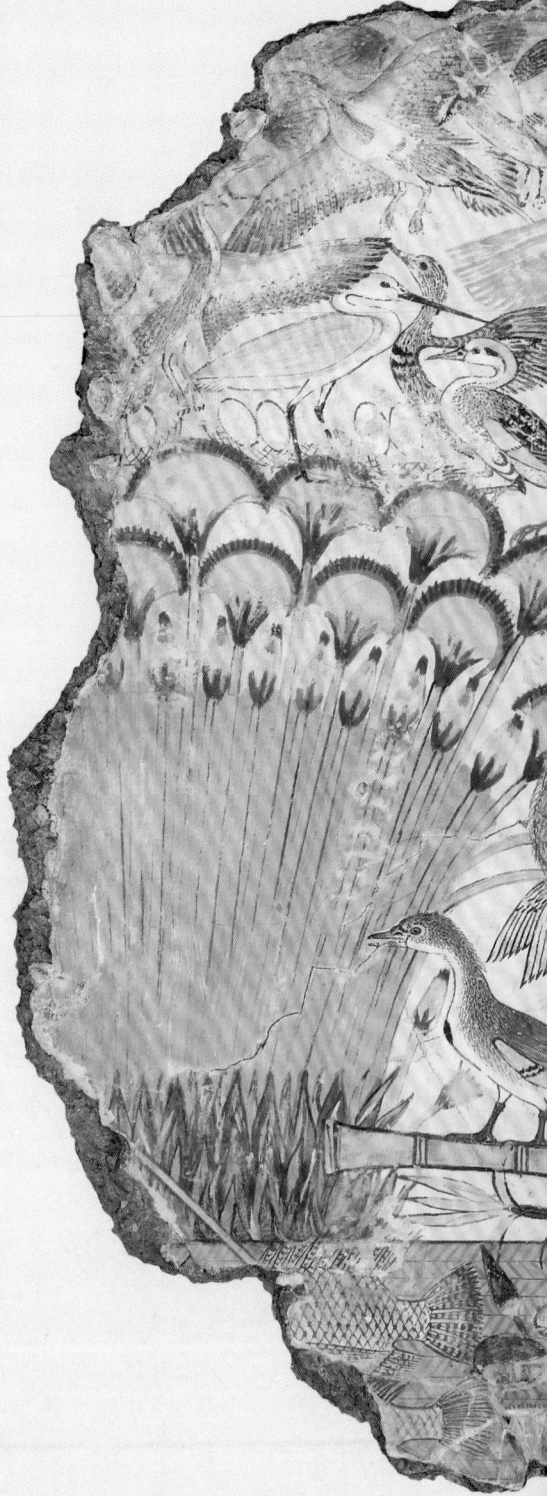

Nebamun was a middle-ranking official who worked as a scribe and grain-accountant at the Great Temple of Amun-Re at Karnak. He built himself a small tomb and associated chapel in a necropolis of comparable burial places on the west bank of the Nile near Thebes in about 1350BCE.

Although the location of the complex is now unknown, pieces of its decoration have survived because they were removed before the site was lost. The tomb was probably typical of its era: cut into the rock of the hillside, an entrance forecourt would have led to a two-chambered tomb-chapel, with a burial chamber positioned several feet beneath them. There, Nebamun's mummified body would have lain, sealed off from the outside world and accompanied by everything necessary to make the journey to the afterlife. The chapel above remained open, so that it could be visited by relatives or, indeed, passers-by. The tomb-chapel as a whole was the point of contact between the living and the dead, a miniature version of the great tomb-temples of the pharaohs.

Nebamun's chapel was richly painted. Immediately after the entrance there was a space large enough to stage elaborate banquets (one such scene was painted on the walls), which were at once liturgical events and sumptuous feasts. Nebamun's mummified body would have been present at such a banquet immediately before it was interred. Beyond this space was an inner sanctuary, its floor positioned directly over the shaft that led to the tomb-chamber. Here would have stood a statue of Nebamun and his wife Hatshepsut (not to be confused with the queen of that name), surrounded by richly painted glimpses of what they aspired to in their afterlife. Nebamun hunting in the marshes (right) is one of these wall paintings.

Like most Egyptian tombs, Nebamun's was a far more permanent structure than the home he occupied in life. Although it stood on the side of the Nile associated with the dead, it probably faced out towards distant grain fields, and indeed the Great Temple of Karnak itself (see pages 79–81) on the east bank of the river.

▶ "FOWLING IN THE MARSHES"

*c.*1350BCE, WALL PAINTING FRAGMENT, TOMB-CHAPEL OF NEBAMUN, THEBES, EGYPT

The Nile marshes were a central feature in Egyptian cosmology, reminiscent of the watery chaos out of which the world was created and the perilous journey that each soul took across a sacred river to the perfect, eternal Egypt that constituted the afterlife. In a scene that had by now been a standard feature of wall paintings in Egyptian tomb-chapels for more than a thousand years, Nebamun is depicted hunting in the afterlife, a figure of commanding power amid the chaos of the natural world, playing his role in maintaining *maat*, or divine order, in a vividly detailed composition redolent with themes of love, fertility, rebirth and divinity. For all its "realism", the depiction of a hunting trip is also layered with symbolism and captures several complex religious ideas.

❶ Nebamun is the largest figure because he is the main occupant of the tomb. He is depicted as young and healthy; every limb is visible and shown in profile, conforming to the conventions of Egyptian art. Such flawless representations were believed to be efficacious in the afterlife.

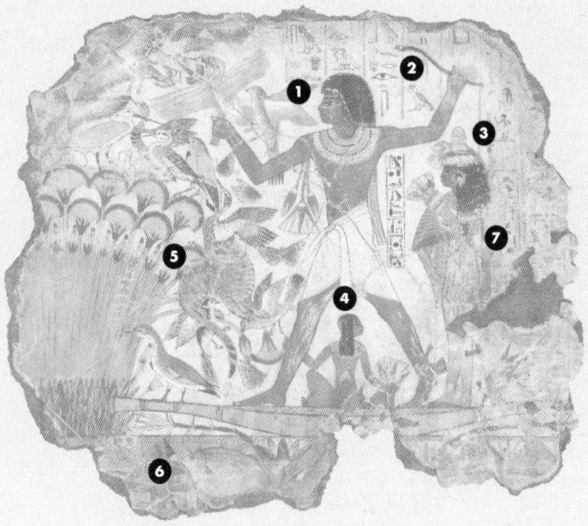

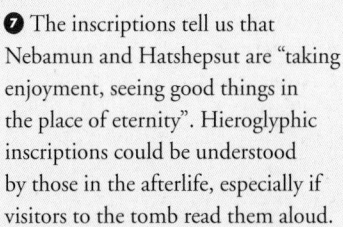

7 The inscriptions tell us that Nebamun and Hatshepsut are "taking enjoyment, seeing good things in the place of eternity". Hieroglyphic inscriptions could be understood by those in the afterlife, especially if visitors to the tomb read them aloud.

6 The tilapia fish was a potent symbol of rebirth because when its young are in danger, it hides them in its mouth until it is safe to release them again. The tilapia was believed to accompany Amun-Re in his nightly journey through the land of the dead. To the left can be seen the shaft of a spear from a lost adjacent scene, in which Nebamun was spearing such fish.

5 The cat is causing chaos among the startled birds, whereas a dog might have been a more reliable form of retriever. Gold has been used to pick out the cat's eye, reminding the viewer that this is also the cat goddess Bastet, daughter and defender of Amun-Re, and with whom gold was associated.

2 Nebamun is using a throw-stick to stun birds so that they can be captured and fattened or used for breeding. However, the throw-stick is shaped as a snake: it is a ritual object rather than a thing for practical use. The word for the verb "to throw" (*qema*) had the same sound as that for "to create".

3 Hatshepsut wears finery with symbolic meaning. On her head she wears a cone of fragrant myrrh decorated with flowers, often worn at funerary banquets. In her hands she bears a bouquet of lotus flowers and a ritual musical instrument known as a *menat*. These associate her with Hathor, wife of Amun-Re and goddess of the afterlife, sexuality and femininity.

4 Nebamun's daughter, balanced on the skiff, steadies herself by clinging to his shin. She would have expected to visit his tomb for days of celebration such as those held at New Year or the summertime Beautiful Feast of the Valley, and to be buried in a comparable tomb after her own death.

CLASSICAL GREECE

For many, a column-lined Greek temple is the epitome of civilized elegance. So it is a shock to picture it as the brightly painted backdrop to a noisy, communal act of slaughter. Yet such acts were typical of the rituals performed outside ancient Greek temples – and not by an elaborate priesthood, such as existed in Mesopotamia and Egypt, but by a wide range of ordinary people. Each temple was the home of a divinity – embodied in the image within the building – and before the temple stood an altar, accessible to all, where sacrifices were offered up. Temple interiors, which might include a separate fire altar, were more exclusive spaces, especially those belonging to secretive mystery cults.

A human-centred world

The Greeks shared with the ancient Egyptians and Mesopotamians the idea that the temple was the home of a deity, who could inhabit a sacred image within it and might be beneficent if given the right offerings and sacrifices. But there were no cults of divine kingship among the Greeks, who developed some of the first decision-making assemblies of citizens to govern the hundreds of autonomous city-states

composing the Greek world. Although no less terrifying, powerful or immortal than Marduk or Osiris, the Greek gods were anthropomorphic: that is, it was imagined that they looked like people. The writings of the poet Homer, dating from the eighth century BCE, depict such divine figures as Zeus, father of the gods, and Hera, his wife, to be human in sensibility, with all the individuality and complexity of emotion of the ordinary mortal. Here may lie the key to the role Greek religion played in making possible the remarkable achievements of Greek art, which for all its precocious humanism is first and foremost religious in purpose.

The rise of Greece

The roots of Greek civilization, and its religion and architecture, can be traced to the earlier Mycenaean culture, which collapsed in about 1200BCE. After a Dark Age of several centuries, what is known as the Archaic Period, from the eighth century BCE, marks the dawn of ancient Greece.

Around this time a simple form of temple developed, initially built using timber or mud-brick, that was to last throughout the history of ancient Greece, imperial Rome and beyond. These temples had a rectangular plan with one or two simple rooms (the most important being the *cella*, or sanctuary, in which the image was housed) and were approached through an open portico. All this was covered by a single roof, with wide eaves supported on all sides by posts (a form known as peristyle). In front of the porch stood an open-air altar, which was the main focus of ritual activity. Besides sacrifices, prayers were noisily said here, and votive offerings dedicated to the resident deity were presented. These offerings were then placed on display, either in

◑ STORIES BROUGHT TO LIFE

*c.*540BCE, CERVETERI, ITALY

Homer's poetry offers epic tales of gods, men and women, and supernatural beings. These stories were known throughout the Greek cultural sphere and inspired some of the first narrative scenes in art. This Greek vase, recovered from an Etruscan tomb, depicts Herakles. He has captured the many-headed dog Cerberus, on the orders of King Eurystheus, only to find the king hiding in a jar.

the building or in the open air, within the sacred enclosure known as the *temenos*.

Between the eighth and the fifth centuries BCE, Greek culture developed rapidly. In spite of the many tensions between them, the Greek city-states began to see certain cultic sites – such as Olympia, Delphi, Delos and Nemea – as sacred places which all Greeks shared in common. Major Panhellenic complexes of temples and other buildings were erected here. The city-states also began to establish Greek colonies around the Mediterranean and the Black Sea, spreading their culture and becoming a major force in the region.

Harmonious treasuries, temples and sanctuaries

During this time, temples became more permanent and sophisticated. The invention of the roof tile meant the pitch of the roof could be shallower, while the additional weight of tiles resulted in buildings being given stronger supports – that is, walls and columns of stone. The exterior of the building – especially the pediment or gable-end, which formed a backdrop to the open-air altar, and to a lesser extent the frieze,

⬥ SACRED WAY

SIXTH CENTURY BCE, DELPHI, MOUNT PARNASSOS, GREECE

The remains of an Ionic column stand alongside the Sacred Way to the sanctuary at Delphi, the most important oracle site in ancient Greece and also a major centre of Apollo worship. In the background is one of several treasuries lining the route, the Treasury of Athens, built to commemorate the Athenian victory at the Battle of Marathon in 490BCE. Such treasuries often held offerings made to Apollo after a victory – usually a share of the spoils of war.

which masked the position of the beams inside the building that were needed to support its wooden roof – began to be enriched with sculpture, initially of mythological beings and produced in terracotta, but gradually replaced by scenes from mythological narratives carved in stone. Everything was boldly painted, creating a vivid and decorous impression.

Although such images were significant, the most important was that within the temple's *cella*, which, being the potential habitation of a god, was the *raison d'être* of the building. Some of the greatest examples, such as the enormous statue of Zeus at Olympia, were made of gold and ivory on a wooden core. Votive offerings also included the standing naked figures, several metres high, known as *korai*, many of which represent the worshipper in idealized form. These were originally close to the stylized forms of Egyptian sculpture, but developed into extraordinarily accurate, if impossibly perfect, depictions of male and female human anatomy. Temples and their precincts thus came to be dominated by sculpted human forms, both mortal and divine. At the great Panhellenic sanctuaries, city-states housed such offerings in miniature side-temples known as treasuries.

Greek architecture is structurally simple and is based on columns and lintels, but over time its proportions became elegant and restrained, and its stylistic decoration highly refined. Two broad cultural regions of the Greek world in particular, the Dorian on the Greek mainland and the Ionian on the islands and shores of the Aegean Sea, refined their local traditions until the roots of their motifs, which lay in Mycenae and the Middle East, became difficult to trace.

The tendency in the Ionian area was towards a poised, almost feminine quality, epitomized by the scrolled volutes of Ionic capitals. Those motifs in the Dorian areas were powerful, brusque and masculine, although the architecture around them retained a magnificent richness. For example, on the frieze above the capitals were placed sequences of sculpted features known as

◑ THE CALF-BEARER
c.570BCE, ATHENS, GREECE

This life-size marble *kourous*, or male votive statue, represents the dedicator Rhonbos, son of Palos, as named on its base. He is nude except for a cloak. Ironically, this piece was saved because it was buried in a pit after the Persians destroyed the Acropolis.

triglyphs and metopes, ultimately derived from the beam-ends of wooden buildings.

These approaches became codified systems called orders – the Doric and Ionic, later joined by the Corinthian – in which it was prescribed how each decorative and structural element should appear. The outcome was a near-modular configuration of architecture. Although in ancient Greece secular buildings were never as ambitious as religious ones, the Greek architectural language can, in theory, be applied to a huge variety of building types.

The glory of Athens reborn

In the sixth century BCE, the city-state centred on Athens began to come into particular prominence, showing its self-confidence by initiating grand new ritual events such as a great Panathenic festival held in honour of the city's patroness, Athena, and a festival of sacred performances dedicated to Dionysius. These were votive acts, rituals aimed at pleasing a deity, but they also included competitions, like the games already being held at Olympia and elsewhere. In the following century the Athenians built a venue for these activities, an open-air theatre made out of marble and dedicated to Dionysius, which was at once a place of religious congregation and the setting for what we now call "drama".

Most Greek cities – repeating a pattern that was common throughout the eastern Mediterranean – were dominated by an acropolis, a defended hilltop that was also a sacred enclosure. Athenians believed their city to be protected by the goddess Athene, but in 480BCE the Persians sacked Athens and left the great temples on the Acropolis in ruins. Not until 448BCE, after peace terms had been agreed with Persia, did a rebuilding programme begin, inspired by the Athenian statesman Pericles.

All the new temples on the Acropolis were made of solid marble, and were adorned on the exterior with bravura displays of sculpture on the pediments and friezes around the colonnade. Much of the work was by the brilliant Phidias, one of the leaders of a movement in which sculpture completed its transformation from stylized monumentality to the vivid depiction of narrative and the human form, perhaps inspired by drama.

Language to please the gods

Many other magnificent buildings were produced throughout the Greek world during this classical golden era. These include the unfinished temple "G" at the colony of Selinunte (Silenus) in Sicily, the largest ever built at 110m by 50m (361ft by 164ft), with its sober Doric massiveness; and the colossal Temple of Artemis (*c*.356BCE), at the cult centre of Ephesus, which exemplifies the Ionic order. The Temple of Apollo (after *c*.430BCE) near Bassae has an unusually ornate interior focused on a single innovative column. This may itself have been the temple's cult image and it became the model for a new, ornate third order, called the Corinthian.

However, perhaps the ancient Greeks' most profound contribution to the history of Western religious architecture is the demonstration that a building could be used to subtly choreograph the emotions of the approaching worshipper. On the Acropolis, the Propylaea, or porch through which Athenians entered the upper *temenos* of their sacred rock, deployed Ionic and Doric in different areas to just this effect.

By such means the Greeks had discovered that architecture's forms have many moods and calibrations, like music or painting – that, in fact, it can have a grammar almost as complex, rich and eloquent as language. The result must have pleased the gods indeed.

From the mid-fourth century BCE, the city-states were conquered by a royal dynasty from Macedonia to the north, which took Greek culture in a new direction. New cities and sanctuaries emerged, for example at Pergamon in Aeolis (Anatolia, modern-day Turkey), and sculpture became even more expressive and vivid. Under Alexander the Great, a vast Greek empire stretched eastwards to the Hydaspes in the Punjab, modern-day Pakistan, spreading late Greek art, language and religion across much of the ancient world. (The great sanctuaries of ancient Greece would not be closed until 393CE, when Christianity was supplanting Greek religion.) However, to the west a polity was rising in southern Italy, based in the city of Rome, that would borrow and modify much of Greek civilization's art, architecture and religion.

◖ THOLOS

c.380–*c*.360BCE, DELPHI, MOUNT PARNASSOS, GREECE

Only three restored Doric columns stand out of the original twenty on the exterior of this once-roofed, and lavishly decorated, circular stone structure within the sanctuary of Athena Pronoia ("Athena before the temple"), which protects the route to the main shrine to Apollo less than a mile away at Delphi. The site was occupied during the Neolithic era, when it was probably dedicated to the worship of an Earth goddess.

THE GREAT PROCESSION OF ATHENA

*c.*447–*c.*406BCE, ACROPOLIS, ATHENS, GREECE

Once the location of a palace from the Mycenaean era, this sheer-sided outcrop of limestone came to be sacred to the goddess Athena, divine sponsor of the city-state of Athens, and a temple stood here from at least the eighth century BCE. As the city prospered, a magnificent series of limestone temples was constructed from the 560s BCE, only to be destroyed by the Persians in 480–479BCE.

The traumatized Athenians buried the architectural remains in great pits on the hilltop. Then, from 447BCE, everything was lavishly rebuilt in marble, which was then brightly painted. Many rites were held on the Acropolis, the slopes of which were peppered with sacred sites. The highlight was the New Year Panathenaea, an annual festival of ancient origin, which from 566 was marked with grand festivities every fourth year. The birth of Athena was celebrated, games were held at a nearby stadium, and the city's gods and social order were renewed.

▶ TEMPLES ON THE ACROPOLIS

*c.*447–*c.*406BCE, ACROPOLIS, ATHENS, GREECE

The Acropolis today is dominated by the remains of the Parthenon, dedicated to the warrior-maiden Athena Parthenos, which represents the essence of Greek temple architecture. Its entablature was once covered in sculpted marble friezes featuring myths and battles, as well as a depiction of the Panathenaea procession (opposite, inset). Remains of other structures survive too, including the Propylaea, the temple of Athena Nike and the Erectheion. Pagan worship on the site ceased in the fifth century CE, and the buildings were converted to other uses (the Parthenon has been a church and a mosque).

❶ The great procession of citizens and animals, which was the culmination of the Panathenaea, entered the sacred precinct through the Propylaea, a monumental gateway (built 437–432BCE, by Mnesicles) whose columns maximized the visual impact of the temple precinct beyond.

❷ The procession passed through the area beyond the gate, which was filled with statues and other objects dedicated as offerings by citizens, who would have visited the hilltop throughout the year. The area was dominated by a 10m-high (33ft) bronze image of Athena.

③ The procession brought a newly made robe to the Erectheion (built from 421), and presented it to the *xoanon*, an ancient olive wood cult image of Athena Polias, protectress of the city, sent by Zeus himself. The *xoanon* had been bare for two months, ever since an earlier procession had taken the previous robe to be washed. Some sources, including the historian Pausanias, writing in the second century CE, claim that further sacred relics housed there included Poseidon's trident.

④ With the removal of the *xoanon*'s robes, a period had begun when the hilltop was temporarily abandoned by its gods. Over several weeks, a series of unusual rites was celebrated. One consisted of a vertiginous night journey made by two girls, the Arrephoroi, from their house in this corner of the enclosure, down the cliff to a spring in a cave where they took part in a mysterious exchange of objects.

⑤ The fire at the great altar of Athena was lit when a great torch race came to the hilltop at dawn on New Year, the twenty-eighth day of the month of Hektombaion, bringing the return of the gods. Later in the day the Panathenaea procession arrived, driving with it 100 sheep and cows, which were slaughtered and burned at the altar.

⑥ The procession was depicted in the brightly painted *cella* frieze on the Parthenon (sculptures by Phidias), which culminated on the east side beneath pediment images of Athena, emphasizing the military prowess with which she had blessed the Athenians.

⑦ The Parthenon was probably the largest building on the Greek mainland. A 12m-tall (40ft) gold-and-ivory statue of Athena dominated the interior, behind which stood a small room used as a treasury to store gifts to the gods.

⑧ The temple of Athena Nike (420s BCE, by Callicrates) celebrated Athena as a bringer of victory. The temple's prominent location advertised its triumphant message across the city.

CLASSICAL ROME

By 200BCE, republican Rome had conquered all of Italy and much of the Mediterranean coast, including Greece and its colonies. Within a couple of centuries, this empire controlled much of inland Europe and North Africa, the Near and Middle East, and its emperors had claimed divine status.

A home for all gods

Roman religion, in its public form, was civic, highly organized and intensely focused on the identity and origin of the city of Rome itself. Its practices and gods had much in common with those of Greece, but with a heavy reliance on auguries: every major decision, from the start of a military campaign to the founding of a city, was preceded by a ritualized search for signs of the gods' favour, often carried out by members of a priesthood, which played an important role in the institutional life of the city. Alongside this state cult that sought divine help for the benefit of Rome, domestic religion involved daily observances that would ensure good fortune for families and individuals.

As the city expanded its influence geographically, Romans came into contact with many different belief systems and architectural traditions. Some local cults spread throughout the Roman empire. These included those of Isis from Egypt, Mithras from Persia and Dionysius from Greece. Judaism and its rapidly growing offshoot Christianity resisted the making of sacrifices that accompanied official cultic practices, and this often brought these monotheistic religions into conflict with Rome. Many cultic complexes throughout the empire were rebuilt on a lavish scale, using a combination of Roman architectural motifs and existing local traditions. Spectacular examples of such Roman places of worship include the Temple of Jupiter at Heliopolis (Baalbek) in the Lebanon, and the oracular temple of Fortuna Primigenia at Palestrina, to the east of Rome. Other cults created more intimate congregational venues for their initiatory rites – such as the Mithraeums, small but richly decorated temples that were often placed underground.

The focus within

The imperial capital was a kind of holy place, its boundary marked by a ritual border known as the *pomerium*, which according to tradition had been drawn by the city's founder, Romulus (several leaders expanded it, despite its sacred status). Auguries were only valid within this line, where political and civic life was dominated as much by gods as by people.

Emperors were expected to dedicate the booty of foreign wars to these deities by beautifying the city, which resulted in waves of imperial construction. For example, the ancient Capitoline temple, dedicated to Jupiter Optimus Maximus, Juno and Minerva, the most important temple in the city (and the repository of the oracular Sibylline Books), was rebuilt several times, but always honouring its sixth-century BCE plan. The Temple of Venus and Roma (*c.*121CE), in the

○ *SOL INVICTUS*

THIRD CENTURY, NORTHERN ITALY

The Unconquered Sun (*Sol Invictus*), a Middle Eastern deity, reached Rome in 102, reviving an ancient Latin cult of Sol. Within a century, Septimius Severus (reigned 193–211) had added a rayed nimbus to his image. In 274, Aurelian (reigned 270–275) made the sun god an official cult, with a festival on 25 December. The solar motif was also carried into Christianity.

⬧ LIGHT TRIUMPHS OVER DARKNESS

*c.*118–*c.*125CE, PANTHEON, ROME, ITALY

This temple to all the gods of pagan Rome is one of the world's great ancient buildings, but how it was used is unknown (it has been a church for more than 1,300 years). The Pantheon has the largest dome ❶ to have been built before the 1400s. The perfect geometry of its interior, in which a regular semi-circle sits on a regular half-square of the same width, appears to be part of an attempt to embody, architecturally, the harmony of the cosmos. The interior would

contain a sphere 43.3m (142ft) in diameter ❷. It is basically a colossal sanctuary whose only light source is the 8.3m-wide (27ft) oculus ❸. The temple entrance faces north, so that for most of the year the interior is dark. At the equinoxes the sunbeam via the oculus hits the doorway and on 21 April (by tradition, the day Rome was founded) it fully illuminates the front door ❹. The building certainly played an important role in the cult of the deified emperor as the sun god.

heart of the Forum, was the largest ever built in the city, at 145m (475ft) long by 100m (328ft) wide. Its enormous main space, beneath a coffered vaulted ceiling, was once flanked by dozens of 15m-high (50ft) white marble columns.

These buildings were near-copies of Greek temples and usually employed the ornate Corinthian order. Some architectural features, such as high platforms and deep porches, were derived from existing local traditions. The Doric-like Tuscan order was also used on occasion. These grand civic temples dominated the great public forums at the heart of each Roman town, but the theatres, bathhouses and basilicas (large, covered meeting halls that were often used as law courts) of these settlements were almost as impressive.

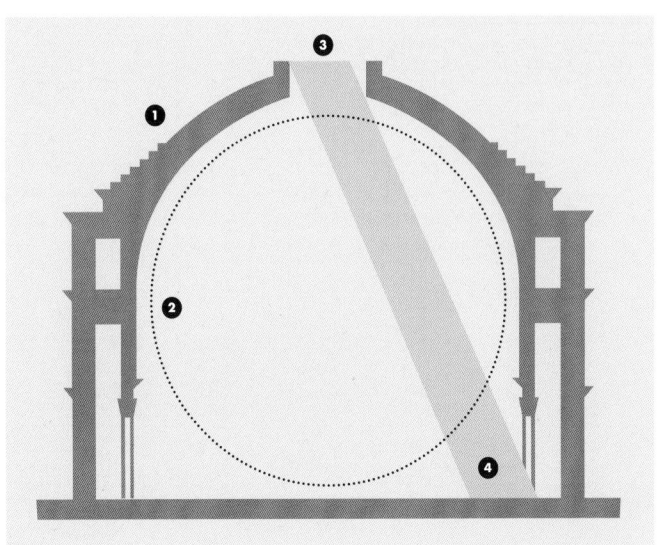

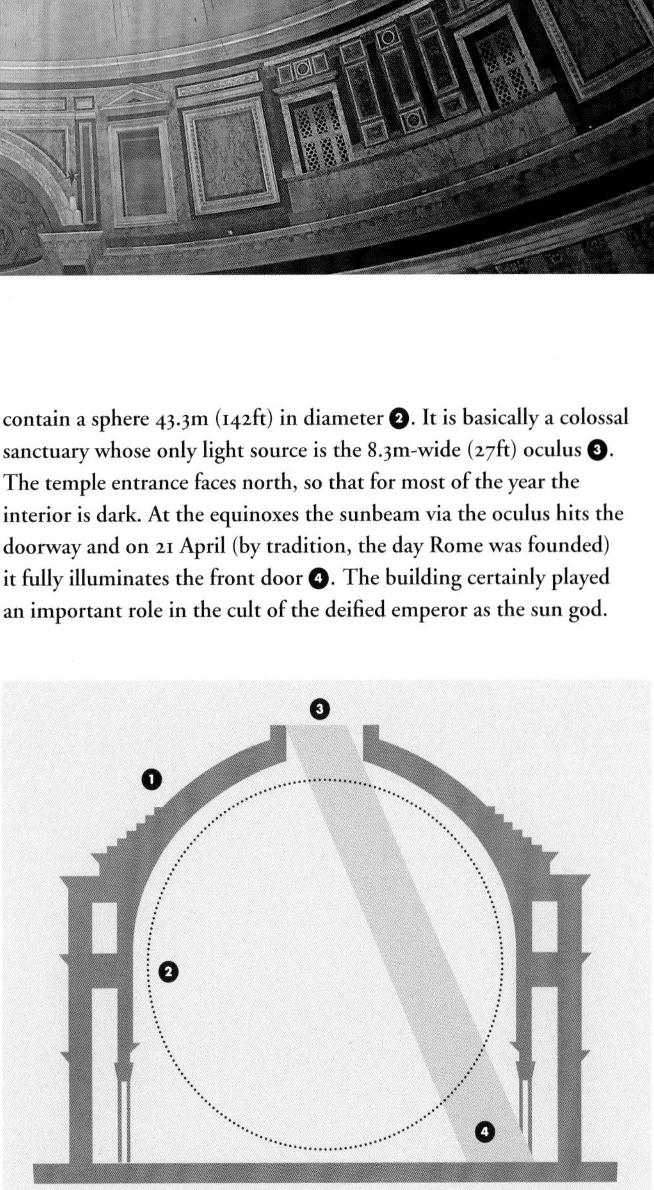

In the Roman world, very unusually, the architecture of secular buildings vied with temples in ambition and often outdid them in inventiveness. In their palaces, public baths and other secular buildings, Roman designers made technical innovations that would be fundamental to the story of religious architecture thereafter. In particular, they perfected two things, both of which had existed in a simple form for some time: concrete and the arch.

Concrete, made of lime and water combined with ash and rubble, could be poured into a variety of shapes before it set, which made it possible to create curved surfaces that were structurally sound. Arches introduced a vocabulary of repeated semi-circular forms into architectural compositions. The curved ceiling vault was one result, the dome was another, and the arcade was a third. All three became fundamental to Jewish, Christian and Islamic architecture.

These features meant it was now possible to create apses, buildings with semi-circular ends, and niches, in which statues could be set. They stimulated an architectural revolution, peaking for the hundred years from the mid-first century CE, in which interiors became works of art in their own right, their walls and spaces interlocking and interpenetrating in complex ways. Although they were explored chiefly in secular buildings, these innovations resulted in one hugely impressive religious structure. The Pantheon is the most celebrated surviving Roman temple and one of the most influential buildings of all time. It was built for Emperor Hadrian (reigned 117–138) to replace an earlier temple built in 27BCE by Augustus's friend and deputy Marcus Agrippa. Equally influential was the basilica, a meeting hall with aisles either side of a higher central space that ran axially to an apsed end that was used by dignitaries, which had originated in the first century BCE and was gradually perfected.

◖ TEMPLE OF JUPITER
27BCE, BAALBEK, LEBANON

When Augustus decided to build this monumental imperial temple in Heliopolis, as the city was then known, he did so on ruins at a site where a religious structure had stood for millennia. Pilgrims flocked to this city to pay homage to a Phoenician cult that became Romanized as a triad of deities: Jupiter, Venus and Mercury. The Temple of Jupiter was the principal place of worship of the triad.

The great achievement of the Egyptian temple builders was to discover the enormous power and permanency that building in stone gave to a religious building. The Greeks discovered the full expressive range of architectural form. The Romans unlocked the true power of the interior. The rest of the story of sacred architecture, in Christianity and Islam at least, flows from these innovations, and the Roman manner became the principal underlying source of stylistic inspiration for buildings in the Western tradition for almost two millennia. Its main source, the religious architecture of ancient Greece, came largely to be forgotten.

◗ SACRIFICING BEFORE THE TEMPLE
176–180CE, ROME, ITALY

This marble relief depicts Marcus Aurelius (reigned 161–180) acting as chief priest (*pontifex maximus*) about to offer a public sacrifice. In the background is the fourth incarnation of Rome's most important temple, Jupiter Optimus Maximus, dedicated to the triad Jupiter, Juno and Minerva. Founded c.509BCE, it dominated the Capitoline Hill.

THE AMERICAS

The ancient architecture of the Americas developed in isolation and effectively ceased when the existing faiths were replaced by Christianity. Pre-Columbian religious architecture is found in three areas: the Andes mountains of South America, where some of the world's earliest buildings were created; the region known as Mesoamerica, stretching from modern-day Mexico to Honduras, where impressive architecture is accompanied by written texts; and in the Puebloan and Mississippian cultures of the southwest and midwest of what is today the United States.

In general, the indigenous peoples of the Americas inhabited an environment believed to be alive with sacredness. Their great religious complexes were often associated with astronomical phenomena, mountaintops and caves. The Puebloan Indians had elaborate networks of paths which ran in straight lines across the landscape and these may be comparable to the *huaca*s, holy places, linked by lines known as *ceques*, that ran across Inca Peru, or the sacred force known as *teotl* by the Mesoamerican Aztecs for whom it was present in all things.

The settlements of many of these cultures were focused around sacred enclosures dominated by large pyramidal mounds, grouped orthogonally around open plazas. Sculpture and decoration reached astonishing levels of achievement, and all this was created, with notable exceptions, without the use of metal tools or a writing system.

The Andes

The mud-brick architecture of the ancient Andes dates back to the third millennium BCE and is as impressive as any of the contemporary structures of the Middle East. Sites such as Aspero, Caral in the Supe Valley, Sechín Alto and El Paraíso, all in what is now Peru, feature circular plazas and flat-topped mounds up to 40m (131ft) high.

A succession of civilizations followed. They include the culturally influential pilgrimage site at Chavín de Huántar (*c.*1000–*c.*200BCE), with its Castillo – a group of broad platforms and courts. At Moche, Peru, the Huaca del Sol (*c.*100–*c.*600CE) was a place of lavish royal burial, as well as of human sacrifice: it is the largest (40m/131ft high) mud-brick building in the Americas. In the centuries either side of the start of the Common Era, an extraordinary sacred landscape was laid out in the Nazca area, on the Peruvian coast: in addition to further monumental mounds, the desert floor bears outlines of giant geometrical forms, including colossal outlines of spiders, hummingbirds and other beasts, some of which are up to 285m (935ft) in length. By about 580CE, at Tiwanaku, Bolivia, the first true Andean buildings of cut stone are seen.

◖ PYRAMID MAYOR
*c.*2600BCE, CARAL, SUPE VALLEY, PERU

Covered with rocks and then abandoned after a millennium, Caral's biggest platform mound is so large (at 200,000 cubic metres/7,063,000 cubic feet) that it was long believed to be a hill. From the positioning of the structures in the surrounding valley, scholars infer that the city may have been configured as a monumental calendar. Caral is the largest of nine inland urban centres (dating from *c.*3200BCE) in the Supe Valley – all part of the first pre-ceramic civilization. It has six major platform mounds and three circular sunken courts or plazas. Not only do the mounds echo the foothills of the Andes mountains in the distance, they were built using stones brought from there.

◯ PYRAMID OF THE SUN

*c.*150CE, TEOTIHUACÁN, MEXICO

Viewed from the Pyramid of the Moon, the Avenue of the Dead forms a long, 40m-wide (131ft) ritual way that runs 4km (2½ miles) from its pyramid-lined plaza, passing the great Pyramid of the Sun (left), as well as the Temple of Quetzalcóatl. Such features of the layout symbolically connected it to the surrounding rain-bearing mountains and agricultural lands.

However, it is from Spanish contact with the great empire of the Incas, from 1519, that we derive most of our information about the religion of the region.

By 1493, the Inca empire ran the length of the Andes. Pyramidal platforms known as *ushnu* existed in many settlements. Other ceremonial structures had exquisitely curved walls. In the temple of Coricancha in Cuzco, Peru, a sanctuary with gold-lined walls held images of the sun god Inti and his sister the moon goddess Mama Kilya, flanked by the mummies of their descendants, the Inca kings and queens.

Mesoamerica

The earliest ambitious architecture in the central area of the Americas started around 1250–900BCE, in what is now Mexico, with the Olmec civilization. Cities such as Teopantecuanitlán have temple-pyramids: steep-sided structures, each topped by a small sanctuary. These were built as part of pyramid-and-plaza complexes, which incorporated ballcourts – rectilinear enclosures that were the setting for a heavily ritualized game. Later, around 500–750CE, the Zapotec culture developed writing, as well as an architecture of cut stone. The central plaza of their city of Monte Albán was 300m by 200m (984ft by 656ft) north to south, and around it were arranged brightly painted pyramidal temple-mounds and smaller temples, as well as a ballcourt.

Between *c.*700 and *c.*900 the Zapotec empire collapsed, by which time Teotihuacán, the great metropolis of the ancient Americas based in the Valley of Mexico, had reached its zenith. Built on a complex grid-like plan that conforms

⬥ A HILLTOP HIERARCHY

683, PALENQUE, CHIAPAS, MEXICO

The Temple of Inscriptions (centre, left), burial place of
the Palenque ruler Lord Pakal (603–683), has nine levels
and five doorways – numbers with cosmological significance.
The great palace (centre, right) also had a partly ceremonial
function. Deep ties to royal power, as well as astronomical
and topographical allusions, typify Mayan sacred sites.

with a solar alignment and the surrounding mountains,
this ritual complex of dozens of pyramids is dominated
by the Pyramid of the Sun and the Pyramid of the Moon.
Teotihuacán was abandoned between 650 and 750, following upheaval during which its temples were damaged but its
residential areas were left intact. Thereafter it played a role in
the Mesoamerican psyche not dissimilar to that of Athens in
Western culture. Its name derives from the Aztecs, who discovered it abandoned and named it "birthplace of the gods".

Meanwhile, further to the south the Mayan-speaking peoples had developed a sophisticated civilization, centred on the
Yucatán peninsula. Early in the Common Era, their city of
El Mirador, in what is now Guatemala, was already one of
the largest in the Americas, with a main temple-pyramid, the

Danta, 70m (230ft) high. The Maya had a writing system and
the efforts of scholars to decode it mean that we can now read
about many events recorded on the sculptured upright stone
slabs, or stelae, often found at Mayan temple-pyramid plazas.

Many of these temple-pyramids survive, such as the group
around a plaza at Palenque (the Temple of the Cross, Temple
of the Foliated Cross and Temple of the Sun, 684CE). This is
the best preserved of ancient American religious architectures,
and while it shows considerable variety, certain common
features may be identified. The temple-pyramids have pronounced bases and stepped sides with steep flights of ceremonial stairs. There is often a small sanctuary at the top. *Talud-
tablero*, a series of alternating sloping and vertical surfaces separated by emphatic horizontal mouldings, is one technique
used to exaggerate the stepped profiles of the structures. A distinctive vertical roof comb rises from many of the pyramid-
topping sanctuaries. Surfaces may be lavishly carved, or covered with richly sculpted and painted stucco decoration.
Within, the rooms of the little temples may be high (over
5m/16ft) but are always narrow, with steep corbelled vaults.
Although columns are sometimes used to support openings,
this is an architecture of exteriors, of masses in the landscape.

Public sacrificial rites took place in front of such sanctuaries, or at altars in the adjacent plazas, where large numbers of people could witness them. Kings might be buried in elaborate vaults deep within the pyramids, as at Palenque. Complexes are interlinked by ceremonial ways.

The last dated Mayan stele was erected in 909, but the culture survived, as evidenced by thirteenth-century cities such as Chichén Itzá. These were contemporaneous with a rising power, the Aztecs, who created a mighty empire based in the Valley of Mexico in the fifteenth century CE.

Unlike the religious architecture of the Maya, the invading Spanish systematically razed much of that built by the Aztecs. The remains of the city of Tenochtitlán, established in the fourteenth century on an island in a lake, Texcoco, now lie beneath Mexico City. Aztec beliefs, however, are known in some detail, including their foundation myth that records how a speaking idol of their hero and war god, the feathered Huitzilopochtli ("Hummingbird of the South"), led them to the site where the city was established.

The Spanish conquistador Hernán Cortés, who saw Tenochtitlán in 1519, described it vividly. Grand causeways ran in a great cross-shape, connecting the city to the shore. At its centre was a ritual enclosure, 350m by 300m (1,140ft by 990ft), marked by a wall carved with serpent's heads. This mighty precinct contained seventy-eight buildings, as well as a sculpted skull rack (*tzompantli*), used as a form of altar to display human heads to the gods. There stood the city's Great Temple, known as Coatepetl. Like other Mesoamerican temples, it had been enlarged many times between the fourteenth century and 1511 (the structure actually contained seven successive layers of addition). This 60m-high (197ft) pyramid was topped by a pair of temples associated with the forces of life and death: one, painted green, was dedicated to the rain god Tlaloc, and the other, in red, to the war god Huitzilopochtli. Viewed from these temples, the sun rose between two sacred volcanoes on 21 March, the spring solstice.

North America

In spite of the survival of indigenous religions to this day, little is known of the religious practices of those who built the great earthworks of what is now the United States. These

◐ TEMPLE OF COATEPETL RELIEF
*c.*1490, TENOCHTITLÁN, MEXICO

This large (3m/11ft in diameter) stone relief was recovered from the base of the Coatepetl (Templo Mayor or Great Temple), dedicated to the Aztec gods Huitzilopochtli and Tlaloc. The carving depicts a foundation myth, which tells how the goddess Coyolxahuqui was killed on a hilltop by her brother Huitzilopochtli, who threw her dismembered remains to the ground. The temple was built on the very same hill, and the carved relief meant that the myth was built into the structure of the temple.

begin as early as *c.*3500BCE, with mounds such as those at Watson Brake, Louisiana. During the first millennium CE, numerous animal-shaped effigy mounds were built in the Midwest and their function often included burial. The greatest of them is the 328m-long (1,254ft) Great Serpent Mound, Ohio. By the end of the first millennium, various peoples in a very broad area around the Mississippi basin had built large settlements centred on palisaded enclosures, within which were carefully placed earthen mounds – and some of these provided the platform for a timber building. The largest is Monks Mound at Cahokia, Missouri, which is 30m (100ft) high. The function of these buildings included both burial and high-status residence. Much further south, peoples were creating masonry towns known as *pueblos*, which gave the culture its name. In these settlements the chief ceremonial structures were circular, half-subterranean buildings known as *kiva*s: the one at Casa Rinconada is about 19m (63ft) wide and more than 3m (11ft) deep.

Ritual sacrifice

The temple-pyramids and plazas of many of these places were the venue for offerings to a wide range of gods, and although most tribute probably consisted of animals, maize and other foodstuffs, the most important sacrifices were human. In the Andes, the Inca buried children alive on the tops of mountains. The Maya and Aztecs believed that the gods required human blood for their sustenance. War was thus a sacred duty, waged to create a flow of live human captives for ritual execution. The game played in the many ball-courts was partly a ceremonial re-enactment of the struggle to exist, which was believed to lie at the heart of the cosmos, and it culminated in the death of the loser. Rulers and priests also practised rites of auto-sacrifice, during which they pierced their own bodies to release blood as an offering (see pages 40–41). Drug-induced hallucinogenic trances also played an important role in religious life.

The coming of the conquistadors

In spite of their achievements, these peoples were unable to withstand the arrival of Europeans who were carrying viruses for which the indigenous peoples lacked immunity. The territories controlled by the Aztec, Maya and Inca states were conquered between 1521 and 1546. The North American mound-building cultures had already passed their prime by the time that their peoples were decimated by colonizers. However, the indigenous peoples of the Americas, north and south, remain very much alive and a faith of shamanic trances, offerings and close spiritual links between people, ancestors and holy places is still maintained by many. They include some groups of Maya, whose ancestors created some of the mightiest architecture of the ancient world. It is as if their practices have reverted to those from which all the first religions sprang.

◗ SACRED MOUNTAINTOP PLAZAS
*c.*1450, MACHU PICCHU, URUBAMBA, PERU

The high-altitude Inca royal estate settlement of Machu Picchu, which echoes its mountainous surroundings, was almost certainly a *huaca* – somewhere pervaded by sacred power. It was a perfect location for holy astronomical observation and more than half of the structures appear to have had a spiritual use. Huayna Picchu, the mountain overlooking the site, holds further temples.

onginneð   ✝ Iohannis aquila   eапп
incipit   god rpel   epē   iohan
euangelium secundum Iohan

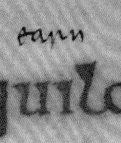

IN PRIN
CIPIO

ERAT VERBUM

ET VERBUM ERA

APUD DM DX

PEOPLES OF THE BOOK

ONE GOD & ONE SACRED WORD

───────────◯───────────

By the beginning of the Common Era, Egypt and Mesopotamia were part of a world in which other polytheisms, particularly those of southern and southeastern Europe, were equally influential, and in which Rome was the most powerful political force. Within this territory, Judaism was notable for rejecting the idea of many gods. Judaism was to have a formative influence on Christianity and Islam, which share with it a group of sacred texts and stories. Muslims call the followers of all three faiths the "peoples of the book". These Abrahamic traditions are practised today by two-thirds of the people in the world, having replaced most of the ancient polytheisms of the Middle East, North Africa, Europe and – much later and further afield – the Americas. Many of the world's greatest buildings are places of worship belonging to one of these three creeds.

◐ ST. JOHN'S GOSPEL

*c.*700, LINDISFARNE, NORTHUMBRIA, ENGLAND

"In the beginning was the Word" – these initial letters I, N and P
("*IN PRINCIPIO*") are from the Lindisfarne Gospels, which is one of the greatest books of the early Middle Ages. It seems likely that the artist-scribe was Eadfrith, who became bishop of Lindisfarne in 698. Ornate signs and symbols – many bearing Hiberno-Saxon, Byzantine and Islamic influences – imbue the book with meaning and convey a spiritual message. Monks believed that such work offered the scribe the possibility of glimpsing the divine.

JUDAISM

THE FOUNDING MONOTHEISM

Judaism is characterized by a belief in a universal, unitary God and the existence of a binding contract, or covenant, between God and the Jewish people – a relationship that originated with the patriarch Abraham (meaning "father of many"). Other central elements of the faith include the divinely inspired text known as the Torah (meaning "teaching" or "law"), also called the Pentateuch, and the biblical idea of a Promised Land, the land of Israel. Repeated experiences of exile and return have helped to shape Jewish spirituality. The religious architecture that resulted was to profoundly influence both Christianity and Islam.

The Ark of the Covenant

The Torah tells how Moses led many Israelite slaves out of Egypt following their release from bondage by the pharaoh. God then revealed himself to Moses,

DIVINE WRITINGS

Judaism, Christianity and Islam share a deep concern for the primacy of a sacred text. Copies of these texts – the Torah, the Bible and the Quran – are among the most lavish and beautiful objects created by the faithful. Their significance also has wider artistic and architectural consequences: in a synagogue, the Torah scrolls are the holiest object in what is otherwise a prayer hall. A comparable idea has shaped mosques, in which written passages from the Quran have become an art form. The significance of the Bible to Christians led to the invention of the book.

The Torah scroll is the most sacred object in Judaism. The protective "mantle" in which it is housed is often richly decorated.

◗ SZEGED SYNAGOGUE
1903, SZEGED, HUNGARY

Chief Rabbi Immanuel Löw guided the sumptuous decoration of this synagogue. The 10m-wide (33ft) dome over the congregational space, like much of the interior, has beautiful stained glass – here strewn with stars – and inscriptions, emphasizing the morality of work, culture and good deeds. The twenty-four columns symbolize the hours of the day.

instructing him to build a Tabernacle – a tent-like shelter – and furnish it with specific items. Within this Tabernacle, screened off from the outside world, the priesthood of the "children of Israel" performed an elaborate series of sacrificial rites before an innermost enclosure in which God was believed to make himself present.

Unlike most other such spaces in the ancient world, this sanctuary did not contain an image, it contained a text: the Ten Commandments, which had been given to Moses by God. This was housed in an ornate receptacle, the Ark of the Covenant. A simple tent was the setting for some of the most influential ideas in history: it represented devotion to a single god, the rejection of idols and images, and their replacement with a divinely revealed legal, moral and religious code.

Jerusalem and the Temple

Archaeologists question whether these events happened or not. What is certain is that the children of Israel settled in an area known as Canaan and, under King David and his son Solomon, the kingdom of Israel was united and a capital established in Jerusalem by c.1000BCE. The Ark was taken with great ceremony to the royal city and later placed within the inner sanctuary, the "Most Holy Place", of the Temple built for it by Solomon – a permanent structure and focal point of worship, with a massive bronze altar.

The layout of the Temple echoed that of the Tabernacle – and it also had much in common with the other temples of the Middle East. The priesthood alone had access to the sanctuary, at the heart of which stood the richly decorated room containing the Ark, and made sacred by the presence of God. The people of Israel gathered in large outer courtyards to make offerings and sacrifices (these were not considered valid anywhere else), and for important communal festivals such as Passover.

Exile and synagogues

After Solomon's death, his realm split into rival states with a kingdom of Israel in the north and a kingdom of Judah in the south. In 586BCE the Babylonians defeated Judah. Solomon's Temple was destroyed and many Jews were exiled, but kept the national religion alive in spite of the absence of the Temple. Babylon was defeated in turn by Cyrus the Great in 539, and many Jews returned to Jerusalem, where they rebuilt the Temple.

Between then and the third century BCE, many features present in modern Judaism emerged. In particular, a type of

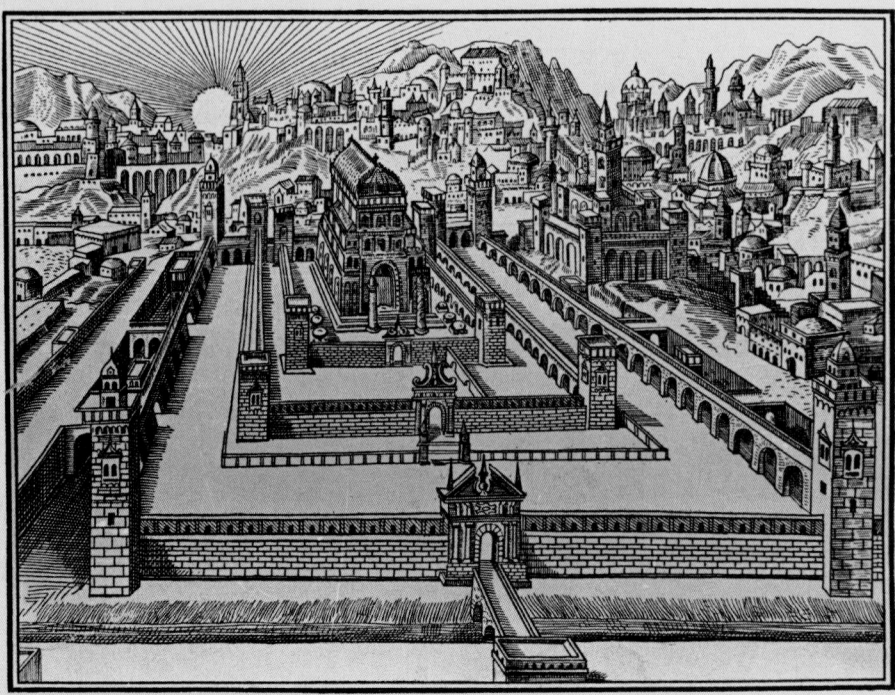

◖ SOLOMON'S TEMPLE
*c.967–c.960*BCE, JERUSALEM, ISRAEL

A seventeenth-century impression of Solomon's Temple, inspired by the description in 1 Kings 6. Building it took seven years and 180,000 men. Solomon presided over the dedication ceremony. As that reached its climax, smoke filled the Temple to signify God's glory residing there. Only priests could enter the building itself, and only the High Priest, once a year, entered its inner sanctum, the Holy of Holies, which contained the Ark of the Covenant, a gold-covered box in which was believed to be stored the original text of the law transmitted to Moses by God.

local place of worship was developed (we know it existed by the middle of the third century), where people could meet to pray and study the Torah. These synagogues (from the Greek for "assembly") were maintained by local communities, among whom there emerged respected teachers known as rabbis. As venues for gatherings of an entire community – for example, on the weekly Sabbath day – the synagogues are the earliest true congregational places of worship.

A synagogue is effectively a prayer hall: the Torah scroll is the only thing in it that is sacred. The Temple remained Judaism's great sacred space, the setting for sacrifices, its interior visited only by the priesthood. In the first century BCE it was expanded and rebuilt on a grand scale by Herod the Great, before being destroyed by the Romans in 70CE during the suppression of the Jewish Revolt. The Jews were ejected from Jerusalem, and a great new wave of exiles joined the already well-established Jewish communities living in various parts of the polyglot ancient world. Without the Temple, sacrifice ceased and the priesthood was effectively redundant. These losses made synagogues central places of worship in Judaism and from the third century CE in particular large numbers appear to have been built.

It may only be in this period after the loss of the second Temple that there emerged a consistent arrangement for the interior of the synagogue: the space is usually rectilinear, with its longitudinal axis pointing towards Jerusalem. In the middle of the Jerusalem-facing wall is a sanctuary area containing an elaborate fitting, the Holy Ark, or *Aron Kodesh*, within which is a copy of the holy Torah. Also on the axis, but varying in its location *vis-à-vis* the Ark, is a platform from which prayer is led, called the *bimah* or *tevah*. The sides of the room are occupied by worshippers, who sit on ledges on the walls. This arrangement has distinct echoes of the hierarchies of sacred space – culminating in an enclosure within which sits a sacred text – seen in both the Temple and the Tabernacle.

Although some beautiful old medieval synagogues have survived, the vast majority have been lost and only ruins exist from earlier eras. Like all religious buildings in the Mediterranean world between the second and sixth centuries CE, the first wave of post-Temple synagogues were

○ MOSES AND THE ROCK OF HOREB
c.245CE, DURA EUROPOS, SYRIA

The discovery of art within the synagogue at the abandoned city of Dura Europos in the 1930s meant that Judaism's prohibition on imagery had to be reinterpreted. The many paintings were probably used as displays to teach the history and laws of Judaism. This image depicts a story from Exodus, in which Moses obtained water for the Israelites in the wilderness by striking the rock at Horeb.

in the Roman style of architecture. They were sometimes richly decorated, with handsome figurative mosaics, or even biblical scenes painted on their walls – a type of imagery that in general has been avoided in Jewish art because of its idolatrous implications, but which is spectacularly preserved at the early (mid-third century CE) synagogue of Dura Europos, now in the National Museum of Damascus. Later synagogues, of which more survive, continued to follow local stylistic practice, be it Christian Gothic or Moorish Islamic – or, indeed, Indian or Chinese, for there were ancient Jewish communities throughout Asia.

In many parts of Europe a virulent anti-semitism developed among Christians. Jewish settlement was restricted by the authorities to specific areas and the activities of Jews were controlled. While there were (and are) Jews who opposed architectural grandeur for religious reasons, it was more often the cramped and oppressive conditions in many Jewish communities that meant that synagogues could not be large, and some synagogues were even unrecognizable from the outside.

CONTINUES ON PAGE 109

THE JEWISH YEAR

POSSIBLY *c.*518–*c.*527, SYNAGOGUE AT BETH ALPHA, JEZREEL VALLEY, ISRAEL

The third to seventh centuries CE was a fascinating time for Jewish culture, steeped as it then was in the visual traditions of the Greco-Roman world. The significance of synagogues had increased in Jewish religious life and the example of ambitious Christian churches led to a flowering of art in a faith that had mostly avoided depicting sacred scenes, especially in places of worship.

The mosaics at Beth Alpha (or Bet Alfa) are folk art, laid when Palestine was part of the Byzantine empire, and they cover the entire floor of the small synagogue (14m by 28m/46ft by 92ft). The synagogue itself was not new when this mosaic was laid: a simpler mosaic floor lies beneath the current one. A *bimah* was added to the building later on in the sixth century. It was the subsequent collapse of the entire building in an earthquake that saved the floor, including this depiction of the Jewish year, from iconoclastic destruction in the seventh century and preserved it intact. The buried synagogue was rediscovered in 1928 by Jewish settlers in British Mandate Palestine and it is now part of an archaeological park.

❶ Abraham (with nimbus) listens to the voice from heaven commanding him not to kill his son, even as he is holding Isaac over the flame. With its themes of sacrifice and divine destiny, the story was at this time often shown in Christian art. As described in Genesis 22:13, the ram's horns are caught in a thicket. Remarkably in Jewish art, the hand of God is depicted, emerging from a heaven imagined as a place of palm trees.

❷ Helios, the Greek sun god, his head surrounded by rays, is emerging from a sinking night sky, as if at dawn, pulled by a *quadriga* (four-horse chariot). He is reminiscent of Ezekiel's vision of the divine chariot. This emblem of the sun is surrounded by twelve panels, running anti-clockwise and comprising a wheel of the zodiac (*mazalot*). Cancer, marking midsummer, is at the top, depicted as a local breed of crab, *Potamion potamios*. The four seasons are in the corners of the square.

▶ SYNAGOGUE AT BETH ALPHA

*c.*518–*c.*527, JEZREEL VALLEY, ISRAEL

The Beth Alpha synagogue was entered through a courtyard **Ⓐ** and a narthex or entrance corridor **Ⓑ**. It had a broadly basilican plan, with columns running down the interior **Ⓒ**, enclosing a 4.5m-wide (15ft) central vessel. A bench lay against the walls, and there was probably a women's gallery above. An apse in the south wall **Ⓓ** marked the direction of Jerusalem. The entire interior was covered in mosaic decoration, of which the most important scenes filled the central vessel. The visitor entering the building would have seen three scenes: at the entrance, the Sacrifice of Isaac **Ⓔ**; in the middle of the main space, a large zodiac, probably to reflect the significance of the Jewish ritual year **Ⓕ**; and against the sanctuary, a depiction of the sanctuary furnishings themselves **Ⓖ**, dominated by the Ark in which the Torah scrolls were stored. Everything was labelled in Aramaic, and inscriptions on the threshold of the front door commemorated those who donated the floor (the local community, with a special contribution from the rabbi and his son), with the names of its craftsmen, Marianos and his son Hanina, given in Greek.

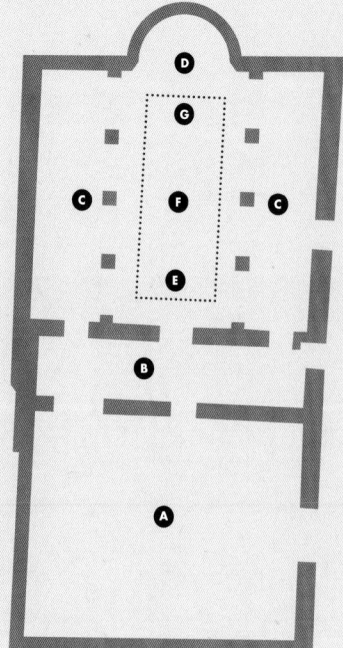

❸ The *Aron Kodesh* ("Holy Ark") is depicted as a tabernacle with richly decorated doors, behind which are the sacred Torah scrolls. Aspects of the Ark's design reflect the Temple in Jerusalem.

4 Items linked with the year's key festivals: the *shofar* ram horn (bottom), blown at Yom Kippur and Rosh Hashanah; and the *lulav*, a palm branch, and *etrog*, a lemon-like fruit, used during Sukkot (the Feast of Tabernacles).

5 At the centre of the Ark's richly decorated gable is a hanging lamp, the *ner tamid* ("Eternal Light"), which is kept burning in front of the Ark as a reminder of God's presence in human life.

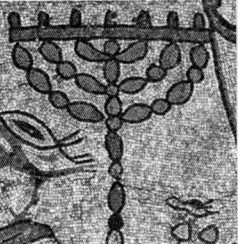

6 This is the seven-branched candelabrum, or *menorah*, used in the Temple at Jerusalem. Two lit candelabra (*menorot*) are depicted in the mosaic and each is decorated with knops and flowers.

From the seventeenth century a more tolerant atmosphere developed in parts of Europe, and during the ensuing Enlightenment, synagogue architecture slowly blossomed. By the twentieth century, following waves of migration by Jews from Russia and eastern Europe who wanted to escape poverty and violent oppression, synagogues could be found in many parts of the world. The grand "cathedral" or "choral" synagogues of that era, such as the New Synagogue in Berlin (1859) and the Temple Emanu-El in New York (1927), are truly impressive places of worship. Some are stylistically adventurous too, such as Erich Mendelsohn's Park Synagogue (1950) in Cleveland, Ohio, with its circular, dome-covered prayer hall. Such synagogues often housed a range of facilities, such as auditoriums, kitchens or schools, in keeping with their role as the focus of community life.

The twentieth century, of course, resulted in a genocide of European Jews, the destruction of thousands of synagogues and the loss of countless precious artworks. Since the founding of modern Israel in 1948, Jews who have settled there have created an extraordinarily varied synagogue architecture.

A profound and complex influence

In many ways, synagogues appear to offer a blueprint for churches and mosques. For example, the arrangement of Ark, *bimah* and congregational space seen in the synagogue, which has its roots in the Tabernacle, is very close to that of the *mihrab*, *minbar* and prayer hall of the mosque and the altar, pulpit and nave of the church. However, the question of exactly which features originated in Judaism and how, when and in what direction architectural ideas moved between the faiths is harder to resolve. Synagogues were profoundly shaped by the loss of the Temple and the experience of diaspora, events which occurred as Christianity was

○ PRINCES ROAD SYNAGOGUE
1874, OLD HEBREW CONGREGATION, LIVERPOOL, ENGLAND

A stylistic blend of Eastern and Western influences, partly influenced by archaeological reconstructions of Solomon's Temple, this synagogue has a standard form, with a *bimah* facing an Ark in a sanctuary (at the Jerusalem or *mizrah* end). There are galleries for female worshippers. Seating here faces the *bimah* rather than the Ark, behind which there is a gallery for a choir.

○ NEW SYNAGOGUE
1859, BERLIN, GERMANY

"Cathedral-synagogues" are among the most impressive places of worship from the nineteenth century. Shaped by the Reform movement in Judaism, these buildings made provision for liturgical music. The influence at that time of the styles of the past meant that Moorish and Egyptian motifs were seen as apt for synagogues.

emerging. The artistic and philosophical traditions of the Greco-Roman world, and indeed the religious architecture of the Near and Middle East, also formed a backdrop to the development of all three faiths.

Nevertheless, the absent Temple (its presumed site now occupied by the Islamic Dome of the Rock) and the sacred city of Jerusalem in which it stands have remained central to all the "peoples of the book": biblical accounts of the Temple influenced church liturgy and architecture, while the Islamic relationship of Ka'ba and mosque is derived from that of Temple and synagogue. Judaism has been influential beyond its size (with about 15 million adherents worldwide), and synagogues can justifiably claim, in the West at least, to be the oldest type of religious building still in use.

CHRISTIANITY

GOD INCARNATED

———————————◯———————————

The great churches of the world were designed as places in which congregations of believers could come together to witness and participate in the sacred rite of the Eucharist. They required two, interconnected, kinds of space: one big enough to hold a large group of people, the other a smaller sanctuary in which a member of the priesthood could perform the rite. These twin requirements have shaped much of the resulting architecture, which is astonishing in its variety.

The dominant form was axial and copied that of the basilica, a Roman meeting hall. Basilicas have aisles either side of a wider, higher, central space, which ends in a semi-circular extension known as an apse. While the main space allowed congregants to gather, the apse provided a sanctuary, exclusive to the priesthood. Its main furnishing was the table-like altar at which the Eucharist was performed. Outside, the church was made visible by the use of a dome or a bell-tower.

EARLY CHRISTIAN ART

The earliest Christian sites, from catacombs and house churches to *martyriums*, are decorated with an emerging language of Christian symbols. Some emblems were new, such as the fish (*ichthys* – from an acronym of Greek words describing Christ), and the *Chi-Rho* christogram. Others, such as Christ as a Good Shepherd, drew upon Greco-Roman imagery of Hermes carrying a ram as the protector of flocks and Orpheus, the charmer of animals, as well as Old Testament motifs, such as Jonah and the Whale.

This depiction of Jesus as a shepherd tending his flock is from the Catacomb of Priscilla in Rome, fourth century or earlier.

⏵ EASTER "MIRACLE OF HOLY FIRE"

325/326–336 AND LATER, CHURCH OF THE HOLY SEPULCHRE, JERUSALEM

The circular Anastasis or Resurrection church, much altered and rebuilt since the fourth century, is one of Christendom's most influential buildings. At its centre stands the Holy Sepulchre, sculpted out of the rock and containing the tomb in which the burial and resurrection of Jesus are said to have taken place. Every Easter, Orthodox Christians flock to witness a fire that they claim is miraculously kindled within the tomb.

⬤ THE SELFLESS SACRIFICE

*c.*1120, APSE MOSAIC, SAN CLEMENTE, ROME, ITALY

Depictions of the Crucifixion, with a grieving Mary
and apostle John on either side, have long encouraged
empathy with Christ's suffering. This cross emerges from
a tree, reaching towards the hand of God in heaven and
symbolizing the growth of the Church.

The second most important plan was a centralized structure, circular or polygonal, usually with an outer aisle around
a central space. This central sanctuary area held the altar, or
perhaps a tomb (this form was derived from Roman mausoleums). Such commemorative structures were, and are,
important in Christianity because of the sacrificial death at
the heart of the faith – that of its founder, Jesus Christ.

Death, sacrifice and resurrection

Jesus of Nazareth was a Jewish preacher in the political tinderbox of Roman-occupied Palestine. Some Jews claimed him to be the Messiah, a divinely "anointed" one (in Greek, *Khristós* or Christ), as prophesied in Jewish scripture, who would usher in a new age of peace. His followers claimed that Jesus was at once fully human and fully divine, an integral part of a monotheistic God who had incarnated as a mortal human being. He had sacrificed himself on behalf of humanity, and had been bodily resurrected three days later. At the end of time, they said, he would return in triumph, to judge the living and the dead, and establish the kingdom of God. In the Eucharistic rite that commemorates this sacrifice, bread and wine are emblems of Christ's body and blood, and Christians live in hope of a similar resurrection.

Christ's sacrifice was also remembered in the symbol of the cross on which he died. The third major type of church plan evoked this: by placing a north–south arm called a "transept" across an axial building, a cross was formed. In this situation, the altar (or a tomb) can be placed either in the centre or at one end of the axis. The lengths of the arms of the building can also be varied: if they are equal (a Greek cross), the plan is centralized; if one arm is longer than the other (a Latin cross), the result is an axial building transected by a cross-arm.

Variety and change

The exploration of multitudinous ways of combining axial and centralized structures is a major theme of Christian architecture, which is marked by exceptional levels of stylistic evolution. This variety partly reflects the varying understandings Christians have had of such ideas as the Eucharist. For Orthodox Christians, this rite is a "Holy Mystery", and the sanctuary is sealed behind a wall-like screen known as an *iconostasis*. Similarly, the chancel arch, roodscreen and altar rails traditional in Roman Catholic churches reflect the interpretation of the Eucharist within this tradition. For some Nonconformist Christian denominations, the Eucharist is merely a shared meal, taken occasionally: a church may be a simple meeting house with no altar. A range of views sit between these interpretations, each affecting the sanctuary.

The sanctuary was particularly important to the Eastern Orthodox and Western (Latin or Roman Catholic) Church traditions, which originated Christian architecture and dominated its development from the third century to the seventeenth or eighteenth centuries CE. Although the resulting buildings can comprise little more than a single room divided by a screen, at their most complex they are vast, labyrinthine structures, with many altars located in interconnected smaller sanctuaries known as chapels, in addition to the main or "high" altar that is the focus of the building.

Image and meaning

Christianity often uses physical forms as analogies for ideas. The English word church derives from the Greek word *ekklesia*, which meant a meeting place for discussion, and came to be applied both to buildings (a church) and to the community of the faithful (the Church). Ultimately, this metaphorical way of thinking may be derived from the symbolism of the Eucharist, and beyond this the idea of incarnation – of God as man – that lies at the heart of the faith.

Heaven is described briefly in the Bible as a vast, yet ordered, city-like environment, lit by a supernatural light and made of precious stones. When combined with the large interiors needed to combine sanctuary and congregation in a single space, these metaphors have provided potent fuel for centuries of architectural invention. Vaults and domes were often used to evoke heaven; or bell-towers were topped by spires that emphasized the proximity of the celestial sphere.

Occasionally, certain motifs became associated with specific meanings, but then tended to lose this focus over time (see box, page 24). Some simple numbers – three for the Christian doctrine of the Trinity (God's three indivisible aspects: Father, Son and Holy Spirit), twelve for the number of Christ's first followers, the apostles – occur frequently, but only on some occasions is this use demonstrably symbolic.

Other specific meanings are associated with images. The function of these is, in theory, to instruct and inform the laity, and to add beauty to the house of God; but they have often become the focus of cultic attention in their own right. Conventional attributes helped people to recognize the subject depicted: St. Peter holds keys; St. Paul holds a sword;

CHURCHES AS EVOLVING FORMS

The basic arrangement of such early churches as 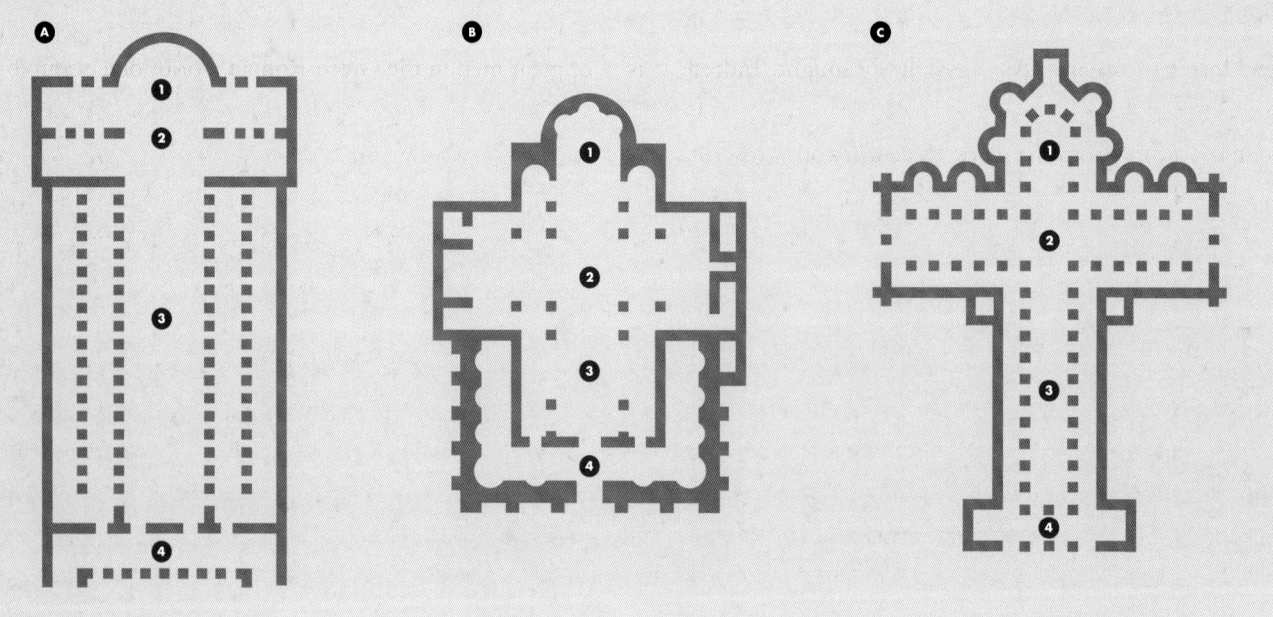A San Paolo fuori le Mura (384) in Rome was based on that of the Roman basilica, or meeting hall: an axial building, entered from an area known as a narthex ❹, which led to a roomy nave with side aisles ❸, culminating in an apse ❶, where the clergy sat during services. However, the designers added a cross-arm, an early form of transept ❷, and located the altar here rather than in the apse; the shrine of the saint stood in front of and below the altar.

In San Marco in Venice ❶ (c.830 and after c.1063), an example of the Eastern or Byzantine mode, the transept ❷ was used to make a cross-shaped or centralized plan, known as a Greek Cross, with an axial emphasis provided chiefly by the larger domes along the main axis ❸ and the ritual apse ❶ beyond, which contains the high altar. This stood above the crypt, which held the shrine of St. Mark. Domes dominated the main spaces, which were surrounded by narrow aisles and chapels. In 1204 the grand narthex ❹ was extended around the nave.

In the Western Church, axiality was the main focus, and vaults were more popular than domes – as in the cathedral at Santiago de Compostela in Spain ❻ (from c.1075). The elements of the plan were less integrated with each other than in the Greek Cross, with a long nave ❸ and transept ❷, both with aisles and – off the transept – apsidal chapels facing east. Further chapels extended around the apse ❶, with its ambulatory aisle and altar, resulting in a complex east end. Once again, the shrine (of St. James) was in a crypt beneath this area. The narthex was replaced with a grand porch ❹, with a towering façade above it. As Romanesque moved into Gothic, these elements were unified: transepts and chapels projected less; east ends varied in layout; there was usually no crypt; any shrine now stood behind the high altar; and buttresses became more emphatic. The Renaissance brought back domes and centralized plans, combining them with axial layouts in new ways. Baroque plans were flowing, breaking down spatial distinctions, although based on the same underlying templates.

the Nativity or Crucifixion have agreed iconographies. Some Christian traditions eschew imagery, pointing out that it appears to be proscribed by the Ten Commandments, and there have been outbreaks of iconoclasm at various points. As a result, deliberately plain churches emerged, decorated with simple symbols or passages of biblical scripture.

Christian sacred landscapes

The ground in which churches sit has (in most traditions) been consecrated, and is sealed from the rest of the world by an enclosing wall. It is usually used for burial. The building set within this enclosure faces east, notionally towards Jerusalem (see page 32). This city was the setting for Christ's death and resurrection, the place where the Last Judgment would begin, and a metaphor for heaven and the Church. A church's entrance façade might also be Jerusalem's walls (see page 48), the interior – and especially the sanctuary – the city itself. Pilgrims flocked to the actual Jerusalem, and both the form of its churches and the physical layout of the hilltop city were enormously influential.

The shrines of Christian saints – exceptional individuals who had imitated Christ in their lives – attracted pilgrims along a network of routes criss-crossing Christendom. After Jerusalem, the most popular pilgrimage destination was Rome, burial place of Christ's early followers Peter and Paul. Major pilgrimage routes were marked by magnificent churches, such as those along the Way of St. James, which still leads from central France to the shrine of St. James the Apostle at Santiago de Compostela in northwestern Spain. Local cults and sacred sites, from miracle-working images to holy wells, were also widespread.

Christianity took the architectural discoveries of the ancient world and reinvented them. It created colossal, open interior spaces and explored the way in which they were illuminated by light, and these ideas were exported globally. Christian architecture originated the idea of "style", in which new forms of ornament are ceaselessly sought. Indeed, it is the very restlessness of this architecture, especially marked in western Europe from the eleventh century onwards, that is as remarkable as the named styles in which churches were built. This restlessness has roots deep within Christianity itself.

The earliest churches

For 300 years, Christianity barely had any architecture. Christians were at first an insignificant group, spread throughout the Mediterranean world, partly because of the exile of Jews that followed the destruction of the Temple in 70CE. Christianity became a major cult, and Christians'

refusal to partake in imperial sacrifices was just one of the ways in which the Roman authorities saw them as a threat. Persecution was sporadic, but could be violent, creating many martyrs and giving rise to the first saints' cults.

Throughout this time, Christians met in house churches and were buried in cemeteries, both in the open air and underground (catacombs), which were architecturally identical to the homes and burial places of people from other faiths. We have a snapshot of such buildings in the form of the remains of a house church at Dura Europos (before 256–257) in Syria, which had separate rooms for teaching potential converts and for congregational worship, as well as an arched recess over a tub for holding water – an early font, a furnishing later ubiquitous in Christian churches. Tombs of martyrs were marked out by small architectural structures, much like the *heroa* monuments that were erected over the graves of great men in the Greco-Roman world: one example is the Chapel of the Popes in the catacomb of St. Callisto, Rome, *c*.250. These were the first *martyrium*s, a type of building, functioning as much as a memorial as a burial place, which would flourish in the fourth century (see also box, page 110).

It is during this time that much of Christianity's distinctive fusion of Judaic and Greco-Roman cultural ideas took place. Many aspects of Christian liturgy are of Jewish origin: the Eucharist is derived from the Seder, the meal shared by Jews to mark the Passover, which was celebrated by Jesus and the apostles shortly before his death (the Last Supper). Like Jews (and, later, Muslims), Christians gathered weekly on a Sabbath or holy day, and their festivals, such as those of Christ's birth (Christmas), and his death and resurrection

⬤ ENAMEL AND COPPER RELIQUARY
c.1185–1195, LIMOGES, FRANCE

Saints' cults once flourished in Western Christendom. Many of the faithful believed that intercession was more likely if they prayed near to the remains of those whose souls were already in heaven. Churches that held the body of a saint created shrines, which attracted pilgrims. More churches owned only small reliquaries such as this, which contained fragments of bone, hair or objects associated with a saint, or saints, and would be shown on special occasions. Reliquaries made at Limoges, the main centre of enamel production in Europe at the time, were often shaped like small churches or houses; in turn, some Gothic churches – such as Sainte-Chapelle (see page 126) – are like enormous shrines.

(Easter), marked significant moments in the past. Much Christian thinking about sanctuary spaces has its roots in the Jewish Temple (and thus, before it, in the Tabernacle).

From imperial Rome came, among other things, a well-developed institutional hierarchy, in which governing bishops had oversight of groups of priests and their congregations. Equally important was the acceptance by Christians of the rich tradition of architectural motifs and sacred images used across the Greco-Roman world. Bishops were marked out within their churches by being given a special seat or throne, in early churches positioned at the far end of the apse, and known in Greek as a *kathedra*. A church that contains such a seat is thus a "cathedral". An architectural hierarchy is suggested by the emergence of a distinction between cathedral and other churches, and it was to be at the top – in cathedrals, and also in major monastic churches – that the full weight of Christian architectural creativity would be focused. Apart from a few purpose-built Christian meeting halls known to have been created by around 300, these "great churches" were invented from 312CE.

The invention of church architecture

In the early fourth century, a chain of events was initiated by the Roman emperor Constantine (reigned 306–337), who during his fight to gain supremacy over the entire empire had come to see Christ as his supernatural sponsor, much as previous emperors had seen Jupiter, Apollo or the *Sol Invictus*. He brought an end to Christian persecution by issuing a proclamation of religious freedom. From 324, in response to the gradual collapse of the western half of the empire, he moved his capital city 1,400km (870 miles) east to a Greek colony called Byzantium, which he began to refashion as a New Rome, and renamed Constantinople.

Constantine's personal commitment to a fully understood Christianity is often questioned; nevertheless he, and to a lesser extent his mother Helena and his son Constantius II, sponsored the creation of several magnificent Christian places of worship. Of these the most significant were those in Rome (including a cathedral, St. John Lateran, from 313, and a *martyrium* church of St. Peter, from 324); in Jerusalem, a city that had been something of a backwater since the events

of 70CE, where a great church (the Church of the Holy Sepulchre, 325/326–336) was built over the places of death and resurrection of Christ; and at Bethlehem, Jesus' birthplace (Church of the Nativity, 333). These were soon joined by important churches in Constantinople (a dynastic burial church, the Holy Apostles, in the 350s, and the cathedral of Hagia Sophia, by 360). The sacred landscape of the empire was being reshaped for Christianity, and in the process a new type of building was invented.

It was Constantine who took the form of large, secular basilican meeting halls and applied it to churches. The apses of basilicas were often occupied by magistrates, and invariably they contained an image of an emperor or a god. At the same time, centralized tombs, especially the grand ones used for emperors – in which an aisle encircled a central burial place – were used for *martyiums*. These innovations were part of an effort to create grand buildings that served the practical needs of worship and pilgrimage, deliberately avoided looking like pagan temples (although they were less dissimilar to synagogues), and associated Christianity with Roman imperial authority.

One of the greatest early basilicas was St. Peter's in Rome, a vast church 119m (391ft) long and 64m (208ft) wide. It was entered through an arcaded corridor known as a narthex: the entrance wall of churches would remain important thereafter. The tomb of Peter, originally located in an open-air cemetery, rose in the middle of its sanctuary. The close association between a saint's shrine and the high altar would remain significant; later on, shrines often sit in a catacomb-like crypt beneath the altar, or are placed directly behind the altar. To provide space for pilgrims, and increase the separation of this sacred area from the rest of the building, a north–south arm was placed between the apse and the main hall: this was one of the first transepts. Old St. Peter's, as it is now known, was not rebuilt until the sixteenth century, and was thus seen by

◑ **THE EASTWARD APSE**

FROM 532, SANT' APOLLINARE IN CLASSE, RAVENNA, ITALY

This basilica in Ravenna's old port (Classe) has glorious mosaics – and once had even more, including the floor. The altar faces roughly east, as was then becoming the norm; this required a western entrance, north and south aisles or transepts, and an eastern apse.

churchmen from all over Europe throughout the period to come. Its dimensions were used to lay out innumerable later buildings, such as Durham cathedral in England (from 1093).

By comparison, the Church of the Holy Sepulchre in Jerusalem was really two buildings linked by a courtyard. A basilica, often simply called the *martyrium*, stood over the place of Christ's crucifixion. The Anastasis, over the place of his resurrection, was more influential: a vast (34m/110ft) circular building with an aisle and a conical, dome-like roof – the tomb in which Christ had been buried, originally excavated into a hillside, now stood exposed in the centre of the interior (see pages 110–111). Many circular churches thereafter are not merely memorial buildings, they are direct evocations of this structure, which commemorated what is arguably the central mystery at the heart of Christianity.

At the same time, an infusion of new images occurred. Constantine transferred to Christ some of the imagery that was associated with Jupiter, Apollo, the *Sol Invictus* and the deified emperors, depicting him as an all-powerful figure. This would have a lasting impact on Christian art: Orthodox churches often display the Christ Pantocrator, the "all-ruler" (see page 119), and the image of Christ in Majesty was to be equally prevalent among Roman Catholic Christians. Many of the older Christian symbols began to disappear. It is also at this time that the Crucifixion began its gradual transformation into the central identifying image of Christianity.

Triumph and divergence

From 380, Emperor Theodosius (reigned 379–395) began trying to create a single, universal – or catholic – Church, and closing pagan places of worship. Buildings proliferated: Milan and, later, Ravenna, capitals of the western part of the empire, were the settings for important churches, such as centralized, complex, ambitious San Lorenzo in Milan (before 378) and basilican Sant' Apollinare in Classe in Ravenna (from 532), with its lavish mosaic decoration, which was then beginning to enrich the interiors of churches. Although the form of these buildings is quite different from that of a pagan temple, the Roman stylistic language remained unchanged. Indeed, many churches were built with reused columns from destroyed temples.

Meanwhile, the northern and western extremes of the empire had effectively returned to a pre-Roman state, and their cities lay in ruins. Because the imperial capital and the emperor had moved east, the bishop of Rome bolstered his claim to supremacy over all Christians by claiming to have the apostolic authority of Peter, and he came to be known as the pope (from Latin *papa*, "father"). By contrast, the eastern part of the empire maintained its ancient urban cultures and Greek-based civilization. Secular and Church authority were closely aligned in the palace and cathedral at the "new Rome", where the Ecumenical Patriarch of Constantinople also claimed authority over all Christendom.

The Eastern Church: Orthodoxy

From his eastern base, Emperor Justinian (reigned 527–565) stabilized the declining empire and in 532 began to rebuild the city's cathedral. Hagia Sophia remains one of the world's most breathtaking buildings, a colossal centralized structure (71m by 77m/233ft by 253ft) with a subtle axial undertow, covered, at a height of 56m (184ft), by a dome to rival that of the Pantheon in Rome. The "great church" had a huge influence thereafter, especially in Eastern Christendom, and, later, the Islamic world (see pages 60–61), not least for its assertion that domes make a vivid evocation of heaven.

It also marked a stylistic departure. For a century or so, the crisp stylistic canon of classical architecture had been disintegrating. The technical achievements of the Romans – the vault, the dome, the arch and arcade (lintels were now rare) – remained in place, but the way in which they were decorated was changing. For example, at Hagia Sophia, the capitals have smoothly curving surfaces rather than the clearly articulated volutes and mouldings of the classical orders, and they are covered in flat, spiky foliage derived but different from the acanthus used in Corinthian columns. Based in Constantinople, emphatically Christian, and with Greek its *lingua franca*, the culture we call Byzantine had developed.

In the eastern, Byzantine, world, the centralized plan was more popular than the basilican. A series of variations on this developed, in which groups of smaller spaces were positioned around a central cruciform one (the most common is a "cross-in-square" plan); domes were used throughout the building. The body of the church was given over to the priesthood, who performed the liturgy under the central dome as well as in the eastern sanctuary, while congregants gathered mainly in the ancillary spaces.

Basilicas, too, were dominated by liturgical activity, with the aisles used by congregants and the central space a burial and ritual area leading towards the sanctuary. However, over time services came to focus on a screened-off area at the eastern end of this space known as the "choir", with the sanctuary beyond the "presbytery". In the Western Church in particular, where basilican churches predominated, the remainder of the central space, today known as the "nave", came to be seen primarily as the congregational space of the laity, although it was still used for liturgical processions and contained important altars and chapels.

Few churches in the ancient Eastern heartlands – from North Africa to the Black Sea, and from Syria to the Balkans – came close to matching Hagia Sophia. Here, doctrinally heterodox Christians, such as the Arians and Nestorians, took the faith to parts of Africa and the East (from Goa in India to Tang dynasty China), but much of the architecture is lost. In Syria (the massive four-armed *martyrium* for St. Simeon Stylites at Qalat Siman, *c.*480–*c.*490), Armenia (at Yeghvard and Ashtarak, seventh to thirteenth centuries) and Ethiopia (Lalibela's twelfth- and thirteenth-century rock-cut churches), the surviving churches are particularly impressive.

The East was also the setting for a new development – the religious community, or monastery, devoted to the service of God. By the second century, a strong ascetic tradition had emerged among Christians. People went into desert wildernesses to devote their lives to celibacy, poverty and prayer; many, like the early martyrs, were later acclaimed as saints (such as Simeon Stylites). In Palestine and Egypt, such

◐ MAGNIFICENCE IN MOSAIC

1011 OR 1022, HOSIOS LOUKAS, BOEOTIA, GREECE

This domed monastic church is an exquisite Orthodox building, its walls lined with marble and rich with mosaic decoration, culminating in a Christ Pantocrator within the central dome, which dominates the cross-shaped interior and the sanctuary with its half-dome beyond (far left). Small ancillary spaces and galleries open off this, forming a "dome-in-octagon" plan. The body of the founder, St. Loukas, was returned to the church (from Venice) in 1986.

people came together within an institution designed to permit a Christian life of perfection in greater security than was generally possible when living in isolation – an alternative, self-supporting society, cut off from the world and rooted in work and prayer, grouped around a church. Regulations, or "rules", for organizing these communities of monks and nuns were developed from the mid-300s onwards, for example by Basil of Caesarea (330–379) in the East and Benedict of Nursia (c.480–c.550) in the West. As centres of holiness and learning, monasteries (in English, divided into larger, more important "abbeys" and smaller "priories" depending on their status), spread throughout the Christian world.

Within a century of Hagia Sophia's completion, most of Eastern Christendom was overrun, at first by Persian and then later by Arab armies proclaiming the new monotheism of Islam. Most of North Africa and the Middle East was lost by Christendom, although Constantinople remained the seat of the Byzantine emperor until 1453 and the Ecumenical Patriarch of the Greek Orthodox Church is based there to this day. Islam abhors any imagery that can be interpreted as idolatry, and from 726 a comparable iconoclastic movement swept through Eastern Christianity. Mosaics and wall paintings were destroyed, to be replaced by simple geometric patterns, images from the natural world or monumental crosses. When, in 843, this policy was overturned, an opposing reaction took place and a deep, mystical devotion to icons (Greek *eikon*, "image") developed. The way in which scenes were depicted was closely prescribed; the very presence of such images was considered spiritually efficacious. To this day, Orthodox icons, filling the *iconostasis* dividing the sanctuary from the rest of an Orthodox church, are kissed reverently by worshippers. Such imagery can be seen in many small-scale monastic churches with beautifully adorned interiors, such as Hosios Loukas (see page 119) in Greece and the Chora church (before 1321) in Istanbul. Architecture on a grander scale was erected in younger centres of the faith.

Russia: the new leader of the Orthodox

In the far north, the peoples known as the Rus' developed important centres in Kiev and Novgorod, and in 988 the kings of Kiev adopted Christianity, swayed partly by a visit to Hagia Sophia. Kiev's cathedral of St. Sophia (1037) adopted the centralized, dome-based architecture of the Eastern Church. Here, however, a large congregation seems to have been particularly important, and there were many small square bays around the central cross, resulting in an exterior dominated by a profusion of small cupolas, clustered together in a pyramidal arrangement. The result looked a little like a model city of many churches, which may have been part of the idea: multi-domed churches that are also images of Jerusalem became a theme in Russian church architecture.

Although Russia absorbed influences from Romanesque Europe and, later, Renaissance Italy, the basic form defined at Kiev remained constant. The clustered effect was enhanced by placing the domes in tight arrangements and raising them on high drums. When Moscow became the capital of Russia, its rulers saw themselves as tsars (from the Latin *Caesar*), inheritors of Constantinople's role as protector of the Orthodox Christian peoples, and they began to conquer lands from the Islamic empires on their fringes.

The first tsar, in 1547, was Ivan IV, the "Terrible". As an offering of thanks for his victories over the Islamic khanates, from 1555 he began the Cathedral of the Intercession on the Moat, just outside his castle-palace, the Kremlin, in Moscow. Much altered in subsequent decades, it is better known as St. Basil's, after the saint whose shrine it contains. Its onion domes were particularly influential and similar

⬤ **MANDYLION OF CHRIST**
*c.*12TH CENTURY, NOVGOROD, RUSSIA

The cloth used by Christ to wipe his face on the way to Calvary was believed to have been imprinted with his image, making it a miraculous "icon not made with hands". Paintings of it were widespread from the twelfth century in the Orthodox world.

◐ ORTHODOX VICTORY
1555 AND LATER, ST. BASIL'S,
MOSCOW, RUSSIA

The onion-shaped profile of
St. Basil's cathedral's eight
domes (additions made in
1586), clustered around a
central, tent-shaped bell-tower
(61m/197ft high), was hugely
influential. Each dome tops a
building that is in fact a separate
church – buildings whose
symbolism simultaneously
evokes Jerusalem, the Trinity
and the triumph of Muscovite
Orthodoxy after the defeats of
Muslim khans at Kazan in 1552
and Astrakhan in 1554–1556.

pyramidal arrangements can be seen throughout the Russian
Orthodox world in many buildings in wood (a medium in
which Russians excelled), brick and stone. The form of the
dome may come from the mosques of Central Asia, or it may
be intended to evoke the Church of the Holy Sepulchre in
Jerusalem, as it was understood to look from engravings.

In Russia, the Orthodox Church has created an architecture of exceptional scale and constant innovation, suffused
with a dynamic energy that is almost mystically concentrated and intense. From the early days of Kiev the image
or analogy of the holy city has been particularly influential.
For example, the Renaissance and Baroque achievements
of the New Jerusalem monastery (1658) – an attempt to
build Jerusalem on the edge of Moscow – or the enormous
Newmaiden or Smolny Convent (designed 1741), built in
St. Petersburg after Peter the Great moved the capital there
in 1712, are convincing reinventions of Russian tradition, as
impressive as any churches in the world.

The Western Church emerges

Much of the western Roman empire, too, was originally on
the edge of Christendom. By the ninth century the area was
largely Christian, and contained many churches, mostly
in local variations of Byzantine practice. When ambitious

Christian polities did start to emerge, it was to Rome that
they looked. Charles the Great, or Charlemagne, built a
large and powerful "Carolingian" empire in which Latin
Christian civilization was actively promoted, and in 800 was
made "emperor of the Romans" by the pope: a direct challenge to the authority of the Eastern Church, and the root
of a Christian imperial institution, the Holy Roman Empire,
which finally came to an end only in 1806.

Charlemagne's Palatine Chapel at Aachen (c.790) was
the first Christian building we know of north of the Alps to
match the achievements further south and east. Indeed, this
centralized building would not look out of place in Ravenna
or Constantinople. As splendid as the remaining chapel is,
developments elsewhere were more significant for the future.
Charlemagne alone is credited with founding or rebuilding
sixteen cathedrals and 232 monasteries, giving rise to many
new architectural ideas, best seen at the abbey church at
Corvey (from c.873) in Germany.

This had striking towers, soon to be topped by spires,
and a complex west end known as a "westwork". Bell-towers
had been an eye-catching element in Christian architecture
since the fifth century; in the West they, rather than domes,
became the prominent external marker showing that a building was a church. In other respects, most churches in the

West were simple, albeit often richly decorated, variants on the basilica. However, they began almost universally to be constructed from cut stone, whereas tile and concrete in the Roman manner remained common in the East. The West was changing in other ways too: towns and cities were growing fast, and required new churches; large monasteries often became major centres of Latin culture and sponsors of ambitious buildings. During the eleventh century, architecture in the West went through a step-change in which Eastern influence began to fall away, and a ceaseless flow of new styles and structural innovations began which continues to this day.

The Romanesque revolution

From the 1020s and 1030s, churches began to display a new kind of complexity, affecting structure and decoration alike. Known as Romanesque, this was the first architectural style to have its roots firmly in western Europe, and it was to outdo the achievements of both the East and ancient Rome.

The resulting changes are exemplified by the eleventh-century cathedral of St. Mary and St. Stephen in Speyer,

Germany. This is a basilican church, 134m (440ft) long and over 37m (121ft) wide, with transepts and an apse: as in any other such church, windows and arcades march in step down the central space. Traditionally, the wall areas between would be filled largely with painted images, but here these bays are the setting for repeated architectural compositions, in which mast-like half columns separate each bay and help support a curved vault 33m (108ft) high. Such ceilings proved to have much potential: while they lacked the dome's ability to bridge enormous centralized spaces, they brought greater visual unity to large, axial, multi-bayed buildings than would have been achieved had they been roofed by long sequences of domes. And like domes, curved stone vaults were visually arresting, vivid evocations of heaven.

All the surfaces in the building would have been whitewashed or painted in colour, perhaps using geometrical patterns or in imitation of marble; sacred scenes might have been depicted over altars. In spite of the complexity of the church plan, with a large crypt and space for several chapels at both the eastern and western ends of the building, this consistent use of repeated architectural motifs, supporting a series of curved stone vaults, gives the interior great internal unity. Externally, the result is a large building with a dramatic, many-towered profile.

By 1100, such ideas were being explored in many parts of western Europe. In France, the mighty monastery at Cluny, rebuilt from 1088, may have been the largest building under a single roof in the world at 183m (600ft) long and 30m (100ft) wide. Plans had become highly complex: all the main liturgical functions were now located in the east end, where, beyond the chancel arch and separated by screens there was a nesting of holy spaces – choir, presbytery, saint's shrine – surrounded by aisles and side-chapels. A monastic template had also emerged, with communal eating (refectory), sleeping (dormitory) and meeting (chapter house) rooms positioned around a courtyard of corridors known as a cloister.

◖ CATHEDRAL OF ST. MARY AND ST. STEPHEN
*c.*1030–*c.*1061, SPEYER, GERMANY

Built as the burial place of German kings, Speyer acquired its rib vaults after 1082, resulting in the grouping of its bays into pairs. Most of the Romanesque nave was reconstructed from 1772.

◗ NARRATIVE CAPITALS

*c.*1120, VÉZELAY ABBEY, BURGUNDY, FRANCE

Romanesque sculpture replaced the hieratic imagery of Byzantium with an elastic energy. Vézelay's nave has 138 capitals, depicting scenes that teach the faithful. Here, Moses pours grain (the Old Testament) into a mill (symbolizing Christ), and when it emerges as flour it is collected by the apostle Paul (the New Testament).

The desire to vault enormously wide and high buildings in stone, and in ways that enhanced the impression of ordered unity provided by the bays, led to experiments with the very form of these vaults. Slender cross-arches known as ribs were added. The earliest dated example of this technique is Durham cathedral in England (from 1093), an entire great church filled with rib vaults. Other details at Durham, like the fake "blank" arcades that line the walls and the large windows, are harbingers of the twelfth century, in which ornament became ever more lavish and delicate, windows and other openings became ever bigger, and rib vaults became a feature expected of all ambitious churches.

These developments fuelled further explorations, against a backdrop of reform, renaissance and expansion in the Western Church. Formal schism with the Eastern Church took place in 1054, and in 1095 the Crusades were launched to retrieve the Holy Land from Islam. The Church of the Holy Sepulchre, destroyed by a caliph in 1004–1013, was rebuilt from 1131. Contact with Eastern learning led to a cultural and intellectual resurgence, and there are signs of a widespread religious revival at this time. Thousands of local, or parish, churches were built or rebuilt. Saints' cults, particularly the burgeoning one surrounding Mary, Christ's mother, seem to have blossomed – many of the great churches on the Way of St. James date from the twelfth century. Intense emotions also focused on the cross on which Christ had been crucified. Life-size sculptures of the crucifix (in English, the rood) came to dominate church interiors, usually set above the stone or timber screen that separated nave from sanctuary.

When the doctrine of transubstantiation was officialized from 1215, an even more charged significance was given to the space around the high altar. Decoration in this part of the church became ever more lavish and, over the ensuing centuries, many churches rebuilt their east ends more than once,

to give the sanctuary a more palatial setting, or to improve routes for processions and the pilgrims who wanted to visit saints' shrines. Plans of east ends became diverse, with the apsidal outline only one of an increasing number of options.

Meanwhile, monasticism began to split into competing, transnational institutions, known as orders, with their own vision of the ideal religious community, sometimes with a distinctive architectural vision. The Cistercians (from 1125) desired ascetic purity and simplicity, exemplified by the Cistercian abbey at Pontigny (late 1130s), with its cool, simply detailed interior. The mendicant, or "begging" orders, from the early thirteenth century onwards, combined a commitment to missionary work in the rapidly expanding cities with a strict personal vow of poverty. Their vast, plain "preaching hall" churches became a striking presence in the urban landscape – an example is SS Giovanni e Paolo, the Dominican church in Venice (from 1333–1334) – standing in contrast to the palatial abbeys and cathedrals and the small, richly furnished parish churches around them.

Gothic: an architecture of light

An extraordinary series of architectural experiments with light and space took place in the churches of the Île de France from about 1140. These combined the idea of the bay

CONTINUES ON PAGE 126

ROSE DE FRANCE

1233–1234, CHARTRES CATHEDRAL, FRANCE

Chartres cathedral has long been a major focus of pilgrimage because it possesses the tunic (*Sancta Camisa*) of Mary, the mother of Jesus Christ. The current church was built immediately after a disastrous fire in 1194. The result was one of the first great masterpieces of the Gothic style, which aimed to flood churches with coloured light.

The new cathedral was designed so that its windows were as large and prominent as possible, and it may have been intended from the outset to be the first building lit completely by large expanses of stained glass, much of which survives.

▶ THE NORTH TRANSEPT WINDOW

1233–1234, CHARTRES CATHEDRAL, FRANCE

The masonry of the north transept window, known as the "Rose de France", had been installed by 1223 and the 10.5m-wide (34ft) window was glazed by 1234. The images depicted in it glorify the Virgin Mary as the inviolate medium by which Jesus Christ was sent to man, and emphasize how the coming of Christ at once replaced and fulfilled Jewish teaching. Most of the figures, apart from Mary and her mother Anne, are from the Old Testament. The window opposite, in the south transept, reflects the New Testament and the role of Christ.

The upper and lower parts of the "Rose de France" explore the theme in different ways. The images in the upper part would easily have been recognized by any viewer, but those in the lower were rather unusual. Chartres was a major intellectual centre at this time, and it is possible that such windows were designed by well-informed churchmen, partly as "teaching aids" to deepen the knowledge of visiting pilgrims. In spite of the anti-semitism prevalent during this period, the window illustrates the profound debt Christianity owes to Judaism; its main patron, Blanche of Castile, is known to have defended French Jews from unfair attacks.

UPPER WINDOW   LOWER WINDOW LANCETS

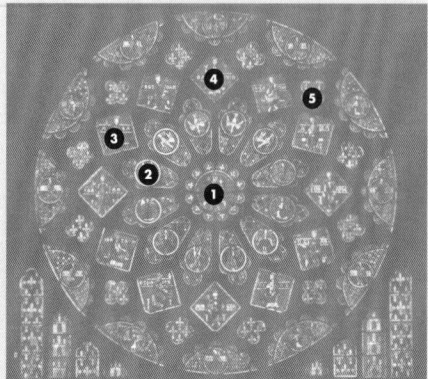

❶ The upper part of the window contains the rose, in the middle of which sits the Virgin Mary, who was believed to have been crowned the Queen of Heaven, with the Christ child on her knee.

UPPER WINDOW SECTIONS

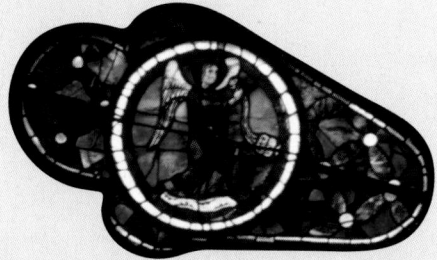

❷ This angel, swinging a censer full of incense, is one of eight (bearing censers or candles) that surround and glorify Mary in the centre of the window. There are also four doves, symbolizing the Holy Spirit and bringing God's grace.

❸ This is Asa, king of Judah, who eradicated idolatry from his kingdom. He is one of twelve model rulers of Judah who appear in the squares arranged in a ring beyond the angels and doves. The twelve outer semi-circles contain representations of Old Testament prophets, all of whom were believed by Christians to be ancestors or precursors of Christ.

❹ This is King David, an ancestor of Jesus through his father, Joseph. The biblical Saviour was seen as a "son" or descendant of David. This belief in Jesus' genealogy meant crowds acclaimed him as the "Son of David".

❺ Heraldic badges from two high-status families fill many of the lights. The dominant images are these yellow-on-blue *fleurs-de-lis*, symbols of the Virgin Mary and of the Capetian royal house of France. The window was probably donated by Blanche of Castile, whose family arms of golden castles on red also appear. Blanche had ruled France as regent and her son Louis IX began to rule in his own right from about 1234.

LOWER WINDOW LANCETS

❻ The window has a row of five lancet lights. The outer two show Melchizedek, priest and king, and Aaron, first High Priest. They embody priesthood, prefiguring the Church, while symbolizing faith and humility respectively. Beneath their virtuous figures is a contrasting vice. Here, below Melchizedek, Nebuchadnezzar engages in idolatry. In the other, below Aaron, a pharaoh embodies pride.

❼ The inner lancets flanking the central one show David and Solomon, embodying kingship at its best, and symbolizing hope and wisdom respectively. David (shown here) holds a harp, emphasizing his role as psalmist. Beneath the virtuous main figure is a contrasting vice: Saul killing himself in despair. In the bottom of Solomon's lancet light (second lancet from the right), Jeroboam worships a golden calf – an act of folly.

❽ The central lancet shows Anne, mother of the Virgin Mary, with baby Mary on her knee. This is an early image of Anne, who does not appear in the Bible, and whose cult developed rapidly in the twelfth century. Chartres cathedral had acquired the reputed head of St. Anne following the Fourth Crusade, when Latin crusaders sacked Byzantine Constantinople, in 1204–1205.

and the newly invented rib vault with pointed arches, borrowed from Islam. A building whose windows, vaults and arcades had a pointed profile resulted in a kind of tense, scintillating harmony; the weight of its vaults was transferred to the ground in a manner that enabled supporting walls to be pared away, leaving space for enormous windows and openings. This was a rapturous evocation of heaven, filled with coloured light, and its potential was explored in a sequence of great buildings, such as the cathedrals of Chartres (from 1194) and Reims (from c.1210). These churches are virtually skeletons of stone, their windows and arches vast, their internal carved detailing relatively repetitive. The high rib vaults at Romanesque Durham (from 1093) had been 23m (75ft) off the ground: those at Beauvais cathedral in 1225, in this new style, were 47m (154ft) from floor level. The unceasing search for an experience of the Heavenly Jerusalem on Earth had created a radical architectural language – that of the Gothic, whose roots in earlier practice were almost indiscernible.

The skeletal nature of Gothic buildings had a dramatic impact on their exteriors as well. Their many buttresses and towers were slimmed down and hollowed out, until they became apparently weightless architectural fantasies, often peopled with sculptures of angels or saints. Façades, often topped by twin towers, were used as the settings for colossal windows and portals, which supported elaborate displays of statuary, painted with vivid attention to detail. Often, the west front was used for liturgical purposes or for visits by dignitaries (see pages 48–49), and ordinary people used other doors to enter the building.

The style in which figures and natural features alike were depicted morphed into something distinct, stylized and elegant. Entire churches were, for the first time, glazed entirely using stained and painted glass; wall surfaces were painted; floors were richly tiled; furnishings increased in elaboration. Specific stone fixtures were created, especially in the sanctuary, where the piscina, a basin, was used for the ritual washing of hands and of Eucharistic vessels; the sedilia was a row of throne-like arches in which the officiants sat; and various images of the Holy Sepulchre, varying from stone tomb-like fixtures set into the wall (the Easter Sepulchre found in England) to entire churches designed to imitate the Tomb of Christ (as at the Jerusalem church in Bruges, Belgium), were developed to enrich Easter rituals. Choirs sat in elaborate timber stalls. Screens and high-status tombs were miniature works of architecture. Gothic fused architecture, sculpture, glass and paint; it blurred the distinction between furnishing and building; the sensory assault that resulted was ravishing. Although heavily restored, one of the best places to

◐ RELIQUARY TABERNACLE
1243–1248, LA SAINTE-CHAPELLE, PARIS, FRANCE

Like a bejewelled cage of light, the palace chapel built for King Louis IX seems to hover over the shrine for the Crown of Thorns, acquired by the king of France from the emperor of Constantinople in 1239.

◑ KING HENRY VII'S CHAPEL
1503–1509, WESTMINSTER ABBEY, LONDON, ENGLAND

At once a chapel to the Virgin Mary, the setting for a putative shrine to Henry VI and a dynastic burial mausoleum for the Tudor dynasty of kings (whose emblems abound), this building, with its magnificent fan-vaulted roof, epitomizes the final phase of Gothic at its most lavish.

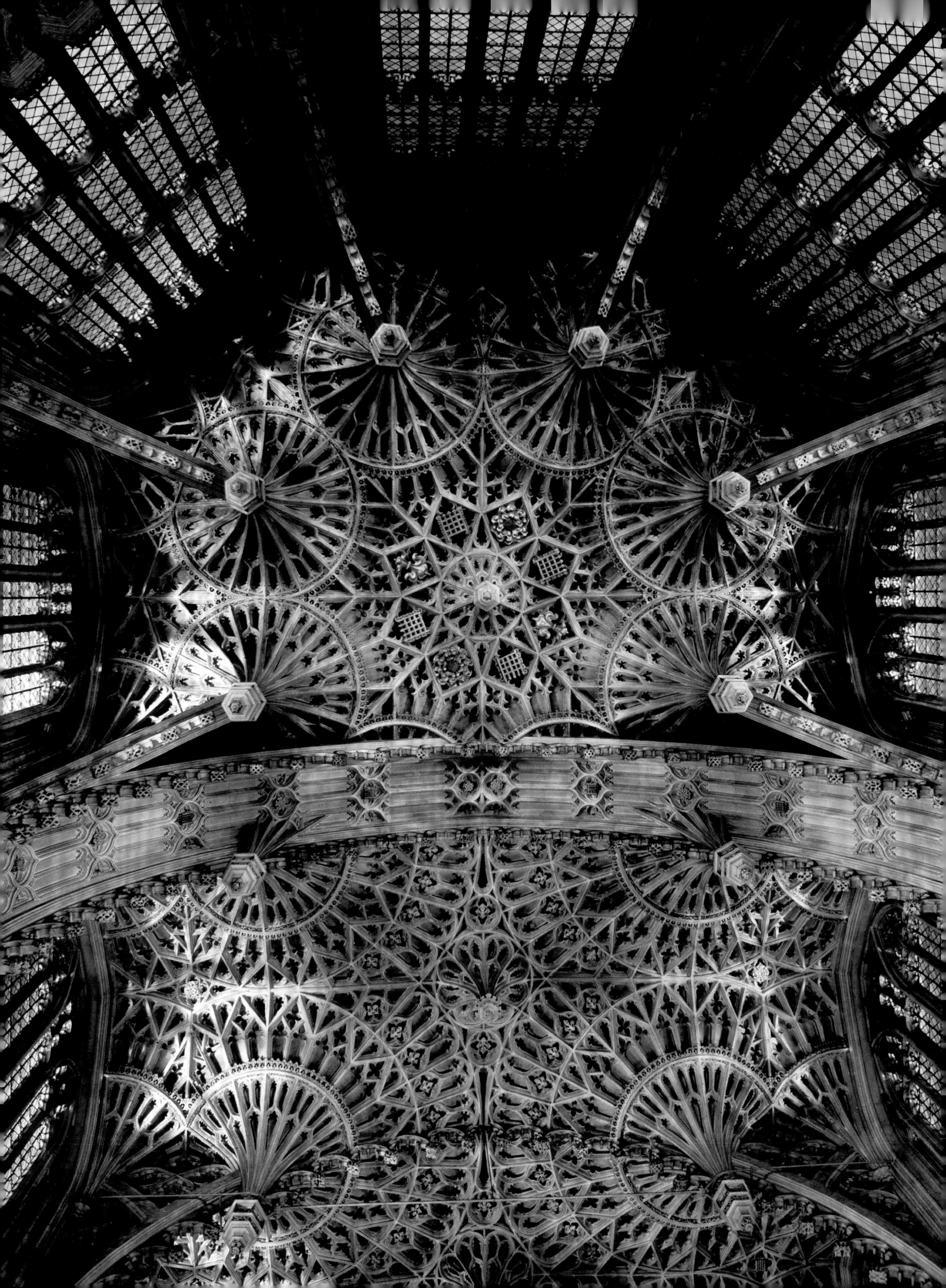

experience this is the Sainte-Chapelle (1243–1248), built by King Louis IX, as part of his palace on the Île de la Cité in Paris, as a gigantic chapel for his collection of relics of Christ's Passion. This building barely has walls at all: it is a simple open space 33m (108ft) high, its plan a rectangle ending in an apse, its walls filled by huge stained-glass windows, its vault supported by a stone skeleton of pointed arches.

By the middle of the thirteenth century the style had spread, first to England and then throughout much of Western Christendom, and it would remain the dominant approach to architecture until about 1500. But it never stood still. To make more of stained glass, windows became yet bigger, and were filled with delicate stone patterns known as tracery (first seen at Reims cathedral in about 1210). The ornamental possibilities were infinite. Large windows were new to architecture: they flooded buildings with coloured light. Indeed, Gothic, perhaps more than any architecture before it, is where designers first fully explored how light itself could be used to create an illusion of heaven. At the same time, extra ribs were added to vaults, further increasing the awe-inspiring richness and apparent weightlessness of these buildings.

The 150 years from about 1350 mark a particularly distinctive phase of Gothic. In 1348 the plague killed at least one-third of Europeans. Western Christians had long believed that the soul after death went to purgatory, where it would be "purged" of sin before entering heaven, and intercessionary prayers or good deeds done on its behalf could help the deceased's soul reach a hopeful outcome at the Last Judgment. Now this doctrine contributed to an enormous upsurge of popular religion. People came together in religious confraternities or guilds, so as to jointly invest in the future fortune of their souls; they rebuilt parish churches and installed huge numbers of elaborate artworks in them. Across Europe, national variants on Gothic emerged: sober Perpendicular, with its rectilinear patterns, in England; the mighty, light-filled spaces of Austrian, Bavarian and Bohemian Sondergotik ("special Gothic"); and the lavish stone patterning, often influenced by local Islamic practice, and massive, shadowy interiors of the Plateresque and Manueline styles in Iberia. Many of these buildings use the ogee arch (see page 156), a curvaceous and decorative type of arch imported from the Islamic east. Some of the biggest churches in Christendom, such as the cathedrals of Milan (from c.1385) and Seville (from 1402), date from this period, the latter demonstrating the triumphalist magnificence that became popular in Iberian architecture as the Muslim kingdoms fell.

Renaissance and Reformation

Meanwhile, a new spirit of independent intellectual enquiry was in the air. In the first decades of the fifteenth century, artists found ways to make sacred images more vividly real, depicting human emotions with new immediacy and closely observing and analyzing the ways in which the world appears to the human eye. Masaccio (1401–1428) and his peers in the wealthy Italian city-state of Florence also studied classical civilization, and developed a deep understanding of Roman

◗ PAZZI CHAPEL

*c.*1442*–c.*1465, BASILICA DE SANTA CROCE, FLORENCE, ITALY

This chapel for the prominent Pazzi family of bankers is also a chapter house for the Franciscan friars of Santa Croce. The crisp proportions of this domed Renaissance building make it one of the most perfectly balanced designs in Christian architecture.

◗ THE HOLY SEAT OF PETER

1506–1667, ST. PETER'S, ROME

A succession of the most important Renaissance architects, including Bramante, Raphael and Michelangelo, worked on this High Renaissance church before the completion of Bernini's famous Baroque audience piazza. This colossal centralized building has been an enormously influential piece of sacred architecure.

architectural and artistic ideas. It was in Florence that this artistic and scholarly phenomenon, called the Renaissance, was first translated into new ways of making sacred buildings. The architect Filippo Brunelleschi (1377–1446) was commissioned to design a series of new churches, buildings that almost completely ignored the previous 500 years of architectural evolution. The Pazzi chapel (c.1442–c.1465) at the church of Santa Croce is just one example: this centralized building has an elegant, measured and reposeful composition, in which flat columns known as pilasters divide the wall surfaces into perfectly proportioned sections, leading to a dome – a motif barely seen in the West for a millennium or more. All the details reveal a close study of Roman style.

The city's cathedral, Santa Maria del Fiore, was incomplete: no one knew how to construct the dome planned for its 42m-wide (138ft) octagonal crossing. Built between 1420 and 1467, Brunelleschi's solution covered this space with a dome 90m (295ft) high, by far the biggest that had ever been built – the proportions still seem to knit the whole city together even today (see pages 62–63). This was a bold statement indeed: a new vision of heaven, a proud declaration of civic and cultural self-confidence, and a deliberate advance on the great domes of the ancient and Eastern worlds. It helped to stimulate a rebirth of the centralized church plan in general, and the dome, now to be constructed on a scale previously unknown, in particular. Western church architecture from the Renaissance onwards is largely an exploration of how basilican and centralized buildings can be combined, often by placing a great dome over a building of cruciform plan, and visually emphasizing the underlying harmony inherent in such a building's proportions.

By 1500, the artistic and architectural transformation first seen in Florence had spread throughout the Italian peninsula. In the course of the sixteenth century it supplanted Gothic throughout the rest of western Europe. But Renaissance architecture itself was moving on. In 1506 Pope Julius II decided to rebuild Constantine's ancient St. Peter's. It would take over a century, but the result was a new claimant to the title of greatest church in Christendom, topped by a world-beating dome, 117m (384ft) high and 41m (136ft) in diameter, designed by Michelangelo Buonarroti (1475–1564). St. Peter's is the grandest building of the mature or High Renaissance style, which adds an air of corporate grandeur to the achievements of the fifteenth century. Further variants of Renaissance architecture, such as (in Italy) the Mannerist style and the works of Andrea Palladio (1508–1580), followed swiftly on. However, for the first time, much of the fuel for these innovations came not from within Christianity but from elsewhere – for example, from palaces. The world was changing: indeed, Western Christendom itself was being transformed.

A radical critique of religious practice had developed. The Englishman John Wycliffe (c.1325–1384), the Bohemian Jan Hus (c.1370–1415) and the German Martin Luther (1483–1546) all criticized many long-established practices and called for a reformation of the Church. By the mid-sixteenth century such ideas had turned into a major phenomenon

CONTINUES ON PAGE 132

QUEEN OF HEAVEN

*c.*1460–*c.*1470, ALTARPIECE OF ST. ANTHONY, GALLERIA NAZIONALE DELL'UMBRIA, PERUGIA, ITALY

The celebration of the Eucharist at the altar of a church was an event of central importance in pre-Reformation Christianity, and as a result the altar was the focus of rich decorations, such as painted altarpieces, which stood behind it. This one was commissioned in about 1460 from the artist Piero della Francesca by a community of Franciscan nuns at the church of San Antonio delle Monache in Perugia. An example as elaborate as this, painted in both egg tempera and oils, and enriched with gold leaf and architectural carving, would probably have been commissioned for the high altar.

The subject is the incarnation of Christ, focusing on the unique role of his mother, the Virgin Mary. Sainthood is also a theme, because Mary was believed to be the greatest of saints and the most merciful of intercessors in heaven. Most of the other saints depicted are gathered around her in an arrangement known as a *sacra conversazione* ("sacred conversation"). The nuns would have selected saints who were their special protectors or were most relevant to their own interests. Piero's depiction gives the figures a three-dimensional quality that was one of the Renaissance's greatest innovations.

▶ ALTARPIECE OF ST. ANTHONY

*c.*1460–*c.*1470, GALLERIA NAZIONALE DELL'UMBRIA, PERUGIA, ITALY

This polyptych, or multi-part, altarpiece has three principal sections: an upper one that depicts the Annunciation, in which the Archangel Gabriel is telling Mary that she will conceive the Son of God; a central main section, entitled *the Virgin and Child between SS Anthony of Padua, John the Baptist, Francis and Elizabeth of Hungary*; and a base known as a *predella*, which depicts miracles associated with three of the saints in the main scene. Adding to the complexity of this structure is a row of small scenes between the *predella* and the central section, which may have incorporated a reliquary behind a door in the middle.

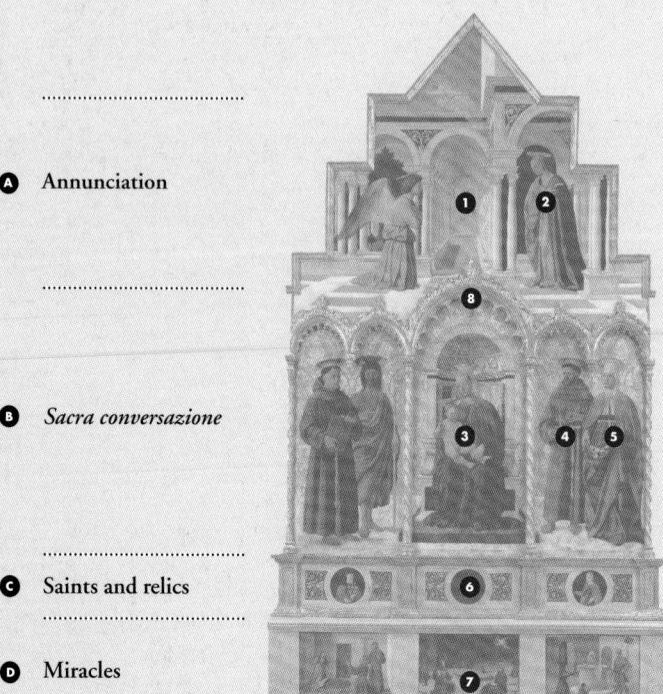

A Annunciation

B *Sacra conversazione*

C Saints and relics

D Miracles

A

1 The setting should be Mary's home in Nazareth, but the artist has depicted the garden of a Renaissance palace. He has used mathematical perspective to create an illusion of actual space, with the arcades receding towards a far-off wall of marble. Piero was a published mathematician and is celebrated for his up-to-date architectural settings.

2 The Annunciation, whereby the Archangel Gabriel told the Virgin Mary that she was to give birth to a divine child, Jesus, confirmed Christ's corporeality and his divinity, while also emphasizing her purity. Mary has her head bowed and her arms across her chest, emphasizing her reflective mood. Nearby, above Gabriel, the Holy Spirit comes down, as a dove, from heaven.

B

3 Christians believed that after her death Mary had ascended to heaven, where she had been crowned as its queen. Here she sits on an elaborate throne, cradling the Christ child in her lap, reminding the viewer that in spite of his divine nature, Jesus was also a real human baby: God incarnate. The throne is a realistically depicted work of Renaissance design, but the golden surface behind it is more abstract (and rather old-fashioned); the intention may have been to indicate a heavenly setting for the group.

4 Francis of Assisi, who died in 1226, was a leading saint, like the group's other innermost figure (John the Baptist). He would have been particularly important to the nuns as their order's founder. He is identified by his grey robes and his cross – a reminder that he miraculously received the stigmata, the wounds of Christ's crucifixion.

5 The outermost figures reflect the interests of the nuns. Elizabeth of Hungary was a queen whose husband, Ludwig, died on crusade, after which the young widow became a Franciscan nun and was later canonized. Opposite is St. Anthony of Padua, a Portuguese hermit and preacher who joined the Franciscans and settled in Italy.

C

6 This empty space may originally have been filled by a depiction of the head of St. John the Baptist, possibly in the form of a door, behind which an important relic was kept. Either side are portraits of St. Claire, the founder of an order of Franciscan nuns, and St. Lucy, an early martyr: two female models for the life of the nuns.

D

7 A night scene depicting Francis miraculously receiving Christ's wounds. Either side are miracles attributed to two other saints depicted in the central section: on the right, Gottfried, a German child drowned in a well, is brought back to life by praying to St. Elizabeth; on the left, St. Anthony cures a child.

8 The centre of the altar is framed by an elaborate Gothic setting. Piero did not use old-fashioned motifs like these elsewhere, and it may be that the nuns insisted on such touches, or that it is intended to be symbolic. A gilt lily, symbolizing purity and Mary, probably once rose from the top.

known as Protestantism. Some states in northern Europe seceded from papal authority. Many of the elaborate rituals, saints' cults and images, which had evolved over 1,200 years or more, were viewed as an abomination by some reformers. In England, Henry VIII (reigned 1509–1547) declared himself the head of the Church, closed all the monasteries, and took down the saints' shrines, confiscating the monks' riches; his successor, Edward VI (reigned 1547–1553), oversaw the destruction of countless thousands of altarpieces, statues and furnishings, and the whitewashing of wall paintings.

Christianity in western Europe now had two competing visions of sacred space. At one extreme of the Protestant tradition, churches became bare and a setting for a liturgy that was focused on the word rather than ritual. Altars were merely tables, and pulpits dominated interiors, to be used for the sermons that were now the centrepiece of the service. However, in those places that remained loyal to the pope – which now called themselves "Catholic", meaning universal – a reaction set in.

Baroque: a global Christian architecture

The Catholic Church initiated its own programme of reform and resurgence: the Counter-Reformation, for which architects developed a new aesthetic mode, which was as grandly theatrical and image-laden as anything in Gothic art. A response to the recommendations of the Council of Trent (1545–1563), it was purposefully designed to appeal to the emotions, with the aim of reinvigorating beholders' faith. The style, known as Baroque, was born in Rome in the 1560s. It spread rapidly, especially in those parts of Europe where Catholicism was strongest, such as Italy, Vienna, southern Germany, Spain and Portugal. By the eighteenth century, Baroque had become the fanciful style known as Rococo. This phase is typified by Balthasar Neumann's Basilica of the Fourteen Holy Helpers (1743) near Bad Staffelstein, Germany. Like many post-Renaissance churches, it is basically a basilican building with a broad transept, topped by a series of domical vaults. But inside, one is barely aware of this: spaces are ovaloid rather than square or circular, and they ripple into one another, creating a sense of interconnected organic volumes. Centralized and axial tendencies are balanced, creating a delicious tension between a high altar in the east and a central one, marking the exact location of a shepherd's miraculous vision (see caption, opposite), which was the focus of visiting pilgrims' devotion. The ravishing, joyous effect that resulted is enhanced by the painted ceilings, in which the illusionistic technique of perspective, a Renaissance invention, is used to make it appear as if heaven itself were opening out of the roof of the church. The underlying language of much of the carved work is classical, but transformed into a multitude of feathery motifs.

European church architecture also spread to new continents. By 1600, Spain and Portugal had empires that stretched from Peru to the Philippines and saw it as their mission to win converts to Christianity. Baroque, a style created in an atmosphere that combined triumphalism and defensiveness, was perfectly suited to this purpose. In the new frontier lands, the incomers built grand stone churches in the swaggering form of Baroque that was popular in Iberia (their decoration sometimes fusing European and indigenous craftsmanship and tastes; see box, page 55). Examples

from across the world include the sixteenth-century churches of Mozambique; Our Lady of the Rosary in Old Goa (1543), India; the enormous Metropolitan Cathedral (from 1563) at Mexico City, which replaced much of the sacred precinct of the former Aztec capital, Tenochtitlán; and the church of San Agustin (1571), outside Manila in the Philippines.

⬥ BASILICA OF THE FOURTEEN HOLY HELPERS
1743, VIERZEHNHEILIGEN, BAD STAFFELSTEIN, BAVARIA, GERMANY

The Basilica of the Fourteen Holy Helpers was the most recent of several churches built on the spot where a shepherd in the fifteenth century had seen a vision of fourteen child-saints. The Rococo interior balances the twin focuses of the central "altar of grace", the object of any pilgrimage to venerate the holy helpers, and the high altar beyond.

Protestant piety

By 1700 two strains could be discerned within Protestantism. Some accepted many aspects of the Catholic Church's hierarchy and ritual but rejected the authority of the pope and certain practices, such as the miracle-cults of saints. Their churches tended to be less richly decorated versions of the Baroque mainstream. Others were labelled Nonconformist – a term that referred to a multitude of smaller independent groups, whose members explored their own visions of the faith. Most of these new groups – from Quakers to Methodists – shared a deep interest in the authority of biblical texts, a suspicion of ritual and of complex hierarchies, and a rejection of architectural and artistic extravagance. Many called the resulting places of worship "meeting houses" or "chapels" rather than churches. Commonly, these are axial buildings, visually similar to traditional churches, but with their fittings designed to make the building more of a prayer hall than a sacramental space: a pulpit often replaces the altar at the end of the axis.

For centuries arguably only one Protestant building matched the greatest churches of older Christian traditions: the rebuilt St. Paul's cathedral in London, England (from 1668), by the architect Christopher Wren (1632–1723). This is another domed building, its style a grand and corporate version of Baroque, its interior balancing the demands of a reformed faith with those of ritual. This is self-consciously a cathedral church for that distinctively English form of Protestantism, the Church of England. This flexible institution reformed Catholic ritual and hierarchy, but ultimately did not abandon them; the major change was that it used English for worship rather than Latin. Northern Europe's colonial adventures were increasingly dominated by England (or rather, from 1706–1707, Great Britain) and the Church of England and its architecture spread globally with Britain.

The English colonies in North America had a varied approach to religion. Nonconformists crossed the Atlantic to escape persecution or to experiment with building ideal communities. Some states, such as Quaker Pennsylvania, were founded with such ideals in mind. From the Anglican (or, in North America, Episcopalian) King's Chapel (1749) in Boston to the First Baptist Meeting House (1774) in Providence, Rhode Island, churches and meeting houses spread fast, their architecture often derived from English models.

Faith in crisis

By the Enlightenment era, a spirit of independent intellectual investigation was picking away at the underpinnings of faith. From the 1840s, laws which discriminated against one religious group or another were being dismantled even as church architecture itself was losing its central cultural role.

This was a turning point of global significance. Since 3000BCE, with few exceptions (China and classical Rome most prominently), the story of religious architecture had largely been the story of architecture itself. Since the eighteenth century, in a process that started in Europe and its colonies, this has no longer been the case. The tale becomes one of interesting religious buildings within a wider architectural narrative whose epicentre is elsewhere. At about the same time, architecture began to consist of reinventions. The

◖ SHAKER SIMPLICITY

*c.*1795, SABBATHDAY LAKE MEETING HOUSE, MAINE, USA

Shaker meeting houses have a numinous sacredness that resides in their very simplicity. This one, near New Gloucester, belongs to the last active Shaker community. Large, simple spaces in house-like timber buildings, well-lit for the study of scripture, such places are a return to the house church, the form with which Christian architecture began.

◐ VOTIVE IN CONCRETE
1961, SACRÉ-COEUR CATHEDRAL, ALGIERS, ALGERIA

Bishop Leynaud vowed to erect this church after the Battle of Algiers in 1944. Built in reinforced concrete, it became the city's cathedral when that of St. Philippe was reconverted to a mosque.

rediscovery of the art and architecture of ancient Greece led to a style called Neo-classical. By 1850 architects applied whichever historical style they felt was most apt. One result was the Gothic Revival, which saw this medieval style become a global marker of a Christian place of worship (see page 22).

Innumerable churches have been built across the world in the modern era and religious architecture has remained a potent source of creative ideas. Since about 1900, architects have sought to define styles that are less dependent on those of the past. The unfinished church of the Sagrada Familia (1882–) in Barcelona, Spain, designed by Antoni Gaudí (1852–1926), coins a fantastical, organic style of its own, deeply inspired by Gothic. The concrete-and-glass skeleton of Notre-Dame (1922) in Le Raincy, near Paris, is a precursor of the Modernist style. For many the pilgrimage chapel at Ronchamp in France (1950) by Le Corbusier (1857–1965) is the greatest work of an architect more famed for his theories, which led to Modernism. Its luminous interior evokes sacredness as powerfully as anything in this book, while abandoning the traditional themes of axial or centralized, domed or vaulted churches. The Second Vatican Council of 1962 led to radical liturgical reforms, as a result of which altars became unencumbered by screens. Many of the Catholic churches of the era (such as the cathedrals of Algiers, Brasilia and Liverpool) combine soaring bare concrete with a centralized plan.

Perhaps more surprising is the belated birth of an impressive religious architecture among Nonconformists. Frank Lloyd Wright's Unitarian Unity Temple (1906) in Chicago translated the idea of the simple meeting house into sophisticated design. Evangelical Nonconformists have built such overwhelming structures as the timber fantasy that is Thorncrown Chapel (1980) in Eureka Springs, Arkansas, and the 126m-long (415ft) glass Crystal Cathedral (1981) in Garden Grove, California. Yet here, and in most other churches of recent decades, it is not hard to detect the lasting influence of the great cathedrals of the past, and the inevitable conclusion that light-filled, axial spaces with ceilings that appear to defy gravity and soaring spire-like forms suit Christian worship well.

With 2.2 billion adherents, Christianity is the world's biggest faith, and its remarkable story continues to evolve. From the Constantinian basilica onwards, it has created expansive, all-embracing internal effects, manipulating space and light in ways matched by few structures in other traditions. Stylistic restlessness has been a defining theme, emerging in Western Christendom from around 1100. Perhaps the very variety of forms and styles seen in the ceaseless Christian search to evoke the "kingdom of heaven" has something to do with the faith itself, and the idea of *becoming* – of man as God – that lies at the heart of Christian spirituality, helping to shape an architecture of incarnation.

☪

ISLAM

SUBMISSION TO GOD

—————————◯—————————

The Muslim holy book, the Quran ("Recitation"), was revealed word for word to a man from Mecca named Muhammad, considered in Islam ("submission") to be the last and greatest of a series of prophets sent by God. In 622CE, fear of persecution forced Muhammad and his followers to move from Mecca; they sought shelter in Yathrib (later renamed Medina), an event known as the *hijra* ("migration"). This is taken by Muslims as marking the foundation of their community of believers, the *umma*. Mosque design has its origins in these events, and is thus caught up in the birth of the faith itself.

The Prophet is said to have built a house in Medina that had a large courtyard, one wall of which was covered with a roof of palm leaves, creating a partially shaded area. This wall marked the direction, or *qibla*, that his followers should face when praying. Originally, Muhammad taught his followers to pray facing Jerusalem, but soon after their arrival in Medina he announced that prayer should henceforth be towards Mecca, where an ancient shrine known as the Ka'ba stood. His house was

HARMONY AT THE HEART OF CREATION

Intricate patterned ornamentation is one of the hallmarks of Islamic art, from painting and calligraphy to architecture and ceramics. These patterns of perfection are not superficial embellishment, but instead they reflect a spiritual belief in an underlying order beneath the apparent chaos of creation. From this perspective, geometric patterns transport the viewer into the presence of the divine.

A fritware tile from Iran (1444) has a floral pattern interlaced with a geometric decoration based on multi-pointed star shapes. The dominant blue glaze suggests life-giving water.

◗ GRAND MOSQUE
638 ONWARDS, MECCA, SAUDI ARABIA

Muslims of many nations gather in October 2011 at Mecca's Masjid al-Haram, also known as the Grand Mosque, during the *hajj* – the great annual pilgrimage that is one of the five principal observances (or "pillars") of Islam.

The mosque has been rebuilt and expanded many times. There are plans to increase the courtyard's capacity from about 770,000 worshippers to two million. The cuboid Ka'ba can be seen in the middle distance.

MYSTICAL MARTYRS

In the 650s, violent disagreement emerged over how the authority of the Prophet should be passed on (see page 145). The result was the main schism within Islam, with those who supported 'Ali (the Prophet's cousin and first male convert) and his descendants forming the Shi'ah-i 'Ali (the Party of 'Ali). The Shi'a were to become a large minority, and over time Shi'ism has developed a strong culture of its own, in contrast to the majority Sunni community, who supported the Umayyads.

Shi'ism is in many ways a cult of the descendants of the Prophet, especially 'Ali, who was murdered in 661, and 'Ali's second son, Hussein (or Husain), murdered in 680, both of whom are martyr-figures of near mystical significance. The authority of Shi'ite *imam*s and *ayatollah*s is in some ways akin to that of a priesthood. There is no specific Shi'a form of mosque, but Shi'a spirituality has strongly influenced the growth of cults and shrines in Islam. Shi'a culture has become distinctive: in Shi'ite areas, images of 'Ali and Hussein are everywhere, whereas an image of the Prophet would scandalize most orthodox Sunni communities. At the festival of Ashura, entire communities unite in grief as they re-enact the murder of Hussein in a dramatic form of outdoor theatre, often performed as part of religious processions. For Shi'a Muslims the tombs in Iraq of 'Ali and Hussein, at Najaf and Kerbala respectively, with their glittering shrines, are second only to Mecca and Medina as places of pilgrimage.

There are also smaller branches of the Shi'a, the Twelver and Ismaili sects, who anticipate the millenarian return of the *imam* or *mahdi*, and among the Nizari Ismailis an esoteric form of Islam is practised in relatively simple places of worship called *jamatkhana*s. Prince Karim Aga Khan is their current *imam* and has done much to further the cause of contemporary Islamic architecture.

◑ 'ALI, DESCENDANT OF THE PROPHET
1125, AQMAR MOSQUE MEDALLION, CAIRO, EGYPT

The arch of the gateway of this Fatimid-era mosque bears this inscription, repeating the name of Muhammad with the Prophet's cousin, 'Ali, at the centre, testament to the dynasty's Shi'ism.

---

altered accordingly. With this building, the essential features of the Muslim place of worship were defined.

A community of faith

A mosque (or *masjid*, a "place of prostration") is a prayer hall in which the *umma* can gather together, oriented towards Mecca by the *qibla* wall. It is the venue for two of the faith's five fundamental requirements, or "pillars". All Muslims must pray five times a day (this does not have to take place in a mosque, but often does), and attend a congregational prayer at midday every Friday. The other requirements are acceptance of a simple formula: "There is no god but God, and Muhammad is his messenger"; the giving of a proportion – usually one-fortieth – of one's income to charity; fasting once a year during the holy month of Ramadan; and, if physically and financially capable, making a pilgrimage (*hajj*) to the Ka'ba at least once in one's lifetime.

Mosques are not holy in and of themselves, although it is important that worshippers are clean before they pray. They exist in great variety, but the most important are those designed for congregational Friday prayers, the *jami masjid*s. This is a faith that stresses the unity of God (Allah), the community of those who accept him, and the finality of Quranic revelation (although it accepts previous revelations, such as those received by Moses and Jesus). There is no formal priesthood: the emphasis is on each member's unmediated communion with God. Caliphs, inheritors of Muhammad's religious and political authority, originally preached a Friday sermon and led prayers, but later this role became a separate one that is conducted by the *imam*; the *muezzin* calls people to prayer.

The Prophet's simple template

By the time Muhammad died in 632, he was a major political and military leader as well as a religious teacher. He was buried in his house in Medina, today much rebuilt and known as the Mosque of the Prophet. The design of this simple building reflected the principles of the faith. The courtyard format gave it an inward-looking quality, serving to draw the congregation together. The *qibla* wall ran in front of the rows of worshippers, emphasizing their equality before God (whereas an axial building tends to emphasize hierarchy by focusing attention on a single point at one end). The mosque is often broader than it is long, and this makes it easier for the lines of worshippers to act in unison, timing their actions by following an *imam*. Finally, having been set by Muhammad himself, the form of the building is a reminder of the Prophet's authority.

By the early 700s, a series of features had been added to this template, and these are almost universally seen in the mosques built thereafter. A niche, known as the *mihrab*, in the middle of the *qibla* wall is the most ornate part of the interior. Although in theory this is merely an additional focus for prayer, popular feeling often gives the *mihrab* and the space around it a sacred charge, and this area is often set aside in a sanctuary-like aisle or bay. If the mosque is a *jami masjid*, a *minbar* – a kind of pulpit – stands near the *mihrab*. If there is a local ruler, the space around the *mihrab* (or a special platform or screened enclosure within it) is often set aside for his use; this is called the *maqsura*. The prayer hall or covered area facing the *qibla* wall may be divided into aisles by arcades or hypostyle columns. The open courtyard (*sahn*) has at its centre a washing place so that ablutions can be performed before prayers. The external walls of the building, apart from any entranceways, are usually plainer than the courtyard and prayer hall within, but the building is made visible from afar by a minaret, from which the call to prayer is made, and a dome, which rises above the *mihrab* bay.

Muslim architects have spent 1,400 years exploring the aesthetic potential inherent in these simple elements, combining and recombining a series of features: the minaret and dome, which were the product of a desire for external enrichment and visibility (sometimes minarets were purely decorative, with little or no practical function); the *mihrab*, and the space associated with it, which becomes particularly dramatic internally when topped by a dome; the expansive space of the prayer hall; and the inward-looking courtyard. Although the paired minaret and dome have become emblematic of Islamic architecture, the spaces within the mosque, with their enveloping sense of a community united in prayer, are equally expressive of Islamic spirituality.

The handling of these courtyards, and the associated prayer hall and *qibla* bay, varies greatly. Where ascetic interpretations of Islam hold sway, the unadorned rows of arches can have a startling purity of form, embodying an austere, prayerful life – as at the Kutubiyya mosque in Marrakesh. Elsewhere, each side of the courtyard becomes an inward-facing façade, the grandest of which is that opening onto the prayer hall and *qibla* wall. When these façades, and the spaces beyond, are enriched with coloured tilework or intense surface patterning, they can have a rapturous intensity, redolent of Sufi mysticism – as at the Friday mosque in Isfahan, Iran (see page 150).

⏷ NORTH AFRICAN ARCHWORK
1147–1157, KUTUBIYYA MOSQUE, MARRAKESH, MOROCCO

The Kutubiyya mosque was once one of the most important in the empire of the Almohads (1130–1269), which stretched from Spain across the western Maghreb. The strict Islam of the Almohads is reflected in a sparse decorative style. Unadorned walls and white arched spaces lend the mosque a distinctively austere beauty.

From *madrasa*s to tomb-shrines

Islam is all-embracing, an attitude of mind, and the architectural forms developed in the mosque may be applied to a wide range of related buildings. It is not unusual to find in a domed, courtyard-format *caravanserai* (a travellers' inn) that the main room has a small *mihrab* in one corner, or that a mosque sits at the centre of a complex of bazaars and schools, which generates income for the mosque or provides the charitable services each Muslim is obliged to fund.

Other types of building include the *madrasa*, a school for legal jurisprudence – itself a religious activity, because Islamic *sharia* law is based on generations of interpretation of the Quran in the light of the actions and sayings (*hadith*s)

◉ ELEGANCE IN ETERNITY

920S, MAUSOLEUM OF THE SAMANIDS, BUKHARA, UZBEKISTAN

This thick-walled (1.8m/6ft) tomb is about 11m (35ft) square, with four openings and capped by a cupola or hemispherical dome. It is believed to house the remains of Ismail Samani, who made the Samanid dynasty a powerful force, together with those of his father and grandson. The entire building, inside and out, is decorated with patterns of baked brick.

of the Prophet. The *khanqa* is a quasi-monastic convent for followers of the mystical aspect of Islam known as Sufism. *Khanqa*s are widespread; they vary in design, but are rarely large or elaborate. *Madrasa*s, by contrast, can be magnificent.

Initially, study took place in mosques, but from the tenth century onwards purpose-built *madrasa*s were founded in eastern Iran, perhaps influenced by Buddhist monasteries. From there they spread rapidly, especially where a regime wished to counter heterodox tendencies among its people. Memorable examples include the stripped geometry of the Mustansiriya *madrasa* in Baghdad (from 1262), or the intimate spaces of the Atarin *madrasa* in Fez (1323–1325), richly finished with carved cedar from the Atlas mountains.

Mausoleums are another major Islamic building type. (This is in spite of the fact that the Prophet had insisted on a modest burial and in its earliest days Islam was opposed to formal commemoration of the dead.) Several things contributed to the development of mausoleums. One of them was a belief in *baraka* ("holiness"), often felt to be particularly intense at the burial place of an individual who had a saintly reputation or had died a martyr's death. The growth of Shi'ism was also a factor (see box, page 138).

The grandest Islamic mausoleums, however, belong to rulers. In a religion that lacked a clear internal governing structure, kings were often the main source of architectural patronage, and many gave themselves a burial place they felt was appropriate to their status, often combined with charitable foundations such as a mosque or *madrasa*. Such rulers often claimed religious authority, and thus might have *baraka* in their own right. The best-preserved early examples of grand mausoleums are in Central Asia and Iran, such as the royal mausoleum of the Samanids at Bukhara (920s) and the Gunbad-i Qabus mausoleum at Gurgan, Iran (1006–1007): these, like most of those that came afterwards, are domed, centralized buildings, following the Roman model for mausoleums. They may also be inspired by the small, domed spaces, open on four sides, which comprised the open-air altars commonly used by Zoroastrians. In Fatimid Egypt (969–1171) there was a huge growth in both the number and quality of mausoleums, explained partly by the commemorative emphasis placed on holy men by Shi'ite Islam.

Major shrines also developed around the reputed tombs of central figures in the faith, such as Abraham and Moses – not to mention Muhammad himself and his early companions. The most important of these shrines often stand alone within a large enclosure, which at the Ka'ba or the Dome of the Rock is called the *haram* (meaning "forbidden" or "sacred"). Unencumbered by buildings (many mosques are surrounded by dense housing) and with centralized plans, mausoleums and shrines afforded an opportunity to develop arresting exterior compositions, from the pinnacle of inside-out *muqarnas* (Islamic vaulting) that towers over the shrine of Zumurrud Khatun in Baghdad (1180–1220) to the ineffable poise of the Taj Mahal in Agra (1631–1647).

A geometry of the spirit

The development of Islam's distinctive stylistic mode unfolded some time after the basic elements of the mosque had been defined, emerging gradually from Roman,

◗ PRAYER HALL *MIHRAB* AND *MINBAR*
1356–1362, SULTAN HASSAN MOSQUE, CAIRO, EGYPT

The mosque-mausoleum built by Sultan Hassan is one of the greatest in all Islam. Around the mosque courtyard are suites of residential and teaching rooms, each a *madrasa* assigned to a school of Islamic jurisprudence. The *mihrab* niche and adjacent *minbar* are the main focal points of the prayer hall, their design exemplifying Cairene style: surfaces covered in geometrical designs and calligraphy; patterns formed by stones of contrasting colours.

Byzantine and Sassanian antecedents. It unites buildings of all kinds, as well as everything from textiles to metalwork, under a single overriding aesthetic, at once varied and unmistakable. At its heart is Islam's devotion to the holy word.

For Muslims, the authority of the Quran is beyond dispute. Many can recite by heart its 114 *sura*s or chapters, each an individual revelation given to Muhammad verbatim by God. As a result of these divinely inspired words, Quranic calligraphy has become Islam's chief art form, and the act of writing these Arabic texts is often a religious experience in itself.

CONTINUES ON PAGE 144

IN PRAISE OF GOD

1416–1418, MASJID-I GAWHAR SHAD, MASHHAD, IRAN

The most important building, historically, in the Shi'a shrine complex of *Imam* Reza is the Friday mosque, founded by Gawhar Shad, daughter of a powerful emir and the wife of the Timurid emperor Shah Rukh (reigned 1405–1447), a Sunni ruler. Although it was not unusual for women to patronize architecture, the scale of Gawhar Shad's mosques is remarkable. Masjid-i Gawhar Shad is at a major pilgrimage site, the most sacred place in her domain, and most of its inscriptions are in Arabic rather than Persian. It may partly be designed to promote orthodoxy at the holy man's tomb.

The mosque is designed to be both the city's main place of congregation and an access point for the shrine, which is located to the north. The building comprises a 55m by 45m (180ft by 150ft) courtyard, overlooked by four *iwan*s (arched openings), with that facing the *qibla* wall topped by a dome and flanked by two small minarets.

▶ *MAQSURA IWAN* TILEWORK

1416–1418, MASJID-I GAWHAR SHAD, MASHHAD, IRAN

This ceramic call to prayer decorates the area around the *maqsura iwan* (see pages 150–151), which has an unusual design. Rather than leading to a separate, sanctuary-like space that contains the *mihrab*, the mosque has a vast open arch, beyond which a *mihrab* that dominates the *qibla* wall is visible from many parts of the courtyard. The dramatic focus on public prayer implied by this arrangement is emphasized by the messages in the tilework, many of which are on the theme of prayer. The arch would have been the setting for Friday sermons. Its calligraphy is by Gawhar Shad's son, Prince Baysunghur.

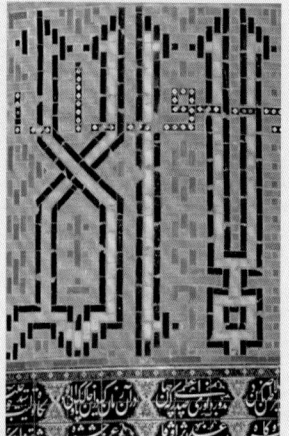

❶ A series of sayings from the Hadith ("report") – accounts that record the words, teaching and deeds of the Prophet Muhammad – that exhort the value of prayer. One saying is attributed to his cousin 'Ali, perhaps as a concession to local Sh'ia sympathies.

❷ In this enormous inscription at the base of the minaret, the two phrases of the Shahada, the Islamic statement of faith, are turned into a near-abstract graphic display. "There is no god but God [Allah]" is in large yellow vertical letters outlined in black, while "and Muhammad is his messenger" interlaces with it horizontally, in an orthogonal script in black studded with white dots.

❸ The repeated use of floral motifs throughout the mosque is a reminder that heaven was, according to the Quran, like a beautiful garden.

4 The main inscription, in white Thuluth script, lines the *iwan* arch. It extols the virtues of the foundress, quoting phrases from the Quran and the Hadith. Floral motifs spiral behind the words, with the repeated phrase in blue Kufic, "the kingdom belongs to God". Panels credit the architect and the calligrapher.

5 A Tree of Life is framed by a quotation from the Quran (*sura* 62, 8–10), extolling the importance of Friday prayers. The text frame rises up to make a series of interlaced zigzags containing the repeated phrase "God is eternal". The Quran mentions a tree growing in heaven, and mystical Sufism made much of this image.

6 The letters of a golden inscription in Kufic ("praise be to God" repeated) rise to become a series of interlocking stars, each containing in white Thuluth a series of phrases in praise of Allah.

7 Tiles are set into plain bricks in a technique known as *banna'i*. The tiles repeat the many names of God.

8 These patterns, developed from the complex interpenetration of polygons and multi-pointed stars, reveal sophisticated mathematical knowledge and reflect the underlying geometric harmonies of the created world.

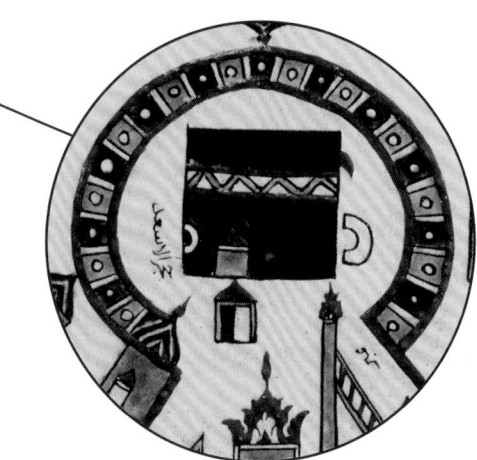

Even to those who cannot read them, such texts are works
of extraordinary abstract linear beauty. Out of various styles
of script, two in particular – stocky, monumental Kufic and
graceful Thuluth – were often used in architectural inscriptions, and their aesthetic qualities have played a key role in
Islamic style (see pages 142–143).

Types of abstract pattern were found to complement cal-
ligraphic inscriptions perfectly. These were mostly vegetal
("arabesque") or geometrical – forms, notably stars, derived
from shapes such as circles, squares, triangles and polygons.
Spread over surfaces, these ornamentations provided a setting for the holy word while suggesting the underlying order
and beauty of creation. This was a culture where God himself was beyond depiction, and the abstract perfection of creation suggested by such patterns is a key to many aspects of
Islamic architecture: for example, the *muqarnas* vaults often
seen in mosques can be interpreted as attempts to translate
the patterns into three dimensions.

Although Muslims believe God is beyond representation,
the Quran does not forbid depictions of the human form.
Indeed, Islamic manuscript illumination, painting and palace decoration have often included exquisite narrative scenes.
However, many Muslims have eschewed the use of imagery,
wanting to avoid anything that could be interpreted as idolatrous, and it is not seen in mosques. The deepest reason for
the focus on inscription is not so much avoidance as an overriding devotion to the beauty and authority of the holy word.

From Arabia to the larger world

This emphasis on pattern and word has not resulted in an
architecture that is homogenous and lacking in creativity.
Quite the opposite: Islam's extensive geographical spread,
and its lack of internal structure, have made it very open to
regional variation and to outside influence. This is a story in
which a simple template for the architecture of a new faith is
transformed into a vast range of magnificent buildings.

After Muhammad's death, a series of four caliphs (from the Arabic *khalifa*, "successor") assumed his political and religious authority (although not his Prophethood). Under their leadership the *umma* expanded its power, and its very success in doing so confirmed to many the truth of the founder's message. Before long, these new believers, men from desert Arabia, whose roots were in a culture that had been on the fringes of the ancient world, had conquered Jerusalem (638) and ruled everywhere from North Africa to Central Asia as far as the Oxus. They supplanted the Byzantine Roman and Sassanian Persian empires (the latter dominated present-day Iraq and Iran) and acquired governance over many ancient urban settlements with significant Christian, Jewish, Zoroastrian and, towards the east, Buddhist communities.

At first the new Muslim rulers exerted control from purpose-built fortified enclosures, such as at Kufa and Basra in Iraq and Fustat near what is now Cairo, where they built the first known mosques after the one in Medina. These were large buildings that adhered to the template of Muhammad's house. The covered area facing the *qibla* wall was enlarged, usually by creating a hypostyle hall of columns: the prayer halls of many mosques thereafter would have this format, which is easy to adapt to any required size. Small minarets or rooftop booths, in which a *muezzin* could stand, may also have developed. Those of their new subjects who were "peoples of the book" – that is, Jews and Christians (and, to a lesser extent, Zoroastrians) – were permitted to practise their faith, but they had some of their citizenship rights restricted, were required to pay a tribute to their new overlords and could not build churches or synagogues that were grander than surrounding mosques.

However, there were underlying disagreements about the line of succession to the caliphate, and these erupted into a civil war and ultimately caused the major divide within Islam: between the Sunni, who accept the legitimacy of the Umayyad dynasty and its successors, and the Shi'a, who believe authority should descend only through the bloodline of 'Ali (see box, page 138).

The Umayyads moved the capital of the caliphate from Medina to the ancient Syrian city of Damascus. Over the next 300 years or so, two succeeding dynasties of Sunni caliphs governed the enormous Islamic empire. During this time, Islamic architecture moved through two phases of development. Firstly, under the Umayyads (661–749) and early Abbasids (from 749), Islamic places of worship were created whose magnificence matched the imperial nature of Umayyad power. The result was the transformation of mosque design, so that it rivalled in elaboration the richly decorated churches and synagogues of the Umayyad realms. In the process, the technical achievements of the Roman

▶ A CATHEDRAL-LIKE MOSAIC FAÇADE
706–715, UMAYYAD MOSQUE, DAMASCUS, SYRIA

The Great, or Umayyad, Mosque of Damascus followed the form of Muhammad's house but aggrandized it with motifs from the Roman and Byzantine worlds. The mosque is the oldest one in Islam surviving in its original form. Much of its courtyard is arcaded and the prayer hall was given palatial decorative treatment. The mosque includes the Christian-era tomb of John the Baptist.

world – the dome, the arch and the vault – became integral features of Islamic architecture.

Two surviving buildings are particularly noteworthy. One is unique, and the other formed a template for future developments. The octagonal Dome of the Rock in Jerusalem is a kind of shrine, standing alone in the centre of a hilltop enclosure, which also includes an important early mosque, the al-Aqsa. The dome (20m/66ft in diameter) covers a bare rock: a spot that had long been abandoned, but which was of the greatest religious significance. For Muslims, this was where the Prophet Muhammad had experienced a miraculous ascent through the seven heavens and into the divine presence (the *Miraj*). For Jews, it had been the location of the Holy of Holies in the Temple of Jerusalem.

Seventh-century Jerusalem was a mainly Christian city. The Dome of the Rock is especially conscious of the rival place of worship nearby – the circular, and thus also centralized, Church of the Holy Sepulchre, the conical dome of which was of almost identical size. Inside the Dome of the Rock, picked out in mosaic, are inscriptions in Arabic, which include pointed assertions of the indivisibility of God and the finality of Muhammad's Prophethood. The message

of the building is clear: the third and final monotheism in the Abrahamic tradition has triumphed. The site remains the third holiest place in Islam, after Mecca and Medina.

The other significant early building was more influential: the Umayyad Mosque, erected in Damascus from 706 onwards. Here, the basic form of Muhammad's house was followed, but – again – it was embellished. Roman corner towers are reused, forming monumental minarets. The prayer hall parallel to the *qibla* wall is given palatial architectural and decorative treatment. The hall is divided into three aisles by arcades. A high central transept, topped by a dome, cuts across these aisles and leads on one side to an ornate *mihrab*, which is one of the earliest known. This richly decorated space appears to have been for the exclusive use of the

⬙ TRIUMPH OF A NEW FAITH
684–691, DOME OF THE ROCK, JERUSALEM

The Dome of the Rock was an audacious attempt by the Umayyad leaders of the new faith to create an unforgettable architectural statement. Built within living memory of the Prophet, this shrine contains the earliest passage of Quranic text to have survived. Inscriptions would remain a central element in the decoration of Islamic sacred space thereafter. The sacred spot covered by the Dome has a role in the story of all three "peoples of the book".

caliph and his court. The surfaces of the building are covered in slabs of veined marble and beautiful mosaic depictions of cities and gardens.

Neither Umayyad building features depictions of human beings; instead, the garden-like paradisiacal scenes, lavish surface patterning and (at the Dome of the Rock) Quranic inscriptions represent the seed ideas of what, over the next two centuries, would become Islamic style.

The birth of Islamic style

In 749/750 the Umayyads were supplanted by the Abbasids, who moved the capital to a new city at Baghdad. There the architectural heritage was more Mesopotamian and Sassanian than Byzantine, feeding a series of new motifs into the architecture of Islam.

The Abbasids presided over an extraordinary flowering of literature and learning. At the same time, Arabic – the language in which God had communicated his final revelation – began to replace Greek and Persian as a *lingua franca*. A final authorized text for the Quran was created. The caliphs must have felt themselves to be at the centre of civilization, and their empire's economic might fuelled the spread of their faith. By the ninth century, travelling merchants and others were taking Islam to China and western Africa.

Little is known of the architecture of Baghdad, which was laid out to a circular plan with a mosque and palace at its centre. However, Samarra, which briefly (836–883) replaced Baghdad as capital, survives as a ruin in the desert. Its Great Mosque (848–852) was the largest then in existence, at 155m by 238m (508ft by 781ft). The spiral form of its minaret (see illustration, page 33) appears to imitate ziggurats; many forms of arch are employed, perhaps influenced by those used decoratively in many parts of the post-classical Near East; and the Sassanian tradition of covering walls in dense stucco patterns was adopted. Gradually, this patterning was to become more linear and abstract.

In other ninth-century mosques these ideas were developed further. The result can be seen at two ninth-century mosques in Kairouan, Tunisia. The arches that dominate the façade of the Mosque of the Three Doors (866) are pointed and stilted – that is, they are raised up on straight segments before the curve of the arch itself begins. Above them rise layers of complex patterning and Arabic inscriptions. The linear rhythm of the geometrical decoration complements the sacred words without upstaging them. Such mosques can be spare internally, with any ornamentation focused on the *mihrab*, its associated bay or aisle and its dome, and the *minbar*. That at the Great Mosque (from 836) is the oldest dated example, and it is covered in dense patterns, set in a grid of wood panels, creating an effect of electrifying intensity.

By the eleventh century an extraordinary variety of such patterns might cover wall surfaces, until their underlying massiveness can seem to disintegrate. A hitherto unmatched variety of arch-types had developed. *Muqarnas* vaults appeared, in which decorative scoop-shaped forms were piled up in geometric arrays over door heads, in the areas of transition between a wall and a dome, in the top of a *mihrab*, and elsewhere. Domes, in turn, were soon to become increasingly prominent, acquiring a variety of pointed profiles. Such motifs ensured that every part of the building was drawn together under a single, unitary aesthetic. A new architecture had been born.

From Iberia to Iran

Within a century of the Prophet's lifetime, then, an empire had been built that stretched from modern Pakistan to Iberia, and a monumental architecture coined from a template set by the faith's founder. Over two further centuries, an Islamic style had developed. But by the tenth century, the political unity of Islam was disintegrating. Many local rulers openly rejected Abbasid authority. Shi'a-led regimes began to appear. Strong regional architectural styles developed, some containing innovations that would be of huge import when, from the fifteenth century, imperial powers again came to dominate the Islamic world.

An early example of these distinctive regional styles produced one of Islam's great buildings. At Córdoba, southern Spain, the only surviving Umayyad prince had established a kingdom. From 961 the Friday mosque in that city, first built in 785–787, was massively extended, resulting in a building whose magnificent opulence deliberately echoed that of the Umayyad Mosque in far-off Damascus. Stylistically, however, the building is an offshoot of the regional style of North Africa, which featured long rows of horseshoe-shaped arches, often in alternating red and white stone; domes with their surfaces covered in bulbous ribs; and minarets with a square profile, their surfaces covered in deep-shadowed brickwork patterns. The seventeen aisles that fill the prayer hall of the Great Mosque of Córdoba seem to contain infinite expanses of such horseshoe arches, often piled one on top of the other.

The ensuing centuries are familiar to many as those of the Crusades. From the thirteenth century, Christian forces began to reconquer significant parts of Iberia. The expulsion of Islam from Spain, which was total by 1492, was to an extent compensated for by the consolidation and expansion of Islamic influence further eastwards, from Central Asia to India. One result of this was that non-Arab cultures became more dominant. These included the Turkic-speaking tribes from Central Asia, the ancient civilization of Persia with its Sassanian and Zoroastrian monotheistic inheritance, and the

◗ *MIHRAB* SANCTUARY

FROM 961, GREAT MOSQUE (LA MEZQUITA), CÓRDOBA, SPAIN

The Great Mosque at Córdoba was built for Al-Hakam II (reigned 961–976), who claimed the caliphate and intentionally attempted to outdo the famous Umayyad Mosque in Damascus. This bay immediately in front of the *mihrab* is arguably the most architecturally complex sanctuary-like space in all Islam. It was entered from the *maqsura*, an area few were admitted into.

animist, nomadic Mongols who conquered and destroyed Abbasid Baghdad in 1258, but whose empire later split into separate khanates, with many of the khans embracing Islam. It was in areas controlled by such peoples that the most influential architectural innovations took place, as mosques were transformed by local architectural traditions.

For example, the Seljuks were Turks originating from Central Asia who ran a decentralized state in which much power was dissolved to local emirs. Having conquered Iran, from the 1070s the Seljuks ejected the Byzantine Christians from much of Anatolia, which thus began its slow

◖ ORDER UNDERLYING ORNAMENTATION

1228, DIVRIGE COMPLEX, EASTERN ANATOLIA, TURKEY

From the 1070s, the Seljuk Turks overran much of the Byzantine empire in Anatolia. Mosques here were particularly varied. The vegetal and geometrical fantasies carved on this gate to the combined mosque and hospital complex at Divrige were probably inspired by contemporary Armenian churches. Their wildness is given order by a strict underlying geometrical framework (above).

⬤ HONORIFIC PORTAL

TWELFTH CENTURY ONWARDS, FRIDAY MOSQUE, ISFAHAN, IRAN

A view of the *iwan* known as *shofa-e shagird* ("of the student"), with the colossal scoops of its *muqarnas* vault, seen from the fourteenth-century Muzzaffarid *madrasa* or the *iwan* of Umar. Several of the four *iwan*s inserted in the Friday mosque's large, 65m by 55m (213ft by 180ft), courtyard appear to have been used for teaching. The most important *iwan* opened to the *qibla* bay.

transformation into what is now Turkey. The Seljuks called this territory Rum (Rome) and mosques here were particularly varied (the complex at Divrige is one result). Most significantly, perhaps because of the wetter climate or the influence of local domed and centralized churches, mosques that were entirely roofed were created, usually with a prominent dome (such as Ince Minareli *madrasa* in Konya, 1258).

Buildings in Anatolia developed further under an emirate founded in 1288 by Osman, whose successors became the area's dominant rulers: the Ottomans. Some of their mosques were simply square halls covered by a large hemispherical dome; each was fronted by a porch and had a sharp-topped, pencil-thin minaret alongside it (as at Ala' al-Din in Bursa, built 1358). This architecture spread with the Ottoman regime as, from the mid-fourteenth century, it expanded into the Balkans. This would remain a regional speciality for a century or so. In the longer term, its impact would be enormous.

Earlier developments in Iran had a more immediate impact. At the Seljuk capital of Isfahan, the largest dome in Islam at that date (15m/49ft in diameter and 30m/98ft high) was inserted in front of the *mihrab* of the Friday mosque in 1088, presumably as a venue for the sultan. Then, in stages during the twelfth century, a great square-topped structure was inserted into the centre of each courtyard façade. Each of these structures contains a vast, scoop-like arch; superficially like porches, the openings that lead from them are comparatively small. These are known as *iwan*s, and, used in combination with prominent *mihrab*-marking domes, their influence would be rapid and widespread.

The origins of the *iwan* lie in the monumental entrance porches constructed outside the audience halls of Sassanian kings, one of which survives at Ctesiphon, their capital in Iraq. The *iwan* at Isfahan brought a new dimension to mosque design, turning each side of the courtyard into a fully fledged architectural composition. The number of *iwan*s in a mosque can vary, although the grandest always have four. The most important is that leading towards the *mihrab*.

The use of *iwan*s spread rapidly, partly because the Seljuks sponsored a massive *madrasa*-building programme as part of a concerted drive to counter Shi'ite influence. An important fourteenth-century example, built by a regime of Turkic origin near the historic heartlands of Islam, illustrates the result. In 1249, following an Abbasid succession crisis, the Turkic mercenaries who had served the Abbasids founded a regime in their own right. Its capital was at the great city of Cairo (al-Qahira, "the triumphant"), which had been founded in 969 upriver of Fustat and was rapidly supplanting Baghdad as the prime cultural metropolis of the Islamic world. The Mamluks, as they were known, filled this city with magnificent monuments, arguably the greatest of which is the mosque-mausoleum built by Sultan Hassan (reigned 1347–1351 and 1354–1361; see page 141).

The *umma* in Asia

Meanwhile, other important architectural developments were occurring in the Indian subcontinent, Central Asia and further afield. Muslim forces acquired a permanent presence in India with Qutb al-Din Aybak's capture of Delhi in 1193. In 1206 the powerful Delhi sultanate was established, ruling a largely Hindu population.

Almost immediately, work began on the Quwwat-al Islam ("Might of Islam") mosque, using materials from earlier local buildings. Its mighty Qutb Minar minaret, covered in inscriptions, was the tallest in the Islamic world at 73m (238ft). The mosque fused Hindu and Islamic traditions while boldly stating the latter's primacy. India eventually became part of a vast area of Persian cultural influence, with a marked architectural character of its own, mainly thanks to the *iwan*-mosque and subsequent developments.

In Central Asia, from about 1370 a capital was established in the city of Samarqand by Timur, a descendant of the Mongol khans and founder of the Timurid dynasty.

The grand series of buildings created were entirely of the Persian type, and they illustrate how that tradition had developed since the innovations of twelfth-century Isfahan. Domes were further emphasized by being given a pointed profile and raised on a drum. *Iwan*-dominated façades were enhanced with tiles, which covered the surfaces of walls with inscriptions and complex geometric patterns composed in striking colour schemes: turquoise, ultramarine, yellow, white and black. Some mosques were set in paradisiacal gardens, in which flowing water moved in cross-shaped channels between rectilinear beds (see page 34).

All these Timurid enhancements can be seen at mausoleums (Ahmad Yasavi, built 1398), mosques (Gawhar Shad, Mashhad; see pages 142–143) and *madrasa*s (that of

⬇ TOWER OF VICTORY

*c.*1199–*c.*1368, QUTB MINAR, MEHRAULI, SOUTH DELHI, INDIA

This tapering five-storey sandstone minaret of the Quwwat-al Islam ("Might of Islam") mosque is the tallest ancient stone tower in India, at 73m (238ft). Much of the stone is from razed Hindu and Jain temples. An unfinished minaret was intended to rise to 145m (476ft).

Ulugh Beg was the first, in 1417, of the three that overlook Samarqand's Registan Square).

In East Asia, at the end of the Silk Road trading route, lay the great imperial civilization of China. It is claimed by some that the oldest mosque in China is the Huaisheng ("Memorial of the Holy Prophet") mosque in Guangzhou, said to date from 627. More certain is the date of origin for Quanzhou's Shengyou Qinzhensi ("Mosque of the Holy Friend"), which was first built in 1009–1010. Other impressive mosques in China are the Great Mosque of Xi'an (rebuilt 1392 and later) and the Niujie ("Ox Lane") mosque in Beijing (1368). These mosques are, like all religious buildings in China, works of the classical Chinese style (see pages 202–206), adapted to meet the ritual requirements of

▼ MUD MINARETS
1907, GREAT MOSQUE, DJENNÉ, MALI

Dating to the fourteenth century, this mud-brick and palm-wood mosque was rebuilt and remodelled under French direction in 1907. Real ostrich eggs top the towers, symbolizing purity and fertility.

congregation and orientation in Islamic practice. They have also received an Islamic imprint by means of small domes, stone-built prayer halls and prominent pointed arches.

Elsewhere in the region, the oldest mosques (such as Masjid Agung, Demak, Java, Indonesia) date from the fifteenth century, a time when Malacca (Malaysia) and eastern Java were the ruling seats of small Islamic states. Mosques in this region were covered by a single great roof – a pagoda-like stepped timber pyramid known as a *tajug*.

Islam in Africa

To the south and west of Islam's heartland in Arabia, sophisticated local vernacular Islamic architecture developed in Africa. In east Africa, there are many fine mosques from Zanzibar (Kizimkazi mosque, 1107) to Mogadishu (Fakr ad-Din mosque, 1269). In west Africa, Guinea has Islamic places of worship (Great Mosque, Dingueraye, 1849–1893) with extraordinary thatched, *stupa*-like domes – each of them covering a Ka'ba-shaped building. Nigeria is famous for

its arch-dominated mosque interiors (Zaria, 1830s/1840s), wherein the arches are often made of mud-bound palm leaves, and it has highly distinctive Baroque-influenced mosques built by freed slaves returning from Brazil (Shitta mosque, Lagos, 1894). All these buildings are less celebrated than the great earthen mosques of Mali (Djinguereber mosque, Timbuktu, 1342–1347, and the Great Mosque, Djenné, reconstructed in 1907). These mud buildings have grown almost organically in the annual cycles of maintenance necessary to prevent their disintegration.

By the late fifteenth century, then, Islam had extended its influence from the Atlantic to the South China Sea, and its distinctive architectural approach appeared in these territories in an assortment of regional styles. These varied from fully covered, single-domed mosques in Anatolia to a grand Persian sphere of influence, with *iwan*s and prominent domes, which reached from Iran through Central Asia and into India. Within this area, the Persian language achieved a status approaching that of Arabic: for example, passages of Persian devotional poetry were sometimes used for mosque inscriptions. The stage had been set for a flowering of traditional Islamic religious architecture under a trio of great imperial powers: the Safavids in Persia, the Mughals in India, and the Ottomans in what is now Turkey.

Three great empires

On the day in 1453 that Constantinople fell to Ottoman forces, Sultan Mehmed II entered Hagia Sophia, threw dirt on his turban to signify his humility, and ordered its conversion to a grand Friday mosque. The Christian high altar and *ambo* were disposed of (along with much ritual paraphernalia), a *mihrab* and *minbar* installed, and the construction of minarets began. The building was otherwise little changed (see pages 60–61). The city itself was renamed Istanbul.

In 1463–1471 the sultan commissioned the architect Atik Sinan to build a mosque to replace Constantine's Church of the Holy Apostles on the imperial city's most prominent hilltop. The Fatih Cami ("Victory Mosque") conformed with the local tradition of a prayer hall covered by a single dome, but it was built on a scale that rivalled Hagia Sophia. Around the mosque stood a planned complex of ancillary

⬤ **LIGHT-FILLED INTERIOR**
1550–1557, SULEYMANIYE MOSQUE, ISTANBUL, TURKEY

The Ottomans developed the *kulliye*, combining educational, charitable and other institutions in a great complex dominated by a huge mosque, such as that at the Suleymaniye, the spacious interior of which adopts the Byzantine template of Hagia Sophia. The adjacent mausoleum of Suleyman is a holy place for many Turkish Muslims.

services: a primary school, a library, a Sufi *khanqa*, a hospital, a *caravanserai*, public baths and markets, and a garden containing a royal mausoleum.

By the 1520s the Ottomans were building an empire that ruled Anatolia, North Africa, Egypt, the Middle East, Greece, the Balkans, much of the Caucasus and Hungary. It survived until 1922. Sultan Suleyman I "the Magnificent" (reigned 1520–1566) and his chief architect, Mimar Sinan, who was of Armenian Christian descent, set about turning Istanbul into a city befitting its status as the new Rome, now reborn for a new faith.

Sinan's inspiration was probably his predecessor and namesake's Fatih Cami. A complex with additional services also surrounds Mimar Sinan's Suleymaniye mosque in Istanbul (1550–1557) and the Selimiye mosque at Erdine (1574). Both these buildings copy Hagia Sophia's use of a dome supported by two sizable half-domes, resulting in extraordinarily voluminous internal effects. But they eschew the shadowy galleries which surround Hagia Sophia's main space. The effect was to replace an architecture suited for a theatrical and hierarchical liturgy with one of space, clarity and light: a bright covered hall for prayer. Sinan designed twenty-two surviving mosques and to this day the Istanbul skyline is punctuated by a series of his great buildings, with their carefully composed arrangements of domes and sub-domes surrounded by minarets. Later Ottoman buildings, such as the Sultan Ahmed I mosque (1609–1617), the "Blue mosque", brought these complex and carefully crafted exteriors to a peak of perfection.

The Safavids made Shi'ism the state religion of Persia – one with which Iran is strongly identified to this day. The Safavid capital was Isfahan, where they built a new royal suburb around a great square, the Maidan, off which was positioned an enormous new Friday mosque called the Masjid-i Shah (now the Masjid-i 'Ali), completed from 1611/1612 to 1637/1638, and the beautiful mosque of Shaikh Lutfallah (1603–1619). Such buildings are the culmination of Persian design traditions, combining the dome, the *iwan, muqarnas* vaults and coloured tiles to create effects of breathtaking intensity of pattern and form.

In India, the Timurid ruler Babur founded a dynasty in 1526 that was to govern much of the subcontinent until the nineteenth century. Its leaders called themselves the Mughals in reference to the tribe of Turco-Mongolian peoples from which the Timurids had come. Under Shah Akbar (reigned 1556–1605) and Shah Jahan (reigned 1627–1658) in particular, the Mughals developed a synthesis of existing Indian traditions with Persian–Timurid models. In terms of sacred architecture, the culmination of this story is a series of great

◗ IMPERIAL "BLUE MOSQUE"

1609–1617, SULTAN AHMED I MOSQUE, ISTANBUL, TURKEY

This enormous mosque complex or *kulliye*, close to Hagia Sophia, is one of the most mature works of Ottoman architecture. Such buildings have exteriors whose climbing sequences of domes and half-domes are as aesthetically satisfying as their internal spaces. Only the largest mosques built for the emperors were permitted six minarets (this viewing angle means that just five are visible).

● PRIVATE PERFECTION

AFTER 1658, MOTI MASJID, DELHI, INDIA

The Moti ("Pearl") Mosque is within the Red Fort in Delhi. It was probably a private mosque for the pious emperor Aurangzeb (reigned 1658–1707). Its bulbous domes may originally have been plated with copper, but otherwise the entire building is of marble. The tiny minarets are purely decorative.

new Friday mosques in Delhi, Lahore and Agra, and a succession of centralized mausoleums, culminating with that at Agra known as the Taj Mahal, after Mumtaz Mahal, the much-loved wife who is buried therein (see page 34).

Mughal architecture used marble and red sandstone to create an effect that balances grand colourfulness with imperial sobriety. Marble was inset into sandstone, usually to form frame-shaped motifs and inlaid flower patterns; marble also clad important parts of a complex, such as a shrine or a dome. Notable examples include the mausoleum of Shaykh Shalim Chishti in the mosque at Fatehpur Sikri (1568–1578). Motifs from both Hindu and Buddhist architecture – the lotus flower and the *chatri*, a freestanding, domed pavilion – were integrated into Mughal style. Hindu temples were also built in the same manner. Enormous onion domes pull the architectural compositions together. At the Taj Mahal, the entire structure is clad in white marble, set off against the red sandstone of the rest of the complex. The Taj's fame ultimately resides in its combination of exquisite detail and perfect proportions.

The Taj Mahal is one of the greatest buildings in the world. The Safavid and earlier tiled *iwan* mosques are arguably the greatest expression of the potential of the courtyard-and-prayer-hall format.

Today's global *umma*

Today, the Ottoman single-domed prayer hall, often given a Persian and Mughal inflection by means of pointed arches and onion domes, is the default pattern for countless mosques worldwide as, during the modern era, Islam has spread into Europe, North America and elsewhere. Many new countries have created grand "national" mosques. Some of these, such as the Faisal mosque in Islamabad (1976–1986), are aggressively modern; others, although of monumental proportions, are local and traditional, such as the Hassan II mosque in Casablanca (1993), which was briefly the largest in the world. Many simply feature a mixture of updated traditional motifs, as seen at the Al-Akbar Surabaya mosque in Indonesia (2000).

Meanwhile, in Arabia, the birthplace of Islam, the great shrines of Mecca, Medina and elsewhere have been lavishly rebuilt by oil-rich regimes, not least to help manage the

enormous number of pilgrims who visit them. The result has been a vapid, if traditionally inflected, grandeur, although the simple cuboid Ka'ba, which was last rebuilt in 684, retains its status as the focus of one of the world's great pilgrimage events. Islamic religious architecture remains abundant, varied and, occasionally, brilliantly contemporary. From Rome (mosque and Islamic Cultural Centre, 1984–1995) to Dhaka (Islamic University of Technology mosque, 1986), the best architects have sought inspiration in Islam's architectural traditions, giving new life to them using modern materials and

● ISLAMIC MODERNITY

1984–1995, MOSQUE AND ISLAMIC CULTURAL CENTRE, ROME, ITALY

Designed by Paolo Portoghesi and Vittorio Gigliotti, this mosque synthesizes modern, Islamic, Roman and Baroque aesthetic themes. The prayer hall, which has separate galleries for women, can hold 2,400 worshippers and has a dome that is 20m (66ft) in diameter. The complex includes educational and community facilities.

techniques, helping to draw together the congregated *umma*, curently 1.6 billion strong, in further reinterpretations of the template set by the original House of the Prophet.

MAN & COSMIC ORDER

SOUTH ASIAN CYCLES OF REBIRTH

—————————◯—————————

India, like the Middle East, is one of the world's great fountainheads of religious ideas. However, its most ancient faith traditions have not died. Instead, the complex tradition known as Hinduism has transformed them over many centuries. In the course of Hinduism's evolution, some teachers made innovations so radical that they resulted in new religions: Buddhism, Jainism and, much later, Sikhism.

Buddhism and Jainism, from around the third century CE, created South Asia's first permanent and monumental religious buildings. Buddhism has since had a huge impact on societies throughout Asia. Hinduism, although deeply rooted in its homeland, also spread to Southeast Asia, and during the fifth century CE it too created a monumental architecture.

These faiths share a conviction that death is not final. The soul may be reborn many times, and one of the aims of religion is to liberate the soul or help it to progress through various cycles of rebirth, sometimes making use of certain forms and patterns to bridge the gap between man and the divine. The ideas that flow from these concepts have shaped Hindu and Buddhist art and architecture, influencing in turn religious art throughout Asia and beyond.

◖ **THE WHEEL OF LIFE**

AFTER *c.*1679, SONGZANLIN MONASTERY, DEQIN, YUNNAN, CHINA

Buddhism and Hinduism see existence as a cyclical process. The Buddhist wheel of life depicts gods, humans, animals, ghosts and others trapped in endless rebirths, ended only by freeing oneself from bad *karma* and moving towards enlightenment.

ANCIENT INDIA

Indian religion has ancient roots. Some of its practices appear to be present in the Harappan culture, which emerged from around 2600BCE across a large area of northwest India and Pakistan. Although its cities, such as Harappa itself and Mohenjo Daro (now in Pakistan), were highly impressive, their religious life is not well understood. Harappans built artificial water tanks, and their art included images of a figure comparable to the god Shiva, suggesting continuity with later beliefs, but the evidence is too thin to draw firm conclusions. This civilization collapsed in around 1800BCE.

Equally important was a major infusion of ideas from outside India, bringing to the north of the subcontinent a range of new religious beliefs and a language. Sanskrit is broadly Indo-European, and probably came from an area to the northwest of modern India. The question of whether Sanskrit-speakers built the Harappan culture, lived alongside it or replaced it, is much debated. If Harappan culture predates their influence, it may have continuities with the distinctive cultures of the Indian south, which appear to have aboriginal roots.

The Vedic Age

By early in the first millennium BCE Sanskrit was being used by a hereditary priesthood, known as the Brahmins, based in the vicinity of the Ganges basin. It was the language of the *Vedas* ("books of knowledge"), the sacred hymns that these priests transmitted orally from one generation to the next. These rites continue to this day and the divinely revealed *Vedas* remain the core of the faith now known as Hinduism.

The *Vedas* contain hymns to a range of deities and prescriptions for rituals which took place in the open air or in the home. The focus is on sacrifices, offered up to deities in fire. This Vedic or Brahminical faith had little need for architecture or imagery, but aspects of it would be profoundly influential on the religious art of both Buddhism and Hinduism. The precise geometrical arrangement and construction of open-air altars was closely specified in the *Vedas*, suggesting that the patterns they formed were themselves considered efficacious. Cosmological concepts appear to be encoded in these forms: Meru, the axis of the universe (imagined as a mountain), and Purusha, the primordial man with whom

FAITH OF THE "FORD-MAKERS"

The intellectual challenge to traditional Indian religion in the sixth century BCE produced Jainism, but like Buddhism this began to fade as devotional Hinduism and then Islam became influential. However, there are still several million Jains in India, and more worldwide. Like Buddhists, Jains hold that certain types of behaviour will lead to liberation from the cycles of suffering that characterize death and rebirth. Their concern for the welfare of every being in the universe commits them to a life of extreme nonviolence. The founder of Jainism, who is considered the last sage of the present age, is Vardhamana Mahavira ("Great Hero", c.599–c.527BCE). He is held to have been preceded by twenty-three other, equally authoritative, sages or *tirthankaras* ("ford-makers"), the first of whom was Adinath.

These sages are the focus of Jain worship. Their teachings, the Agama, form the Jain sacred texts. The sages are perfected souls, not gods. Although Jainism accepts that there are supernatural beings, who themselves need liberating from the cycle of rebirth, it does not acknowledge the existence of a creator or god. Jainism has no priesthood, but it does have orders of monks and nuns.

Jain temples vary depending on whether they belong to the strictly ascetic Digambara order, whose members refuse to wear clothes or to decorate their statues, or to that of the Svetambara, whose temples

and ritual practices may be very elaborate. Many are only visually distinguishable from a Hindu temple by their iconography – Jain sages are often depicted as naked, standing or sitting in meditation. Although activity in a Svetambara temple may look very like that in a Hindu one, the aim of Jain worship is not to seek blessing from a deity, but to focus on the example set by a sage and so progress the evolution of one's own soul.

Some Jain temples have a distinctive layout. A courtyard lined by small shrines surrounds a central temple that is approached through a series of *mandapa* halls, evoking the heavenly preaching hall or *samavasarana* to which Mahavira went after his enlightenment. This is the form taken by the *mandapas* at the temples on Mount Abu, an important pilgrimage centre for Jains.

⊙ ADINATH – THE FIRST *TIRTHANKARA*

*c.*1032, VIMAL VASAHI TEMPLE, MOUNT ABU, RAJASTHAN, INDIA

Famous for its carved white marble, this temple is one of the five Dilwara temples on Mount Abu, sacred to Jainism. Vimal Vasahi is dedicated to Adinath, also known as Lord Rishabdev, whose idol, identifiable by its long hair, sits in the Gudh *mandapa*.

◆ THE GOD IN THE *GARBHAGRIHA*

SHRI SWAMINARAYAN MANDIR, LONDON, ENGLAND

The Hindu priesthood, known as the Brahmins, has ancient roots. Modern temple life focuses on images of deities, which are believed to be vessels for the living presence of the gods themselves. The representations are housed in room-sized sanctuaries known as

garbhagriha. His Holiness Pramukh Swami Maharaj (above) is the Spiritual Leader of BAPS Swaminarayan Sanstha, a Hindu organization that has built several temples outside India in recent decades. He is standing before images of the Hindu teacher Bhagwan Swaminarayan (1781–1830) and two of his disciples. Bhagwan Swaminarayan is acclaimed as a god by his followers.

DESIGNING A HOUSE FOR GOD

As early as the Vedic era, the square was a form with sacred significance in India – an emblem of the universe and of *brahman*, from which all things emanate. It was often used as the basis for the *mandala*s from which Hindu temples and much Buddhist architecture are derived.

*Vastupurushamandala*s, for example, are subdivided squares used to create the plans of Hindu temples. These are derived from Vedic stories about existence (*vastu*) having originated out of the body of Purusha, the vast primordial man, who was ritually sacrificed and dismembered. Each part of the *Vastupurushamandala*'s grid pattern is dedicated to different parts of the human body, as well as to different gods: the main, central, square belongs to Brahma and also to Purusha's heart.

Although in practice individual temple plans may not conform precisely with the specifications set out in a *Vastupurushamandala*, the final temple design will be the result of a process of subdivision and fractal expansion within grids, with squares arranged in complex, interlocking patterns. The resulting building is not only an image of the universe, it also embodies the image of man.

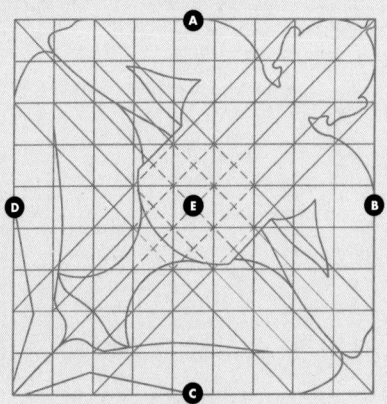

Ⓐ *Northern deities and devatas; upper parts of the body.*

Ⓑ *Eastern deities; right side of the body.*

Ⓒ *Southern deities; the legs and nether regions.*

Ⓓ *Western deities; left side of the body.*

Ⓔ *Centre point (Brahma) or middle body, surrounded by inner divinities.*

---

creation began. The idea of the spiritual pattern (*mandala*) – in which certain abstract forms are symbolically meaningful, and can in themselves be spiritually powerful – would play a major role in Hindu and Buddhist religious architecture.

An ordered universe

Brahmins believe themselves to be the highest element in human society, which is part of a great spiritual hierarchy that places gods and goddesses of colossal power at its apex, includes four human *varna*s (castes or social classes), and has the animals at its base. Brahmins must remain ritually pure, never marrying out of their *varna*. The universe is a continuum, an expression of an immanent underlying divine essence known as *brahman*, a oneness of existence which can accommodate many deities and a complex cosmological picture of space and time.

For Brahmins, the soul does not die, but merely enters into a cycle of rebirth (*samsara*). The idea of *karma* has developed in association with this: the soul acquires merit or de-merit, according to the actions one takes, which affects its fate in the next life. For example, a Brahmin who neglects his obligations, or pollutes his caste, might be reborn in a lesser caste or even as an animal.

Suffering, it was clear, was everywhere. Things might get worse as well as better over multiple lifetimes, and much pain might result. Some argued that ascetic practices increased the chances of rebirth into a more exalted existence, or could even liberate one from the experience of suffering itself.

Visionaries of a new age

By around 500BCE, life in northern India was changing rapidly. Urban life had re-established itself after the collapse of the Harappan civilization. Some teachers rejected the authority of the *Veda*s; others denied the validity of caste; and many argued for the efficacy of various kinds of religious discipline. Two of the most influential of these teachers were Vardhamana Mahavira, called the Jina ("conqueror"; see also box, page 160), and Siddhartha Gautama, who became the Buddha ("enlightened one", c.565–c.485BCE). Each had a clear and persuasive vision of how human beings could liberate themselves from suffering. The Jainism and Buddhism that they established are two of the earliest religions with an explicit founder and a proselytizing mission. Both began to gather adherents in large numbers, and then to produce monuments, which may have been the earliest permanent religious buildings in the landscape of India. The resulting architectural ideas would interact with each other, and with the emerging ones of Hinduism, over many centuries, producing a series of brilliant interpretations of ancient Indian notions about rebirth and the significance of sacred pattern.

BUDDHISM

THE MIDDLE WAY

By the middle of the first millennium BCE, a rich merchant class was developing in the cities of the northern part of India, eager to engage in religion but excluded from Brahminical life. The Brahmins, too, may have been seeking forms of religious practice that offered more than simply obliging them to enact and transmit ancient rites. It was into this world, in about 565CE, that Siddhartha Gautama, a prince of the Sakya people, was born.

The Buddha and his teaching

Siddhartha Gautama grew up in a world of comfort and luxury, and he was moved by his first encounters with human suffering. In response, he left his comfortable home to take up a life as an ascetic, wandering holy man. Having attempted all manner of privation, he came to advocate a Middle Way between rejection of and engagement with worldly life.

TIMBER PAGODAS

The *stupa* is the defining Buddhist building and the pagoda is its multi-storeyed Chinese form, ubiquitous throughout East Asia. The sixth-century example at the Yongningsi in Chang'an (Daxing, modern Xi'an) is said to have reached 161m (528ft), which would have made it one of the highest buildings anywhere. Over time, while *stupas* remained important elsewhere, the significance of pagodas in East Asian architecture went into decline and many temples had no pagoda at all.

The five-storey Horyuji pagoda at Nara, Japan, is one of the oldest wooden structures in the world, c.607.

⊙ DAIBUTSU

743, TODAIJI TEMPLE, NARA, JAPAN

Known in Japan as Daibutsu, or Big Buddha, this massive, 15m-high (49ft) statue at Nara's Todaiji temple (745–749) represents Dainichi Nyorai, or Vairocana, the cosmic *buddha*. It is the largest freestanding bronze statue in the world. The lotus throne is original but the figure, originally covered in gold, has been recast several times (much of it dates from 1692). His right hand is raised in the fear-allaying gesture (*abhaya mudra*).

In his thirty-fifth year, Gautama sat in meditation beneath a tree on the banks of a river near the city of Gaya. Here he experienced a transformation so profound that it completely reconfigured his consciousness. He had become a *buddha*, an "awakened one". His growing band of followers called him Shakyamuni, the "sage of the Sakyas".

The Buddha taught that his enlightenment had broken the wheel of suffering and his soul was thus liberated from the cycle of death and rebirth; it had entered a state beyond description known as *nirvana* ("blowing out", meaning free of ignorance and desire). This state was achievable by anyone and it was his earthly mission to pass this knowledge on to others. Caste was to be no barrier to acceptance of this teaching. His followers were to commit themselves to "Three Jewels": the Buddha, their spiritual exemplar; the Dharma, his teaching; and the Sangha, his community of followers.

Buddhism shared a great deal of its cosmology as well as many ideas about reincarnation with Jainism and Hinduism. Although Buddhism does not require the existence of gods, it accepts that there are supernatural beings, such as *devas*, and other divine entities. Buddhism also developed a huge body of literature, much of it concerned with the life and previous lives of the Buddha (*jatakas*), widely depicted in temple art. Gautama had been a *bodhisattva*, a being on the verge of enlightenment. The near-infinite compassion that *bodhisattvas* possessed meant that people entreated them to intercede and assist, much in the manner of a saint or a deity in other faiths.

There are three major branches of the faith. Alternative *buddhas* and *bodhisattvas* were emphasized in a tendency that became known as Mahayana ("Great Vehicle"). This had early roots, but only became self-consciously separate around the fourth century CE. Mahayana recognizes a vast pantheon of highly realized beings, often ascribed godlike power, and is rich in both imagery and liturgy. It stands in contrast to the older (and liturgically simpler) Shakyamuni Buddha-centred Theravada ("Little Vehicle") Buddhism. Within Mahayana Buddhism, between *c.*500 and *c.*1000CE there developed the Vajrayana ("Diamond-Thunderbolt Vehicle") school, which advocated magical practices believed to advance the adept rapidly towards *buddha*hood. Today, Theravada Buddhism

is dominant in Sri Lanka and Southeast Asia; Mahayana Buddhism dominates East Asia, with Vajrayana strong in Tibet and Mongolia.

*Stupa*s and sculptures

The creation of the first Buddhist monuments seems to follow immediately from Shakyamuni Buddha's death. He is said to have requested that his body be cremated and the ashes placed in a mound, as was traditional for high-status burials. But he also asked that the mound be located on a crossroads, so that pilgrims could have access to it: this, then, is more than a burial chamber – it is a kind of shrine.

The Buddha's relics were split soon after his death and housed within eight mounds, known as *stupa*s. Emperor Ashoka (reigned 274–236BCE), a ruler of the Mauryan dynasty, afterwards adopted Buddhism and used it to unify his territories. He is also credited with taking its message beyond India, to Sri Lanka, Burma, and what is now Afghanistan and Pakistan. Ashoka distributed the relics across the empire in what were probably India's first permanent religious buildings. None of these early *stupa*s survives in its original form (although Ashoka's inscribed freestanding columns do), but there are some from about a century later, by which time Jains (see page 160) as well as Buddhists were constructing them. The *stupa* is at once a shrine, a cosmological emblem and the physical symbol of the faith. Its form became extremely varied, and it was the overriding focus of creativity in Buddhist architecture.

Monasteries and *chaitya*s

*Stupa*s have no interior spaces. It is from a little after Ashoka's reign that the first true temples appear in India. They start not so much as architecture, but as something more like sculpture: cave temples, excavated within rock. Their most ambitious spaces are ones for assembly, known as *chaitya* halls (see page 25). These are associated with groups of square residential cells, which are remnants of Buddhist monasteries, or *vihara*s, institutions that originated in the Buddha's lifetime. The *chaitya* halls and *vihara*s seem likely to have been modelled on what, by the third century BCE, were presumably freestanding complexes of timber buildings.

⏵ CAVE 26 AT AJANTA

*c.*470, MAHARASHTRA, INDIA

Cave 26 contains one of the earliest giant images of the Buddha, a 7m (22ft) sculpture of his *parinirvana* – that is, a depiction of the moment of his physical death. In such scenes the reactions of his disciples, shown below the prone Buddha, vary. Those who are themselves approaching *buddha*hood are calm, knowing that he is beyond suffering and that physical death is of little significance; less realized souls are grief-stricken.

At Bhaja in Maharashtra, the hall façades imitate a roof made of thatch laid on top of curved beams, bound at the top. The curve of this horseshoe-shaped gable rises to a point at the peak, like an ogee arch. This ogival outline is found on religious buildings of all kinds throughout the subcontinent. It is often called a *gavaksha*, or a *chaitya* arch.

Representing the Buddha

Originally, Buddhism relied on impersonal symbols to communicate its message. But about a century after cave temples started to be carved, and peaking from the first century CE, many images of the Buddha began to be created. This probably reflects an increasing tendency to deify him. The early images are mainly associated with the Kushan empire (*c.*50–*c.*250CE), and produced in two centres: a western area known as Gandhara (western Afghanistan/eastern Pakistan; see page 174), and an eastern one, around Mathura (Madhya Pradesh).

Both regions achieved a convincing vision of *buddha*hood: poised, profoundly conscious and deeply still. The artists of Gandhara, at their best, fused the humanistic qualities of Hellenistic and Buddhist culture to extraordinary effect – and combined Greek and Indian architectural elements. Gandhara's position along routes into Central Asia and China made its art influential, and it survived until the Islamic invasions of the seventh to ninth centuries. In India, Mathuran Buddhas, with their quiet, inward-looking smiles, were important in shaping the next major stylistic development.

From *c.*320CE, until around 550, northern India was united under the reign of the Guptas. Gandharan and Mathuran visions of the Buddha were fused, resulting in a model that would become a pan-Asian prototype.

Although cave temples continued to be carved from rockfaces, most famously at Ajanta, kings replaced merchants, nuns and monks as the main patrons. Increasingly, these monasteries had monks' cells around a rectilinear cloister, with an entrance to one side of an axis and a square image room or sanctuary opposite it that contained an image of the Buddha. *Chaitya* halls began to disappear, and *stupa*s became the dominant feature of a complex, apparently positioned so that laymen and monks alike could gain access.

As Buddhism made inroads into Asia, the places associated with the Buddha's life became centres of pilgrimage. Hugely influential buildings were constructed, such as the temple at Bodh Gaya, site of the Buddha's enlightenment, with its exceptionally high (55m/180ft) *sikhara* spire, and the university at Nalanda with its enormous and elaborate *stupa*. However, by the tenth century Buddhism was in decline in India and many of these sites were destroyed or fell into ruin after Islam came to the north of the subcontinent.

The spread of Buddhism

By the first to third centuries, Buddhism had become well established in the subcontinent and was close to being a pan-Asian phenomenon. The *stupa*, while common to all

CONTINUES ON PAGE 170

THE GREAT STUPA

*c.*250BCE–*c.*50CE, SANCHI, MADHYA PRADESH, INDIA

Sanchi is by far the best preserved of the first generation of *stupa*s (see page 166), and one of the great monuments of the earliest age of Buddhist art. At that time, no images were yet made of the Buddha himself, but his relics had become enormously significant, and the Great *Stupa* is one of many – perhaps 84,000 – built by the Emperor Ashoka across his enormous Indian domain. The Sanchi site was once a monastic complex, which was not abandoned until the thirteenth century CE. Pilgrims approached from the south and circumambulated the 37m-wide (120ft) *stupa*, both at ground level and on a raised platform, from east to west. This inner area is demarcated by the enclosing fence, with its four gates oriented to the cardinal points of the compass; their "L"-shaped entrances also give the structure a sacred plan form shaped like a swastika. Some other early sites have the layout of a *mandala* when seen from above. Every part of the *stupa* has a symbolic meaning. The finial at the top alludes to the axis of the universe, Mount Meru (Sumeru), and evokes the tree under which the Buddha attained enlightenment; its three levels symbolize the "jewels" of Buddhist teaching: Buddha, Dharma and Sangha.

Its perimeter marked by a fence ❶ and its entrance by an adorned stone gateway known as a *torana* ❷, the Sanchi *stupa* consists of a hemispherical dome 16m/52ft in height called an *anda* ❸, which is encircled by a double circumambulatory way system – a path ❹ at the base and a platform higher up ❺. Surmounting the *anda* is a relic receptacle ❻, which is crowned by an honorific umbrella, or *chattra* ❼.

▶ EAST *TORANA*

AFTER *c.*50BCE, SANCHI,
MADHYA PRADESH, INDIA

The four gates, or *torana*s, at Sanchi are among the finest works of early Buddhist sculpture. They were added, along with most of the *stupa*'s architectural features, around the mid-second century BCE, when the *stupa* was doubled in size. The images adorning the east *torana* (opposite) focus mainly on the life of the Buddha, key moments in the history of Buddhism, and scenes from the *jataka*s or stories of the previous lives of the Buddha. The Buddha himself is not depicted; instead motifs such as wheels, Bodhi trees, footprints, empty thrones and riderless horses stand in for him.

❶ The wheel is one of the key images of Buddhist art. Symbolizing the cycle of birth, death and rebirth (liberation from which the Buddha attained through enlightenment), the wheel also embodies the teaching of the Buddha, or Dharma, and the constant process of spiritual development.

❷ As a young prince, Siddhartha, the Buddha-to-be, was deeply upset by the brief encounters he had with human suffering. He abandoned his palace at night and went in search of a spiritual path that would free humanity from pain. A series of riderless horses mark his journey beyond the city walls.

❸ Finally, Prince Siddhartha sent his groom, Chandaka, unwillingly home; the servant bows to his master, here represented by his footprints, before he leaves. The Buddha's footprint is one of the most venerated of all Buddhist icons.

❹ The Bodhi tree at Bodh Gaya, under which the Buddha attained enlightenment, became the first, and most important, site of Buddhist pilgrimage. A visit by Emperor Ashoka was an important marker of his commitment to the faith. Having dismounted his elephant, Ashoka is shown here approaching the tree in an attitude of worship.

❺ This voluptuous tree spirit, sometimes referred to as a *yakshi*, clings to a fruit-bearing tree; she embodies fertility and good fortune and is one of the many protective and beneficent mythological figures and animals on the gates. Throughout its history, Buddhism has absorbed existing local mythologies and cosmologies.

Buddhist complexes, developed in various ways. That at Mirisavatiya in Sri Lanka was 60m (197ft) in diameter, and at Amaravati in Andhra Pradesh, India, the *stupa* was richly coloured and sculpted. Some had simple, chapel-like openings let into their bases for images of the Buddha, and at Takht-i-Bahi, in what is now Pakistan, smaller *stupas* or image-chapels were arranged geometrically around the base. Such changes emphasized Buddha images and enhanced the *mandala*-like symbolic associations of *stupas*. Representations of the Buddha were becoming common as well as increasingly large, suggesting they required an architectural setting of their own. These are the forms that would develop as Buddhism spread to the south, where Sri Lanka played a key role, and to the north, through Gandhara.

Buddhism in Sri Lanka

Ashoka's son Mahinda and his sister Sanghamitra converted the king of Sri Lanka in *c.*250–*c.*210BCE, bringing to the island a cutting from the Bodhi tree, under which the Buddha had become enlightened. Relics – a tooth was acquired in 328

– and pilgrimage sites, many including more tree-cuttings, remained focuses of Sri Lankan Buddhism from then on.

Mahavihara, the "Grand Monastery", was founded in the capital Anuradhapura – a community that became a great storehouse of Buddhist knowledge. The *stupas* (in Sinhalese *dagoba*) built there and at the rival, and more doctrinally varied, monasteries founded by Sri Lankan kings over the ensuing centuries were exceptionally large (the original height of Jetavana monastery, before 301CE, is said to have been 122m/400ft, which would have made it one of the world's tallest buildings). Mahavihara also contained a residential and ritual structure known as the Lohapasada ("Brazen Palace"), which was nine storeys high, clad in copper plaques, and supported by 1,600 columns.

Sri Lankan Buddhism's two great ages of independence and prosperity were from 459 to 993, at Anuradhapura, and from 1073, when a new capital was laid out at Polonnaruwa. The island's competing monastic communities were brought together by King Parrakamabahu I (reigned 1153–1186) under the "supreme order" of the Mahavihara, making Sri Lanka a bastion of state-supported Theravada orthodoxy.

Architecturally, a series of innovations were made in the first period, which were to be explored with vigour in the second. The *patimaghara*, or "temple of the image", is a varied building type dominated by a portrayal of the Buddha. The *vatadage* is a *stupa* surrounded by columns, probably originally supporting a great conoid thatched roof: it is thus a kind of "temple of the *stupa*". Both are found at Polonnaruwa, well known for the statues cut from the cliff at Gal Vihara and the axial, sheer-walled sanctuary of the Lankatilaka *patimaghara* (late twelfth century), with galleries that overlook a standing Buddha 12.5m (41ft) high. These buildings sometimes borrow forms from Indian temples and are often set in large monasteries. A typical example, the

◖ "TEMPLE OF THE *STUPA*"

*c.*1160, POLONNARUWA VATADAGE, SRI LANKA

In Sri Lanka, the *vatadage* circular relic house or shrine places a *dagoba* (*stupa*) in a roofed rotunda surrounded by columns. The four oriented openings have characteristically Sri Lankan semi-circular "moonstones", symbolizing the progression from an outer world of animal desire to an inner one of enlightenment.

Pubbaramavihara, had a moat, a grid of monastic cells, and an inner enclosure – approached by roads arranged cardinally – containing a *stupa*, a *patimaghara*, a chapter house (*uposatha-ghara*) and a Bodhi-tree shrine. Such plans are very *mandala*-like.

Although Sri Lanka's influence was considerable and felt widely – with the Mahavihara monastery becoming the fountainhead of Theravadan orthodoxy, which transformed Buddhism in Southeast Asia and Indonesia – its distinctive architecture of *stupa*s-cum-centralized-temples, image-houses and *mandala*-monasteries was more than matched by the remarkable innovations elsewhere in the region.

From Indonesia to Burma

Ashoka is said to have sent a mission to the Mon peoples in the Irrawaddy Valley area, in what is now Burma (or Myanmar), during the third century BCE, and the earliest Buddhist structures in the region date from around the fifth century CE. Although by about 800 there were many smaller Buddhist monasteries in the region, major Buddhist architecture only

◗ GRANITE-CUT GIANT BUDDHAS

*c.*1153–*c.*1186, GAL VIHARA, POLONNARUWA, SRI LANKA

At Gal Vihara ("stone temple") four shrines have rock-cut figures. The "standing Buddha" (7m/23ft high) is on a lotus pedestal and the "reclining Buddha" (14m/46ft long) is in the pose of a sleeping lion (*simhaseyya*) rather than *parinirvana*. Both were once covered, making this a former image-house. From India to China, similar colossal images appeared almost simultaneously, and the idea of the giant Buddha remains a major theme of Buddhist art to the present.

explodes onto the scene far to the south, on Java. This island was an important staging post between India and East Asia, and became a major centre of Mahayana Buddhism, just as the esoteric Vajrayana tendency was developing.

The result was a series of emphatically Buddhist monuments whose architectural conception is a kind of fusion of Buddhist *stupa*, Hindu temple and architectural *mandala*. Typically, these buildings – such as the Candi Kalasan (778) and Candi Plaosan (825–850) – have cruciform plans, with four entrances (each facing a cardinal direction) and a dark internal sanctuary, above which rises a richly carved spire, rather like a centralized Hindu temple or a hollowed-out

☁ CITY OF MOUNTAIN-INSPIRED SHRINES

c.1050–c.1250, PAGAN, MANDALAY, BURMA (MYANMAR)

Among the 2,217 temples on the plains around Pagan are three of Burma's largest: Thatbyinnyu (centre left, c.1155), Ananda (centre, c.1105) and Gawdawpalin (centre right, c.1227). The Ananda is 53m (174ft) square, rises to a *sikhara* 51–52m (167–170ft) in height, and contains a *mandala*-like network of corridors, in which four entrance routes, crossed by circumambulation paths, run along the cardinal directions to the heart of the interior, where there are four large gilded *buddha*s. The Thatbyinnyu is 61m (201ft) tall and contains a single great image of the Buddha on an upper level and residential quarters for an entire monastery in its hollowed-out base.

stupa. Their spires in particular are very like the *sikhara* of Hindu temples, but made up of miniature sculpted *stupa*s rather than statues of gods. This tradition reaches its climax at Borobudur (c.780–850; see pages 178–179), which is approached along a pilgrim route marked by smaller temples. Although this structure is generally classified as a *stupa* (it is an artificial mound, rising in symbolic stages to a central, spire-like structure, and without an interior), it can equally be seen as a massive, three-dimensional sculpted *mandala*. The size of a small hill, it was probably designed as the setting for extended circumambulatory rites of an immersive and spiritually transformative nature.

Buddhist Java blurs into Hindu Java at the enormous nearby Prambanan Hindu temple (856, see page 197), with its 47m (154ft) *sikhara* and its 240 minor temples, arranged like *stupa*s in a *mandala*-like grid. Borobudur or Prambanan may have influenced the architecture of the Khmer, who built a colossal series of temples (*wat*s) with *mandala*-like plans in the Hindu city of Angkor (notably Angkor Wat by Suryavarman II, see pages 56–57), which had a final Buddhist phase to its story after the ascendancy of Jayavarman, a devotee of Mahayana Buddhism.

King Jayavarman VII (reigned 1181–c.1219) wiped out the city centre built by his ancestors, replaced it with the new city of Angkor Thom and enriched it with Buddhist temples. His mortuary temple, the Bayon, its outer enclosure a rectangle about 125m by 136m (410ft by 446ft) – dominates this city. The main nod to the devotional change, from Vishnu or Shiva to Buddha, comes in the subject matter of its sculpture: in particular, 216 giant faces – fusing the image of the Buddha with that of the king – stared down from its fifty-four *sikhara* (of which only thirty-seven survive).

By this time, an equally impressive city about 1,800km (1,100 miles) to the north had been rebuilt by King Anawrahta (reigned 1044–1077) and his successors. Pagan is both the next stage in the great sequence of Southeast Asian Hindu/Buddhist *mandala stupa* temples and the harbinger of a new phase in the history of Buddhism in the region. From Pagan, founded in 849, Anawrahta united the country and made orthodox Theravada Buddhism into a kind of state religion. In doing this, he effectively brought into being the state of Burma, now known officially as Myanmar.

Over the next century, Pagan was filled with some 2,217 separate Buddhist monuments – today scattered like spaceships across a great plain from which the other buildings have disappeared. One of the first was the sacred Shwezigon Paya, an influential *stupa* (in Burmese, *zedi*), completed in 1090. The largest are the Ananda of *c.*1105 and Thatbinnyu of *c.*1155. Externally, these two buildings resemble a *stupa*: a centralized mound built in levels, with circumambulation terraces and an elegant gilded spire. But both have been hollowed out, turning them into enormous temples (in Burmese, *gu*, which may translate as "cave") with sheer, subtly lit internal walls dominated by massive gilded images of the Buddha.

Throughout the region today, most of the people of Burma, Cambodia, Laos and Thailand practise an orthodox Theravada Buddhism that was largely imported direct from the Mahavihara community in Sri Lanka (see page 170) as part of state-building efforts by various kings. (Java is part of Indonesia and is now mostly Islamic.) Their temples are often placed in enclosures whose general form evokes *mandala*s, with monastic ordination halls, image-halls and massive *stupa*s as their centrepieces. These buildings have sweeping, brightly coloured roofs, and much structural use is made of timber. An aesthetic of strained elegance, with a pronounced vertical emphasis, unites these buildings. Such *stupa*s as the Shwedagon, Rangoon (perhaps fourteenth century), have a swooping, rocketship-like form, articulated by layers of mouldings, and surrounded by smaller *stupa*s or image-houses. Temple complexes such as Wat Phra Keo (1784/1785), sacred heart of Thai Buddhism and adjacent to the Grand Palace in Bangkok, have *stupa*s, multicoloured Thai *prang* (sanctuary towers influenced by Hindu *sikhara*) and ordination halls with eight carved *bai sema* boundary stones around them, embodying the directions of the cosmos and the Eightfold Noble Path of Buddhism.

At Mandalay, which had now become the Burmese capital, King Mindon (reigned 1853–1878) placed 729 smaller *stupa*s around a larger one: each contains a copy of the definitive Theravada version of the Buddhist canon, the text for which had been agreed at a Buddhist council held in the city in 1871.

In summary, it is possible to identify a southern Buddhist tradition, perhaps inspired by models in eastern India and Sri Lanka and extending through much of Southeast Asia and Indonesia, in which various architectural themes recur: the turning of a *stupa* into a temple to create a building with an interior; the conversion of a temple or a *stupa* into a *mandala* to form a colossal sacred sculpture, a manipulation of the landscape; and the combining of Hindu, Buddhist and indigenous religious and artistic ideas. The resulting fusions

⬩ GOLDEN GEOMETRY

FOURTEENTH CENTURY ONWARDS, SHWEDAGON PAGODA, RANGOON (YANGON), BURMA

Legendary holder of eight hairs of the Buddha, this *stupa* is first documented in the fourteenth century and reached its present height of 99m (326ft) in 1774. It is approached on stairways oriented cardinally. At its foot are sixty-four smaller and four larger *stupa*s, used for meditation. The entire structure is covered in gold plate, with gold leaf lower down. At the very top is an orb studded with diamonds.

of *stupa*, *mandala*-like plans and temple are arguably the southern Buddhist tradition's most remarkable contribution to religious architecture, resulting in structures uniquely Buddhist and aesthetically ravishing.

The emphasis in these buildings on ideas about sacred pattern, brought to a height at Borobudur and Angkor, reflects not orthodox Theravada thought but the strong influence of esoteric Mahayana and Vajrayana culture in this area for much of the medieval period. Orthodoxy triumphed in Sri Lanka and Southeast Asia, at about the same time that the great architectural innovations of the Buddhist south came to an end. To the north and east of India, however, Mahayana and Vajrayana Buddhism had a lasting artistic impact.

Buddhism in Gandhara and Central Asia

It was through the northern Indian subcontinent that Buddhism spread along the desert oases of the Silk Road and into East Asia. From the seventh century CE onwards, the influence of the once independent kingdom of Gandhara faded as the region began to fall to the forces of Islam. Much Buddhist art was then either destroyed or left to fall into ruin.

Doctrinally, Gandhara was an early and significant centre of Mahayana Buddhism. Artistically, the area was a crossroads. It is probably from this part of Central Asia that various ideas made their way into Indian, Islamic, Christian and Chinese religious art, including: winged anthropomorphic beings, known in Christianity as angels, in Islam as *malak*s and in Buddhism and Hinduism as *deva*s; the use of the halo to indicate a holy person; and the ogee arch.

Architecturally, the area features carefully planned monastic institutions, dominated by exceptionally ambitious *stupa*s. The one at Guldarra, Afghanistan (second/third century CE or later), is covered in simple Corinthian pilasters and blank arcades featuring Indian *chaitya* ogee arches. The idea that *stupa*s could have complex surface articulation, many storeys and an attenuated outline was hugely influential. Further early experiments with multi-storey *stupa*s are seen in the approximately seventh-century towers standing in the ruins of Jiaohe near Turfan in Xinjiang, China, which are studded with tiny niches for Buddha statues.

Rock-cut *vihara*s are the region's best-preserved Buddhist structures, found at sites such as Bezeklik and Dunhuang,

THE GESTURES OF THE BUDDHA

From the third century CE onwards, depictions of the Buddha and associated beings were guided by clear written rules, sharing their origin and many of their principles with the Hindu *shilpa shastra*s (see page 192). Among other things, these define the hand gestures (*mudra*s) used in depictions of Shakyamuni and other *buddha*s and *bodhisattva*s. *Mudra*s are often combined with a specific pose to illustrate a certain moment in the Buddha's life or represent a generalized quality of importance.

Among the most significant are two often seen on cross-legged, meditating images of the Buddha at Bodh Gaya: *dhyana mudra* **A**, with hands folded in meditation, and *bhumisparsha mudra* **B**, with the right hand lightly touching the ground, calling the earth to

witness the Buddha's deep resolve to attain enlightenment. Various *mudra*s show him while teaching. In the most common of these, the *vitarka mudra* **C**, the thumb and forefinger of one or both hands form a circle, making a point of explanation while preaching. The related *dharmachakra mudra*, "setting the wheel of the law in motion", brings the two hands together close to the chest and is particularly closely associated with Shakyamuni's first sermon, in the Deer Park at Sarnath.

In the *abhaya mudra* **D**, one hand is up, facing the viewer, conferring the Buddha's own fearlessness and spiritual power onto the beholder. In the *varada mudra* the hand is also open, but it hangs down rather than up, indicating the desire of the figure to devote himself or herself to human salvation.

◀ MEDITATION

c.780–c.850, BOROBUDUR, JAVA, INDONESIA

In a state of profound concentration, Shakyamuni, identifiable by the distended earlobes, sits with his hands folded in the *dhyana mudra*.

A

B

C

D

both now in China (in Xinjiang and Gansu, respectively). These monastery cave-temples are famous for their spectacular painted interiors, in which rectilinear spaces are dominated by *buddha* images.

Gandhara was one of the first places where statues of the Buddha were carved, but its role in the dissemination of colossal, cliff-cut images is impossible to assess. Although they are now found across the Buddhist world – from the 13m (43ft) bronze Amida Buddha (1255) in Kamakura, Japan, to the much more recent 46m (153ft) reclining Buddha at Wat Pho in Bangkok, Thailand – the greatest of these rock-cut figures were the two that once stood in mighty niches cut into a cliff at Bamiyan in central Afghanistan, until their destruction by the Taliban in 2001.

These sober seventh-century Gandharan giants, 53m (174ft) and 38m (125ft) high respectively, were originally accompanied by at least one further representation of the Buddha, cut into the valley floor. They were once part of a monastic complex; the cliffside is hewn with some 750 painted and sculpted cells and chapels, originally connected by wooden walkways and corridors on and in the cliff-face itself. Such small and ornately decorated cave-temples show that the giant Buddha images did not stand alone in a rocky landscape. The Buddhas themselves were also, to varying extents, enclosed by decorative wooden or brick image-houses, the fixings and footings for which are still visible. These are works on a monumental architectural scale and form part of the story of religious architecture.

Buddhism in East Asia

In East Asia, Buddhist architecture goes through an abrupt transformation. Temples there are almost entirely of wood, and their overriding focus is on a series of image-halls arranged along an axis. Each successive hall sits across that axis, rather as the prayer hall of a mosque has its longest wall facing the *qibla* direction. The round, stone *stupa* has become the tall, thin – and often timber – pagoda. Buddhist architecture, in short, has adapted itself to the existing principles of Chinese architecture (see pages 202–206), making Buddhist temples – excepting their pagodas – identical to other kinds of temple or high-status buildings.

◑ VENERATING THE *STUPA*
c.75–c.125CE, BUNER/SWAT, ANCIENT GANDHARA (PAKISTAN)

These figures, their depiction influenced by Greek art, are circumambulating an elaborate Gandharan *stupa* with many layers, rich surface decoration and an attenuated form. The monks move clockwise around the sacred object, led by a figure carrying a votive lamp, who is probably not a monk (because his head is unshaven). He may be the patron of the piece.

The distinctive character of Buddhist art in East Asia is partly a reflection of such adaptations, but it is also a testament to the continuity of Mahayana and Vajrayana traditions. Chinese, Korean and Japanese Buddhist temples are dominated by *buddha*s, *bodhisattva*s and other deities, which have become the devotional focus of these complexes, almost replacing the *stupa*-circumambulation so vital elsewhere.

At first, the faith was a minor presence in China, perhaps associated with foreign traders and local merchants, in what was a sophisticated, urbanized society with powerful indigenous religious, philosophical and artistic traditions of its own. We know little about the form of the resulting temples, such as the Baimasi (White Horse Temple), founded in Luoyang as early as 148CE.

The ruling Han dynasty collapsed in 220CE, and the ensuing 400 years were troubled ones. Several rulers promoted Buddhism, such as those of the Northern Wei dynasty (386–534), whose capital was at Pingcheng (Datong) in Shanxi. By *c.*400, it was said that there were almost 2,000 monasteries south of the Yellow River – and Buddhism was, if anything, even more popular in the north. The Buddhism being imported was suffused with the emerging Mahayana tradition, and its cultural impact was felt widely.

Buddhist buildings outstripped the spread of Confucian and Taoist temples (about ten Buddhist temples for every Taoist one is the estimate for fourth-century Luoyang). And the *stupa* was to be the only architectural form in China that was both widespread and uniquely religious in nature. These early pagodas, especially those made in stone, must have been a striking and exotic presence in the landscape.

Buddhism goes native

The unification of China under the Sui (581–618) and Tang (618–906) dynasties led to a period of stability, prosperity and cultural openness, during which the capital of Chang'an (Daxing, modern Xi'an) became one of the greatest cities in the world. A national temple, the Daxingshansi, took up an entire ward of Chang'an. But the acceptance of Buddhism was not a smooth or simple process. Confucians in particular resisted it, and in 845 Emperor Wuzhong banned "foreign cults", resulting in the closure, it was said, of 44,600 Buddhist

chapels and monasteries. The emperor's thoroughness is demonstrated by the fact that (pagodas and cave-temples apart) just one surviving temple is known that predates this: the Nanchangsi (782) on the edge of a village near Mount Wutai in Shanxi. Despite such episodes, Buddhism generally put down deep roots among both the people and their rulers.

Pagodas, stone and timber alike, were widely built; the form of the timber pagoda is borrowed from indigenous defensive towers or *ge*, but their circumambulation platforms and *chattra* umbrella-shaped finials, which top a central pole that evokes the world-axis, betray their origin as stretched-out *stupa*s.

China's rock-cut temples were constructed in large numbers throughout the country from the second century CE. The interiors of these spaces, none of which is large, copy local wooden architecture just as their Indian models reflected contemporary timber temples there. Some are dominated by a single central column, carved into a pagoda-like form and studded with tiny images of the Buddha, creating a restricted circumambulation space. Major rock-cut sculpture was also being made in China as early as anywhere (Yungang dates

CONTINUES ON PAGE 180

◐ MAITREYA IN CAVE 12

483CE, YUNGANG, DATONG, SHANXI, CHINA

The heavenly beings and Maitreya (*buddha* of the future, far left) in Cave 12 form a colourful assembly. They are just a few of the 50,000 carved and painted figures in fifty caves at Yungang, which is one of two – with Longmen, near Luoyang – magnificent Buddhist cave sculpture complexes begun under the Northern Wei dynasty (386–534).

◐ SONGYUE TEMPLE PAGODA

523CE, DONGFENGXIAN, HENAN, CHINA

This twelve-sided, brick-built, 40m-high (131ft) structure, erected during the Period of Disunion (220–581), is believed to be the earliest multi-eaved pagoda in China, and its Gandhara-influenced form is reminiscent of a tall, thin *sikhara*. The stone steeple is distinctly divided into a pedestal, main body and top. The "Sumeru pedestal" is the shape of a lotus flower; the main body of seven discs is crowned by a huge bead.

A PILGRIM'S PROGRESS

*c.*780–*c.*850, BOROBUDUR TEMPLE, JAVA, INDONESIA

As pilgrims made their way along the galleries of Borobudur, with its 2.5km-long (1½ mile) panels of reliefs, they encountered in the middle stage of the *stupa* some 460 scenes from the story of a fellow pilgrim: Sudhana, the son of a wealthy merchant, and his search for wisdom. The tale is found in the Gandavyaha Sutra, written in Sanskrit in the second century CE as the climax to the Avatamsaka ("Flower Garland") Sutra. Here, Queen Maya, Shakyamuni Buddha's mother, tells Sudhana about the battle between the forces of light and darkness which took place as the little-known *buddha*, then a *bodhisattva*, Vimaladhraja approached enlightenment.

The scene's underlying theme is that *buddha*hood involves a profound detachment from worldly concerns. This is similar to the better-known account of the demon Mara, who attempted to use both his armies and his three beautiful daughters to distract Shakyamuni Buddha from his meditation.

▼ THREE-DIMENSIONAL *MANDALA*

*c.*780–850, BOROBUDUR TEMPLE, JAVA, INDONESIA

Borobudur is arguably the supreme architectural achievement of Mahayana Buddhism. At 119m (390ft) square and 30m (90ft) high, it is climbed by means of a labyrinthine path. The journey is an education and a spiritual progression: from earthly desire (*kamadhatu*) at the square base, through the world of form (*rupadhatu*) in the middle, to the *buddha*-inhabited *stupa*s at the top, which symbolize formlessness (*arupadhatu*). Finally, *nirvana* is reached with the empty central *stupa*.

❶ Vimaladhraja, a seated figure with an *ushnisha* or protuberance on his head indicating his potential *buddha*hood, sits beneath a tree in the gesture of meditation (*dhyana mudra*). This ancient position was used by *yogi*s long before the historical Buddha's time.

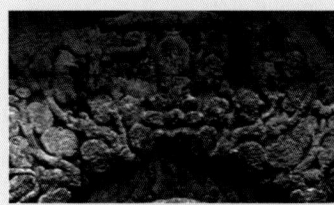

❷ The *buddha*-to-be sits beneath a pipal tree (*ficus religiosa*). The pipal, or Bodhi tree, at Bodh Gaya in northern India was believed to be the sacred centre of the universe, the place that not only Shakyamuni but other *buddha*s-to-be had come before attaining enlightenment. Bodh Gaya remains one of Buddhism's most important pilgrimage sites.

❸ Forces of light and darkness battle around the unperturbed Vimaladhraja.

❹ Queen Maya, mother of Shakyamuni, is present in one of her previous rebirths, as the goddess Netrasri. It is Maya who will later recount the story to Sudhana. She is shown here with a handmaiden doing homage to Vimaladhraja. Maya was believed to have given birth to many *buddha*s in her previous lives.

5 The story tells of a king who intervened to prevent the battle from interrupting the nearby *buddha*-to-be; this king, too, was later to attain *buddha*hood. He may be the royal figure accompanied by two courtiers who appears to be watching in the midst of the tumult.

⬥ WOODEN GUANYIN

1755, TEMPLE OF UNIVERSAL PEACE, CHENGDE, HEBEI, CHINA

Housed in the Dacheng *ge*, or tower-like image-hall, at Puningsi, the giant (21m/69ft) multi-armed Guanyin is believed to be the world's largest wooden statue. It is made out of five types of wood: pine, cypress, elm, fir and linden. Guanyin epitomizes compassion.

countries it brought with it a huge influx of Chinese architectural, artistic and cultural practices. It is in these countries, where Buddhism was emphatically an arm of the state, that the early East Asian Buddhist buildings survive.

The Todaiji (745–749) in Nara, the official head temple of a network that was created in every province of Japan, was an attempt to match (and perhaps outdo) the greatest architecture of Tang dynasty China. As the Tang buildings have gone, the Todaiji (though much rebuilt) is now one of the only surviving temple complexes in East Asia to match for scale the great religious buildings seen elsewhere in the world. However, it is built almost entirely of wood.

The central axis of the temple runs for about 800m (2,624ft) south to north, and is dominated by a single vast image hall, the Great Buddha Hall (Daibutsuden), an exceptional example of a building generally known in Japan as the Golden Hall (Kondo). At the rear of the temple are the monastic quarters and a second great hall, in which monastic teaching took place. Throughout, the experience of moving through symmetrical, orthogonal spaces, rationally arranged and with a cumulative air of great grandeur, is much like that which may be enjoyed – with multiple variations – in temples and palaces throughout East Asia to this day.

to the fifth century, an impressive outpost of Silk Road art, some 3,700km/2,000 miles from its Gandharan point of origin), and it remained a major theme of Chinese Buddhist art until the thirteenth century.

In 713–803, one of the largest sculptures of the ancient world – 71m (234ft) high – was created in China: the Dafu, the Great Buddha, at Leshan in Sichuan. By that time, however, the Silk Road connection was fading. Between the artistically sophisticated Longmen caves (c.494–c.1120) at Luoyang in Henan, the long sequence of sculptures and paintings at Dunhuang in Gansu, and the exquisite late caves at Bei Shan and Baoding Shan near Dazu in Sichuan (last added to in the thirteenth century), the sculptural style loses its Indian and Gandharan roots and becomes part of the mainstream of Chinese art. Buddhism had gone native.

Buddhism comes to Japan and Korea

Meanwhile, Buddhism had spread from China to Korea (fourth century) and Japan (552) respectively, and in both

East Asian image-halls

While Buddhist temple architecture in East Asia remained ambitious, the idea of the architecturally giant complex rarely re-emerged. A large Chinese temple, such as the Longxingsi in Zhending, Hebei (971), sits in an enclosure about 370m (1,215ft) long and less than 50m (165ft) wide, most of which is open space: the main buildings were originally five great halls, encountered in sequence along the axis. Each contained large statues. The worshipper moves through them along the central axis, passing less significant buildings such as the pavilion-like Drum and Bell towers (used to announce prayer times and major festivals) and a *sutra* hall containing a revolving library that is a miracle of carpentry. Monastic quarters are positioned to one side of the otherwise symmetrical plan; meditation halls and lecture halls, also containing Buddha images, are towards the rear. Such features are replicated in many complexes throughout East Asia.

Some Chinese temple buildings included a vertical image-hall known as a *ge* ("pavilion") – a structure several storeys high in which devotees could circumambulate a massive wooden statue, gazing from galleries at the figure as it stood in a central well. One such was built for Empress Wu Zetian (reigned 690–705) adjacent to her *mingtang* ("hall of light"), and the two structures dominated Luoyang.

Increasingly, temples in general were focused on series of halls for colossal images, their interiors dominated by trios of giant *buddha*s, such as Shakyamuni, Amitabha (the celestial *buddha* who established the Pure Land paradise) and Maitreya (the *buddha* of the future). Additional figures fill subsidiary halls, such as the "gate guardians" who stare fiercely down on those who enter the complex, or the

☉ HODO ("PHOENIX HALL")
1053, BYODOIN TEMPLE, UJI, NEAR KYOTO, JAPAN

The traditional wooden construction and the elaborate *kawara* roof tiles of the Hodo ("Phoenix Hall") at the Byodoin are an aristocratic vision of the Pure Land, reflected in a lotus pond that represents the sacred lake of the palace of the Western Paradise.

*arhat*s ("worthy ones"), housed in chambers that can hold up to 500 separate statues. And in front of all the *buddha*s or *bodhisattva*s is an altar table, laden with liturgical objects and offerings, and more monumental than anything in the Theravada-dominated areas. At the same time, while the *stupa* remained the devotional focus of most complexes elsewhere, it did not do so in East Asia, in spite of the enormous size of many early examples (see box, page 164).

East Asian Buddhist architecture developed other distinctive traits too. Korean temples are notable for their use of granite in *stupa*s and sculpture, and for the bold geometry and soft colour schemes of the forms that result. An early Korean *stupa* stands at the Chongnimsa in Puyo. Small in scale, but exquisite in conception, is the Seokguram (Sokkuram) "cave", an eighth-century shrine at the Pulguksa. Its domed subterranean interior is dominated by a single granite image of a seated Buddha, as plain as it is powerful.

Japanese temple architecture also developed its own themes. Colour schemes retained the early starkness of Han and Tang dynasty buildings in China, whereas bright

◐ CHAKRASAMVARA *MANDALA*

*c.*1500, NGOR MONASTERY, TIBET

Vajrayana devotees envision themselves moving stage by stage through the sacred spaces depicted in *mandala*s, gradually transforming their own consciousness. Each *mandala* is secret, transmitted within a given monastic tradition; this one was commissioned by the monk Lhachog Sengge (1468–1535) for his teacher, Kongchog Pelwa (1445–1514). A circular enclosure protects a square sacred structure – at once the human body, a palace, Mount Sumeru, and an entire universe – with a sanctuary at the centre inhabited by a deity.

These monks of the Sakyapa order are depicted to emphasize that it is through their lineage that the primordial *buddha* Vajradhara has transmitted this *mandala*.

This is one of the four gates in the central structure. Together the four evoke a Diamond Thunderbolt – an emblem of Vajrayana's spiritual power.

The male and female aspects of Chakrasamvara, an emanation of the *buddha* Akshobhya, are in sexual union, symbolizing the bliss, power and oblivion of enlightenment. His wrathful appearance indicates the energy of his compassion.

combinations of gold, blue, green and red came to dominate buildings in China. In the Vajrayana temples of the Tendai and Shingon sects, ceilings were inserted between the image-hall and roof, and screens subdivided internal spaces. Those temples might have an exclusive rear area or adjoining building, the *naijin*, containing sequences of separate rooms and aisles, their interiors densely packed with furnishings, statues and *mandala*s – for example, at the fourteenth-century Shingon temple of Kanshinji in Kawaranagano, Osaka.

East Asia's image-rich Buddhist art reflects the devotional needs of the Mahayana and Vajrayana schools, further influenced by indigenous faiths such as Taoism and Confucianism (in China), Shinto (in Japan) and the shamanic traditions of Korea. The area remains predominantly Mahayana (and Vajrayana), unaffected by the Theravada reforms which transformed Buddhism in Southeast Asia.

Images of the *bodhisattva* Avalokiteshvara (Guanyin in China and Kannon in Japan) can seem to upstage those of Shakyamuni Buddha; distinctive Vajrayana images include painted *mandala*s and a pantheon of beings such as the *bodhisattva* Tara and various wrathful deities. Notions of a sacred landscape were layered on top of pre-Buddhist cults relating to Mount Fuji in Japan and the Jirisan mountains in Korea. In China, Buddhists linked particular celestial *bodhisattva*s with four holy mountains: Puxian (Sanskrit, Samantabhadra) with Mount Emei, Wenshu (Manjushri) with Mount Wutai, Dizang (Kshitigarbha) with Mount Jiuhua, and Guanyin (Avalokiteshvara) with Mount Putuo.

Buddhist schools in East Asia emphasized that in spite of the increasing obscurity of Mahayana and Vajrayana mysticism, enlightenment remained accessible to all. These include the Jingtu, or Pure Land school, which claimed that the Amitabha Buddha (Amituo Fo in China, Amida Butsu in Japan) had created a heavenly land where *buddha*hood could be attained with ease. By contrast, from the seventh century the Chan school (transliterated as Zen in Japan) placed the emphasis on meditation and other techniques.

Both these important movements had an impact on architecture. In Dunhuang, eighth-century painted images of the Pure Land depict *buddha*s sitting in joyous, ordered array, surrounded by landscapes of pavilions, parks and ponds (see page 35). Later, actual temples began to be set within artfully designed rural landscapes so that journeys to and around them were partly experiences of the Pure Land (for example, the Pulguksa in Korea and the Byodoin in Japan; see page 181). Also Japanese, but very different in effect, is the sober refinement of the gardens constructed for the contemplation of Zen monks in the monasteries of Kyoto and elsewhere, such as Ryoanji (1499) and Daisen-in (1509–1513).

One final development had a significant impact on Buddhist architecture in China. In 1271, Mongol invaders claimed the imperial throne and, under the Yuan dynasty, brought to court life devotion to the form of Buddhism practised in Tibet and Mongolia (see below). This remained the court religion under the Qing dynasty (1644–1911). One result was an influx of *stupa*s of Tibetan form. A stone Tibetan-style monastery, the Putuozongchangmiao (1767), was built at Chengde (Jehol), the Qing summer capital.

Tibet and Mongolia

Landlocked Tibet contains sites sacred to Hindus and Buddhists alike, such as Mount Kailash (home of Shiva and Chakrasamvara, respectively). Parts of the Jokhang monastery in Lhasa date back to the seventh century, when Buddhism first appeared in the country. The deep-rooted religious culture visible in Tibet today preserves a snapshot of the faith as it might have been practised in many places at the peak of Mahayana and Vajrayana influence.

Several monastic orders, such as the Kagyupa ("Red Hats") and the Gelugpa ("Yellow Hats"), are unique to Tibetan Buddhism, as is the idea that their abbot is a *tulku*, or reincarnate teacher (the order's founder reborn to resume their mission). The Mongol leader Kublai Khan (reigned 1260–1294) adopted this form of Buddhism and it remains the dominant faith in Mongolia. It was his descendant Altan Khan who in the sixteenth century added the word Dalai ("Ocean [of Wisdom]") to the title of the third *lama* in the lineage sequence of the Gelugpa order, and by the seventeenth century the fifth Dalai Lama was ruling Tibet as a theocracy from the Potala Palace in Lhasa.

The Potala (1645–1648 and 1690–1694) is thus both a palace and a monastery (and a mausoleum, containing as it does funerary *stupa*s or *chorten*s to the fifth, sixth, seventh and eighth Dalai Lamas). Like many Tibetan monasteries, it features sloping, cliff-like external walls, gold-covered roofs with Chinese-style sweeping eaves, and *chorten*s derived from Indian models. The Potala apart, the greatest architectural works in Tibet are small-scale but vivid evocations of *mandala*s, such as the 23m-tall (75ft) whitewashed Great *Stupa* of Gyantse (from 1427). Its rising levels, into which are let 70 chapels, culminate in an uppermost shrine room. Such sites are full of offering-bedecked images and esoteric paintings, with devout locals in constant circumambulation.

Tibet's neighbours have also been deeply influenced by the cross-cutting religious influences of the region. A syncretic Hindu–Buddhist fusion thrives in the Kathmandu Valley of Nepal, where Buddhist monks belong to hereditary castes and live in distinctive monastic complexes known as *baha*. The Svayambunatha *stupa* outside Kathmandu may be a much-restored structure of the Ashokan era.

Buddhist architecture today

Buddhism today, in all its variety, claims about 490 million adherents worldwide. It is a defining part of the national identity in such countries as Thailand, Sri Lanka and Japan. In Nepal and India, places such as Lumbini (the Buddha's place of birth), Bodh Gaya (site of the Buddha's enlightenment), Sarnath (the deer park where the Buddha taught his first sermon) and Kushinagara (his place of *parinirvana*, or physical death), include very recent temples built by Buddhist organizations from many nations. Outside Asia, Buddhism has spread beyond diaspora communities, winning local converts and building temples. The booming economies of modern Asia have funded the building of many temples, as well as gargantuan objects such as the 128m-high (420ft) standing Buddha completed in 2002 at Lushan in Henan, China. Such structures as the White Temple (2000) designed for the Zuisenji, near Kyoto in Japan, by Takashi Yamaguchi are exquisite works of modern design. Perhaps a truly contemporary Buddhist architecture would see a return to the plain vision of Ashoka or of the Kushan empire in the last few centuries BCE: a half-egg rising from the ground, or an art focused on the simple image of a man, sitting.

HINDUISM

ONENESS OUT OF MANY

The social and religious changes which, around the sixth century BCE, had resulted in the emergence of Buddhism and Jainism, also had a dramatic impact on the Brahmins. Some of them adopted the ascetic practices that the Buddha had himself followed for a period. More significantly, a passionate devotional culture known as *bhakti* ("partaking of god") gradually developed.

Bhakti transformed religious custom in a complex process that lasted until the middle of the first millennium CE. *Puja*, the making of non-sacrificial offerings to an image of a god, became a centrepiece of worship. Anyone could practise this, providing ordinary people with a role in religion for the first time. While ancient Vedic rituals were not forgotten, sacrificial rites went into decline and Brahmins found a new role as intermediaries between laypeople and divine images. Acceptance of innumerable local deities helped such traditions to spread.

A VAST PANTHEON

Brahmins transformed Vedic practices into Hinduism by absorbing many regional gods. This pantheon, combined with *puja*'s need for images, generated a rich visual culture. Although, over time, three deities (Vishnu, Shiva and Devi/Durga) came to the fore, they all acquired multiple manifestations, often originating as local gods who were now understood as aspects of the power of these greater ones. As part of this process, important figures reached their present form – for example, Krishna, the saviour-manifestation of Vishnu, and Ganesha, the son of Shiva who is depicted with an elephant's head, and is popular for his ability to overcome obstacles and his sponsorship of language and literature.

A stone sculpture (c.1000) of Vishnu in his emanation as Narayana, with the attributes that identify him, including his conch shell and mace.

⊙ PALACE FOR THE GODS

1992–1995, SHRI SWAMINARAYAN MANDIR, LONDON

This 60m-long (195ft) Hindu temple is in Neasden, northwest London. Each *sikhara* spire marks a sanctuary containing an image of a deity – the flags indicate that the deity is in residence. The temple is constructed out of limestone and marble, and accord to the precepts of the *vastu shastra*s, the traditional prescriptions for architectural design, which have their roots in Vedic conceptions of sacred space. It was consecrated in August 1995.

This spread throughout the subcontinent: indeed, *bhakti* itself represents an infusion of southern Indian, or Dravidian, culture into the Indo-European-influenced religion of the north. While the *Veda*s remained the core sacred texts, they were joined by accounts such as the Upanishads and the Puranas, which included, among other things, mythological cycles such as the *Ramayana* and *Mahabharata*.

Hinduism is the result: a drawing together of the religious ideas of a civilization as much as a systematic creed. It recognizes many deities, while emphasizing the essential unity of all things, and sees the universe as characterized by great cycles of divine creation, maintenance and destruction. Gradually, devotion to three deities in particular came to the fore: transcendent, all-pervading Vishnu; the contradictory creative energy of Shiva, the preserver and the destroyer; and Devi or Durga, the Goddess or Divine Mother, whose many different forms are usually either maternally protective or erotic and dangerous. Such deities acquired multiple manifestations, often former local gods who were now understood as aspects of these greater ones (see box, page 184). The intense devotion of some people to one or other major god can seem like an individual religion in its own right: Vaishnavism for devotees of Vishnu, Shaivism for those of Shiva, and Shaktism (after *shakti*, the female creative power of the universe) for those who look to Devi.

The birth of Hindu architecture and art

Construction of the open-air altars of the early Brahmins followed precise ritual prescriptions, as set out in the *Veda*s, which governed their location, the materials used, and their design. These, it seems, helped to make the altars efficacious as transmitters and receivers of sacred energy.

◉ SACRED SCULPTURED TEMPLE

c.756–*c*.773, KAILASA, ELLORA (CAVE 16), MAHARASHTRA, INDIA

Dominating the thirty-four Buddhist, Jain and Hindu structures at Ellora, this is a sculpture of a building on a grand scale – 60m (197ft) long and 30m (98ft) deep, it cuts down into the rock and transplants the sacred mountain from its Himalayan fastness to central India.

Buddhist *stupa*s of the second century BCE provide the first surviving depictions of divine beings, in this case mainly nature spirits, which later became part of the Hindu pantheon. Only later were major deities given cult images: an early example is a wooden image of Vishnu, recorded in 278CE as standing on a stone platform in the open air. Carved reliefs that depict buildings have also survived, their function unknown; but some of them have spire-like towers.

Comparable towers are a feature of the earliest brick or stone Hindu temples, which appear by the fifth century CE. They are varied and experimental in character, and although the sudden appearance of these buildings may partly be a result of the stability and prosperity of the Gupta era (*c*.320–*c*.550), it also owes something to royal patronage. Brahminism had already developed a strong association with kingship – a role viewed as divine – and the building of temples was a particularly lavish way for powerful kings to gain, and to display, *punya*, or spiritual merit. Such support did not necessarily follow tidy devotional lines: throughout the Hindu and Buddhist world, the same patron may have founded buildings for either faith, and deities from one tradition may be depicted in the temples of another.

Gupta sculpture is as important for statues of Hindu gods as for its Buddha images (see page 167). The iconographies begin to emerge by which Hindu deities can be identified, such as (there are many) Shiva in dancing form; Vishnu with blue skin, his four arms holding a conch, discus, mace and lotus (see page 184); and Durga calmly slaying the buffalo-demon.

From the seventh century onwards, temples – always elaborately sculpted – began to appear in huge numbers. This is the first Indian architecture of freestanding cut stone and it profoundly influenced the existing tradition, dominated by the Buddhists and the Jains, of excavating temples from rock. Hindu cave-temples are first seen in the sixth century CE – for example, at Elephanta, near Mumbai (*c*.550–*c*.575). They were initially often hypostyle in form, emphasizing devotion to images rather than promoting congregation. By the eighth century, the spread of freestanding Hindu places of worship had resulted in a radical change to this rock-cut tradition. Rather than excavate caves into the cliff, and then carve their interiors and façades in imitation of a freestanding building, masons were hewing entire three-dimensional temples out of outcrops of natural rock. The extraordinary temples and reliefs at Mamallapuram in Kerala, in the far south (seventh or eighth centuries; see pages 188–189), including the Pancha Rathas, and the great Kailasa temple at Ellora, Maharashtra (*c*.756–*c*.773), are just some of the remarkable results.

The tradition of rock-cut architecture had effectively died by the ninth century, but the building of freestanding masonry temples has continued ever since, with slight variations, both in the Jain tradition (see box, page 160) and in a series of broad regional styles. Although these temples are instantly recognizable buildings, they are set in a landscape replete with sacred sites of other kinds, such as wayside shrines, holy trees, and places known as *tirtha* ("fordings"), where the divine and the human draw closer to each other. Among the most significant are the seven sacred cities, such as Varanasi, which lies on the Ganges, the most holy of several sacred rivers; and the "four sacred abodes" – Badrinath, Puri, Rameshwaram and Dwarka – that

CONTINUES ON PAGE 190

◑ COMMUNION WITH THE SPIRITS

c.1800–1816, DURGA SHADOW PUPPET, JAVA, INDONESIA

Hindu shadow puppetry is a ritual and sacred event as well as an entertainment, believed to channel divine energies which protect the audience from evil. This is a fearsome aspect of Durga, local to Java: Dewi Umayi, wife of Shiva. Performances, led by a *dalang*, or puppeteer-shaman, are often held within temple precincts.

THE PENANCE OF ARJUNA

c.630–c.668, MAMALLAPURAM, TAMIL NADU, INDIA

Usually known as Arjuna's Penance, or the Descent of the Ganges, this rock-face has a narrow cleft in it which forms a centrepiece of the composition. The remains of a cistern above and a pool below suggest that, on certain occasions, water was poured down this fissure, placing a living waterfall in the middle of the scene.

There are two main interpretations of the imagery, both set in the far-off Himalayas. The most likely is that it shows the hero Arjuna, who did penance to Shiva and received in return a supernatural weapon. In another reading, the ascetic is the great king Bhagiratha, who pleaded with Shiva to break the fall of the deity Ganga as she flowed back to Earth as the colossal force of the Ganges. It is possible that the carvings are designed to make both explanations simultaneously possible, in the manner of the contemporary *dvi-samdhi-kavya*, or "double-meaning poem".

In any case, the scene is most vivid in its depiction of the great cycle of life – from the lowest animal, through souls striving for liberation, to supernatural beings and, finally, the gods themselves. The rock-art could thus have served as an introduction to the whole concept of *karma* and reincarnation.

▶ MAMALLAPURAM MONOLITH

c.630–c.668, TAMIL NADU, INDIA

The important seaport of Mamallapuram on India's southern coast was also a centre of pilgrimage for devotees of Vishnu. Under the Pallava kings (possibly Rajasimha, reigned *c.*630–668), a series of large outcrops of granite on the seafront were carved into spectacular freestanding temples, caves and reliefs. The rock-face is about 30m (98ft) long and 15m (49ft) high and its near-lifesize figures would have been visible from the port. The scene contains about ninety figures. A quarter of the carvings are unfinished, and a further unfinished relief of the same scene stands nearby.

❶ Shiva, with his retinue of *gana* dwarfs, has his arm out in a gift-giving gesture known as *varada*. He is about to hand over his cosmic weapon, the Pashupatastra. An ascetic is in a yogic pose before the god. Arjuna won the weapon after just such an act of devotion, and used it to rout his enemies, as recounted in the *Mahabharata*.

❷ A guru and three disciples pray and practise yoga at a temple to the god Vishnu. The shrine itself is a sculpted image of a Dravidian or southern Indian temple. This scene may be depicted to demonstrate that devotion to either Shiva or Vishnu is equally valid.

❸ *Naga*s and *nagini*s, snake-beings associated with water, emerge from the netherworld, suggesting that the cleft in the rock may be meant to represent the sacred Ganges River, with the heavens above.

❹ The sixth-century *Kiratarjuniya*, by the Kanci poet Bharavi, has a verse in which the animals and birds forget their natural antipathy and join a hunter-army marshalled by Shiva in Arjuna's defence. This great retinue dominates the sculpture. It includes elephants with their babies between their legs, as well as anteaters, lions, boars, monkeys, rabbits, turtles and other beasts.

❺ As if imitating the ascetics on the other side of the river, a cat performs yogic austerities, deceiving the surrounding mice into worshipping him. Or perhaps he has genuinely overcome his instincts through Hindu self-discipline?

❻ A crowd of gods, demigods, flying sages and other beings, including villagers and wild hunters (*kirata*s) and music-playing half-human birds (*kinnara*s), are among the gathering crowd.

mark out the compass points of India, and are visited in order, as if circumambulating the country as a whole.

The temple defined

Approached from the outside, the typical Hindu temple stands on a high plinth in a walled compound, serving to maintain the building's ritual purity. Nearby there is often a large water tank, itself sometimes a major work of architecture, where Brahmins or pilgrims can ritually cleanse themselves before entering the complex. Within the enclosure there may be numerous subsidiary shrines or chapels, each a small temple-like structure in its own right; for example, in Shaivite temples, there is often one to the bull called Nandi, Shiva's *vahana* or mount. For offerings, an outdoor altar, the *bali peetam*, sits before the main temple.

The temple itself (see page 195) has a tower with a curved, tapering, roughly pyramidal outline known as a *sikhara* (from the Sanskrit for "mountain peak"), attached to one side of which is the *mandapa*. The result is an axial structure perhaps 15–30m (50–100ft) long, with the entrance usually to the west and a profile that rises towards the *sikhara* in the east.

Inside the temple, the *mandapa* reveals itself to be a small hall in which lay devotees can gather. Beyond the *mandapa*, beneath the *sikhara*, the upper part of which contains a functionless attic space, is the room-sized sanctuary that is the focus of the entire building. This is the *garbhagriha*, or "womb-house", which is just large enough to contain an image and its attendant Brahmins. This space is the focus of the building; indeed, some temples are nothing more than an image-house comprising a *sikhara* over a *garbhagriha*. The image within the *garbhagriha* is the temple's *raison d'être*: the building is primarily a palatial residence for a god.

The representation of the deity can be human, anthropomorphic or abstract. Temples to Shiva are often dominated by a *linga*, an abstract shape that evokes both the phallus and the vulva, and thus the progenerative union of male divinity with female divine energy. But the reason for the temple's existence is not so much the image itself as what it is capable of: for, like those in the temples of many ancient religions (from Mesopotamia and Egypt to Greece, for example), the Hindu temple statue has the potential to be inhabited by – to physically incarnate – the deity it depicts. This capability is the key to temple ritual and temple architecture alike.

Temple ritual

The image is tended by Brahmins, whose rituals are focused on awakening the god or goddess and inviting it into the statue as if it were an honoured guest. In a *puja* that takes place four to six times a day, the priests ritually enter this chamber. Their rites purify themselves and the space, invoke the deity, and present offerings to it, accompanied by bells, hymns, chanted *mantras*, sacred phrases and other formulas, usually in Sanskrit. The statue is anointed, bathed, dressed, fed and adorned, often with garlands of flowers. If the image

◖ THE SABHA *MANDAPA* AND RAMAKUND

1026–1027, SUN TEMPLE, MODHERA, GUJARAT, INDIA

Dedicated to Surya, the sun god, the Modhera temple has three axially aligned elements. The open, multi-pillared (fifty-two – one for each week of the year) hall for sacred music and dance, the Sabha *Mandapa*, has twelve carvings of *aditya*s (celestial deities, one for each month); a connected *garbhagriha*; and the Ramakund, a water tank geometrically arranged into four, stepped terraces incorporating 108 shrines.

is freestanding, the priests may circumambulate it, before the doors to the sanctuary are closed.

There is no need for anyone else to be present during these ceremonies, the main aim of which is to serve the deity, but attendance at them is popular with lay devotees, especially when there is an opportunity – as there is in most services – to view the statue, an experience known as *darsana* ("sight" or "vision"). At the climax of the service, amid the noise of drums and other instruments, the curtain separating the statue in the *garbhagriha* from the *mandapa* is drawn back, Brahmins swing lamps before the image, and these lights are then brought before the faces of worshippers in the *mandapa*, transferring to them the brightness and warmth of the deity. Each worshipper may accept from the priest a mark on their forehead (*tilaka*) made with powdered turmeric, white ash or another substance.

Worshippers may come to the temple at any time, out of private devotion, to seek intercession, or as part of their own search for *moksha* (spiritual "liberation"). People may commission a Brahmin to perform specific services on their

⬥ *PUJA* AT THE TEMPLE SHRINE

*c.*950, MUKTESVARA TEMPLE, BHUBANESHWAR, ORISSA, INDIA

Like most Hindu temples, the Muktesvara has a water tank and many subsidiary chapels, all within a walled enclosure and with the most important structures raised on platforms. The pyramidally layered *pida* roof (centre and right) is an Orissan speciality.

behalf, or leave offerings such as flowers, food, or fragrant oils. Sometimes a circumambulatory aisle, or *pradakshina-patha*, comes off the *mandapa* and runs around the *garbhagriha*, and worshippers may also process outside the temple.

Architecture as sculpture

The temple's internal spaces alone, however, cannot explain its overall form. For example, the *sikhara* is one of its fundamental constituent parts, yet much of it has no practical use. In fact, the *sikhara*, like every other aspect of the building, fufills a symbolic – even magical – function, for the very form of the temple is important to making it efficacious as a place that can be inhabited by the divine. As its name ("mountain peak") suggests, this part – and to an extent the building as a whole – is an image of Mount Meru, making the building an embodiment both of the gods' habitation and of the cosmology of the universe. In other words, the form of the Hindu temple expresses ideas.

This principle extends to its decoration. Every inch of a temple's surface, inside as well as outside, is sculpted. Hindu temples have an underlying architectural grammar comparable to that of buildings of other faiths, in that columns have capitals and bases, and elevations are divided into sections using entablatures; however, the structural aspect of these features is rarely emphasized. Columns are transformed into piled-up decorative motifs of varied form, in which capital and base are sometimes barely distinguishable. Windows are insignificant and ogee *chaitya* motifs (or *gavaksha*) may be used in myriad ways: above images in niches, or repeated in a honeycomb pattern, rising up a *sikhara*.

These decorative motifs repeat each other. Smaller motifs are generated out of larger ones of the same form, in a manner similar to the patterns created using mathematical fractals. This reflects Hindu cosmology, in which *brahman*, an immanent underlying oneness, subdivides in subtly changing ways until infinite spiritual and physical forms have been brought into being. Superficially, these buildings may appear to have an all-encompassing concern with surface decoration, but in fact their underlying proportions are finely judged, resulting in effects of considerable monumentality and elegance, which unite the disparate decorative forms with which they are covered. And everything – from tiny sculpted decorations to underlying proportional schemes – is there to aid the building's role as the home of an image that can be inhabited by a deity. This includes the figurative sculptures on the domical roofs, the carved columns and *chaitya*-headed aedicules with which the building is covered. Usually these adornments compliment the building's dedicatee: for example, the Kailasa temple at Ellora (see page 186) contains a sculpture of Ravana, the demon-king who attempted to uproot Kailash, the mountain this temple represents; his ten arms grasp the base of the temple itself, even as Shiva, the temple's dedicatee, sits above, effortlessly containing him.

All of these elements – the proportions, the elaborate sculpted forms, and the ways in which individual gods and goddesses are depicted – are governed by a tight canon of rules, refined and elaborated over many centuries in texts known as *shastras*. These guidelines have religious authority, although they rarely spell out the metaphysical significance of their content. The *vastu* and *shilpa shastras*, which cover building and sculpture, include instructions for everything from the choosing of a site to the consecration of a finished structure, as well as for the correct appearance of deities.

The *shastras* have at their heart an idea of Vedic origin, in which the plan of an altar is specified as if it were a kind of sacred diagram. A square *mandala*, the *vastupurushamandala*, underlies much Hindu temple design, and it represents Purusha ("primordial" or "cosmic" man), from whom everything was created (see box, page 163). The purpose of an Indian temple, then, like that of a Brahminical altar, is to be efficacious in embodying the divine – to help to incarnate sacred energy. For this reason, the rules for temple design, for (even more so) the depiction of Hindu gods and goddesses, and the guidelines for the performance of rituals by the Brahmins, all show strong continuity with those for other art forms. Sacred dance and drama, the drawing of *mandalas* (a practice that originated in Hinduism and became central to some aspects of Buddhism) and the incantation of *mantras*, are all practices capable of embodying divine energy and therefore of enabling humans to connect with the divine. It was a belief of the early Brahmins that the very sounds of Sanskrit were sacred, and that prayerful phrases or words could be infused with godly power: the Hindu *aumkar* symbol represents the "seed sound" *aum*, or *om*, the deep and resonant sound through which the entire cosmos is said to be manifested.

The aim of this architecture, then, is a profound one: to make buildings that are inhabitable by the divine, and to provide humans with a space where they can come close to their god or gods (for most Hindus the singular and plural elide). The structure symbolizes all creation and the human body. It is form that matters: a Hindu temple is designed as if it were three-dimensional carved stone. Stylistic innovation and structural experiment can occur but they are incidental to this main concern. Unusual designs, such as the thirteenth-century Sun Temple at Konarak in Orissa (1238–1264), partly envisaged as a colossal imitation of the chariot of the sun god Surya, illustrate this sculptural approach to architecture.

However prescriptive the *shastra*s may seem, they rely on a certainty that aesthetics are themselves divine. Simply following the rules is not enough (in practice they are often bent): the gods must be able to find the result beautiful, and their delight is akin to ours, because we are all part of one creation.

This uniquely Hindu vision is equal to the architectural achievements of any major faith. Hinduism attempts to crystallize in stone a series of forms that not only embody the energy, beauty and abundance of the created world but also have the potential to bring the divine into the presence of humans. The temple may be a comparatively late development within the history of Hinduism – and, indeed, within

○ CHARIOT OF THE SUN
1238–1264, SUN TEMPLE, KONARAK, ORISSA, INDIA

The sun god Surya crossed the sky in his celestial vehicle or *ratha*, and this daily journey is evoked in this temple's twenty-four 3m (10ft) wheels. Originally, seven sculpted horses stood here as well as a *sikhara* perhaps 70m (225ft) high. King Narasimha I may have built the temple to celebrate a defeat of Muslim armies.

the story of religious architecture in general – but it is also one of the clearest expressions of assumptions that unite most Hindus, and that appear to have been present in parts of Indian culture from the earliest times (see pages 160–163).

North to south
From its fifth-century CE point of origin onwards, Hindu temple architecture developed strong regional schools under a succession of dynasties in different parts of India. The two most important styles are the northern, or Nagaran, and the southern, or Dravidian. These came to be defined in *shastras*, and as a result knowledge of them could be transmitted widely. It is possible to find examples of a given regional type many hundreds of miles from its native area. For example, the Kailasa temple at Ellora is located several hundred miles further north than other temples in the southern style.

Sikhara design is the easiest way to distinguish a northern from a southern building. The Nagaran tradition has a tapering *sikhara* covered in shallow rectilinear projections, which swoop upwards along its comparatively smooth surface. Atop each of these may be a curved, ribbed motif called

an *amalaka*, perhaps evoking the amla fruit, which had purifying qualities. In the Dravidian tradition, these towers are called *vimanas*; they rise upwards in emphatic steps, resulting in a pyramidal profile, with each step a platform for sculpture. The uppermost storey of these towers is the only part to be called a *sikhara*, the design of which is often like that of a small domed, or *chaitya* arch-ended, pavilion. In the north, any *mandapas*, or porches, are covered by a small *sikhara* too, so that the building looks like a mountain range whose highest peak rises above the sanctuary. In the south, *mandapas* may have a flat roof because the *garbhagriha* is the only part of the building that must be covered by a *vimana*. Surface detailing is less busy and rather more regular in the south, with images arranged neatly between columns and entablatures in a manner reminiscent of Western classical architecture; intervening columns have a restrained and standardized form, a kind of "Dravidian order". Dravidian buildings tend to have regular, orthogonal plans, whereas Nagaran ones feature arrays of offset squares and corners.

Magnificent Khajuraho

For many, the most perfect Hindu buildings are a group of temples constructed in the Nagaran tradition from the ninth century onwards in the capital of the Chandelas, a relatively minor dynasty that ruled a part of north-central India from the ninth to thirteenth centuries. Today, they stand, in various states of preservation, in fields around the village of Khajuraho in Madhya Pradesh. Most of these twenty-five buildings were erected to house Hindu deities, although some honoured Jain sages. The settlement's other structures were made of perishable materials and have been lost.

The greatest of these survivors is the Khajuraho Mahadeva temple built at a point, early in the eleventh century, when the Chandelas had become the most important kings in northern India. Its upward-sweeping energy and poise is so well judged that the dense cascade of sculpted architectural motifs and figures in which it is draped – some 646 figures have been counted on the exterior alone, some of them engaged in gymnastic sexual activity – seem almost to lighten its presence. In spite of all this the building manages a monumental impact far greater than that suggested by its 31m-tall (102ft) *sikhara*.

Ascetism is widely practised, but it is by no means the only spiritual discipline: there are many others, particularly in the esoteric traditions known as the Tantra, which indulge the senses, or flout convention, with the aim of spiritual liberation. Bodily pleasure or other sensuous experiences are thus not inherently sinful; rather, they are the product of innate energies that, when tamed or disciplined, can be directed so as to bring spiritual benefits to the practitioner. For Hindus,

⬣ TEMPLE TO VISHNU

c.1025, DEVI JAGADAMBA TEMPLE, KHAJURAHO, MADHYA
PRADESH, INDIA

Originally dedicated to Vishnu but now to Parvati, the Devi
Jagadamba temple (above right, with a subsiduary shrine, left) is
typical of northern Indian temples. A *sikhara* spire Ⓐ (topped with
an *amalaka* Ⓑ) rises above a dark *garbhagriha* sanctuary; a central
mandapa hall Ⓒ is lit by small windows; and there is an entrance
porch (*ardha mandapa* Ⓓ). The whole structure is elevated on a
platform (*adhisthana* Ⓔ), which itself sits on a raised base (*jagata* Ⓕ).

⬤ KING OF *GOPURA*S

1559, MEENAKSHI AMMAN, MADURAI, TAMIL NADU, INDIA

The four largest of the temple-city's eleven *gopura* towers stand over the cardinal gateways of the outer enclosure, which measures 258m by 218m (846ft by 715ft). This is the southern *gopura*, built by Siramalai Sevanthi Murthy Chetti; it is 49m (161ft) high and is covered in 1,511 mythological figures.

physical beauty is a powerful metaphor for divine insight, liberating enlightenment and spiritual bliss, and beautiful human beings, especially women, are everywhere in Hindu sculpture. As an extension of this, Hindu religious art can be erotic: sex acts, and the blissful union they evoke, can be powerful spiritual metaphors.

The effects of Islam

By the time the last of the temples at Khajuraho was being completed, in the late twelfth century, the north's ability to make ambitious or innovative temples was in decline. A series of powerful Islamic states had culminated in the Delhi Sultanate (established by 1206), and a new ruling class. Some rulers ordered the demolition of Hindu, Jain and Buddhist temples (as some Hindu rulers had earlier treated Buddhist and Jain monasteries), objecting to their idolatrous nature.

Violent iconoclasm also occurred, resulting in blanks in our knowledge of Hindu temple sculpture (for example, in Kashmir). In other places, the shift in power meant that there were fewer Hindus able to patronize architecture. Muslim rulers, of course, built mosques. There were converts too – as the earlier success of Buddhism showed, claims of equality before god and rejections of priestly authority could appeal in a caste-based society. In some cases, common ground was found – for example, between the more mystical Muslim Sufis and the Hindu practitioners of *bhakti*. Emperor Akbar (reigned 1556–1605) did a great deal to facilitate dialogue between the two faiths.

Hindu temples continued to be built, often containing details inspired by those of Mughal architecture, such as the Madan Mohan temple (1590) at Vrindavan in Uttar Pradesh, or the multi-towered temples popular in Bengal – for example, the Krishna Changra temple (1751) at Kalna in West Bengal. However, perhaps the most significant of the attempts to synthesize and reform religion itself were the enlightened ideas of Guru Nanak and his successors, who founded Sikhism (see box, page 199). Its central shrine, the Golden Temple at Amritsar (after 1581), is a gold-covered structure of Mughal onion domes, set in the middle of an enormous Hindu-style temple tank.

Developments in southern India

In the south of India, Hindu regimes remained in charge, and Dravidian architecture made a dramatic developmental leap from around the eleventh century onwards.

Southern temples had long tended to be larger than those in the north. By the early eighth century, the two largest buildings in India were arguably the Kailasanatha temple (before 722) at Kanci in Tamil Nadu, 30m long (98ft) within an enclosure about 57m (187ft) long, the wall of which is itself made up of fifty-eight little shrine-like pavilions; and the

Virupaksa temple (before 746) at Pattadakal in Karnataka, at about 35m (115ft) long with a 17m (56ft) *vimana* (tower).

However, it was only after the Chola dynasty (at its peak from the ninth to the thirteenth century) established its capital at Thanjavur (former Tanjore), Tamil Nadu, that imperial religious buildings of the kind familiar in other cultures were seen for the first time in India. Fusing cults of kingship with a tendency to architectural gigantism, many of these temples include sculptures of Chola rulers, often depicted in close association with a god. Perhaps the greatest of them is the Rajarajeshvara temple (1009/1010, also known as Brihadishvara) at Thanjavur.

Apart from its unprecedented size – its 63m-plus (207ft) *vimana* rises from a 241m-long (791ft) enclosure – this temple was stylistically influential. The perimeter and gates of southern temples had always been architecturally ambitious, but here the gateways were turned into elaborate buildings known as *gopura*s, which were almost miniature temples in their own right, three storeys high and topped by a *vimana* tower. Giant *gopura*s, often of brick on a timber frame, and bristling with life-size, brightly painted images of divinities, became the defining feature of southern architecture. The descendants of the Rajarajeshvara, such as the Nataraja temple at Cidambaram in Tamil Nadu (*c.*1200) or the Meenakshi Amman which dominates Madurai in Tamil Nadu, became multi-towered Hindu temple-cities which are among the most gigantic religious complexes ever created.

Srirangam, a Vaishnava temple-city in Tamil Nadu, has grown gradually from the fourteenth century, and now covers 63 hectares (156 acres). Seven nested layers of enclosing walls are gated by twenty-one enormous *gopura*s. These are the dominant visual element of the complex, reversing the norms of religious architecture by increasing in height as they move further from the sanctuary at the temple-city's centre. The largest is 70m (230ft) high and was completed only in 1987. Within each circuit of walls there are shops, ritual bathing tanks, offices, accommodation for the Brahmins and enormous covered hallways with sculpted columns, as well as "hundred-pillared" *mandapa*s: freestanding halls in which ritual dances, teaching and other functions are carried out. Within the central enclosing wall stands the gold-covered, *vimana*-topped main sanctuary, containing a 4.5m (15ft) image of Vishnu. The sanctuary is dwarfed by the great tower-porches which help to seal it from the outside world.

These *gopura*-dominated temple-cities marked the most radical development in Indian temple architecture between its birth and the modern era. They may be a response to the scale of Mughal architectural achievement or a spiritual defence

◉ *SIKHARA*S OF THE ANCESTORS

856, PRAMBANAN TEMPLE, JAVA, INDONESIA

The Hindu and Buddhist architectural ideas aimed at evoking the sacred axis of Mount Meru were cross-fertilized throughout the Hindu world. This was especially true on Java, where these dual influences were syncretized with indigenous beliefs about ancestor worship (in this case of deified kings). Prambanan Hindu temple, with a *mandala*-like arrangement and major shrines dedicated to Shiva, Brahma and Vishnu, is a fine example.

against the threat from the north, but they may equally be a consequence of the achievements of the Hindu kingdoms that had developed more than 2,000km (1,250 miles) away in Southeast Asia (see below). Meanwhile, in the south, Hindu temple architecture, although it has remained active to the present, ceased to develop from the later eighteenth century. This was when European powers began to make their presence felt in the subcontinent, just as the architecture of the north had tended to ossify after the coming of Islam.

Hindu temples in Southeast Asia

Hindu architecture is found throughout Southeast Asia, as well as in Indonesia, the faith having been imported by travelling merchants. Its earliest survivals are in late sixth-century Cambodia, and thereafter the story of the region's religious architecture is one of the cross-fertilization of Hindu and Buddhist traditions, with a marked indigenous character.

The exquisite temple complex at Banteay Srei (967–968, see page 8), Cambodia, built by the courtier Yajnavaraha, and the enigmatic eleventh-century sculpted cave-sanctuary of Goa Gajah, Bali, are memorable examples. The enormous Prambanan Hindu temple (856) on Java illustrates the regional tendency towards great size and the laying out of plans rooted in the idea of a sacred pattern or *mandala*. From the eighth century, a Hindu dynasty known as the Khmer started to build a regional empire. Centred in the south of what is today Cambodia, by the twelfth century it dominated everywhere from what is now Vietnam to what is now Thailand – and the result was some of the most sophisticated and enormous glorifications of divine royal power ever built.

The epicentre was the capital, Angkor, founded by King Indravarman I (reigned *c.*877–890). Successive Khmer kings built temple complexes that may also have been mortuary palaces – places the king might inhabit after death, his soul fused with Shiva or Vishnu, depending on his devotional preferences. Angkor includes great *baray*s or water tanks up to 8km (5 miles) long, which irrigated the surrounding countryside, and many of its temples are – beneath their sophisticated architecture – pyramidal mountains of earth capped by five *sikhara*s, recalling the form of Mount Meru. The city thus evoked sacred mountains and their hydrological

power, as if it were the centre of the Khmer cosmos. Some temples (Phnom Bakheng, 893) are positioned on actual hills. The form of such temples was a major innovation. The temple-cities of southern India are the only Hindu buildings of comparable scale, but they cannot be seen as a single structure any more than a city is a single building. The great Southeast Asian temples have complex, coordinated plans, marked by sequences of sculpture-lined corridors, aligned on the cardinal directions, leading inwards (and often upwards), towards the *garbhagriha* sanctuaries topped by bud-shaped *sikhara*s. The effect is not that of a single massive interior, as was typical in the giant religious buildings of the Western world, but of a great sacred diagram, a kind of artificial landscape. The idea may have come as much from Buddhism as from Hinduism.

The largest of the temples at Angkor is Angkor Wat (literally, "the temple city"), built by King Suryavarman II (reigned *c.*1113–*c.*1150; see pages 56–57). Not long after Angkor Wat was built, Buddhist monks replaced the Hindu Brahmins at Angkor itself and the local kings began to identify themselves with *bodhisattva*s rather than Hindu deities. Thereafter, Buddhism was to become the dominant faith in Southeast Asia, with Islam the main faith in Indonesia and Malaysia. The illustrious Hindu story of the region remains alive only immediately east of Java on the island of Bali, which is the centre for a devout and distinctive Hinduism to this day.

Hindu temples today

For much of history Hinduism was an entire cosmology, the world view of a civilization, including every conceivable shade of religious activity. In the nineteenth century, teachers such as Ram Mohan Roy, who died in Bristol, England, in 1833, attempted to reform this rich inheritance by drawing out of India's manifold traditions a vision of a consistent, systematized Hinduism with a powerful universal message – and in succeeding in doing so they created the "Hindu Renaissance". One result of this was that some Hindu teachers (not to mention spiritual disciplines such as Hatha yoga) became influential in the West, while Western spiritual movements such as Theosophy reinterpreted Hindu traditions and re-imported them to India.

SIKHISM'S MONOTHEISTIC COMMUNITY

The Sikhs acknowledge a succession of *gurus*, or religious teachers, starting with Guru Nanak (1469–1539), who taught in the Punjab. He opposed caste and elaborate ritual practices, preaching a monotheistic, tolerant and egalitarian faith focused on a life of good moral action and devotion to God. This, Sikhism claims, can result in liberation from the cycle of rebirth. The teaching of the *guru*, who was raised a Hindu, was influenced deeply by both Islamic and Hindu ideas. He founded the first Sikh temple, or *gurdwara* ("the door that leads to the *guru*", in Punjabi), at Kartarpur in 1521–1522. The fifth *guru*, Arjan, compiled and edited the Sikh holy book, the *Adi Granth*, in 1604, and completed the process of creating Amritsar,

a spiritual capital for the Sikh community. Gobind Singh, the tenth *guru*, declared the holy book was itself the final *guru*, renaming it *Guru Granth Sahib*, and installing a copy of it in the Harmandir Sahib, the Amritsar *gurdwara* known as the Golden Temple, which remains the most important place of Sikh pilgrimage.

Congregational devotion to the words of the *Guru Granth Sahib* is the main function of the Sikh *gurdwara*, of which there are many worldwide. Apart from the canopy in which the book sits, the *gurdwara* is unadorned, and the book is treated with the greatest of respect. Every *gurdwara* has four doors, indicating its openness to all, regardless of origin or caste.

○ HOME OF THE *GURU*

AFTER 1581, GOLDEN
TEMPLE, AMRITSAR, INDIA

The foundation of this holiest *gurdwara* is associated with the third and fourth Sikh *gurus*, Amar Das and Ram Das. The installation of the *Adi Granth* there in 1604, three years after the shrine's completion, was carried out by the fifth *guru*, Arjan. A major city grew around the Golden Temple, and it reached its modern form in the nineteenth century, when under Maharaja Ranjit Singh (reigned 1799–1839) the Sikhs governed an empire.

Yet the very philosophy that underlies Hindu architecture has made it resistant to such modernizing influences. Instead, from the late twentieth century in particular, the growth of wealthy Hindu communities, both in India and elsewhere, has resulted in new temples that are traditional in style, if often built on a huge scale, such as the Akshardham (2005) in Delhi. Yet Indian architects such as Charles Correa have demonstrated that the *vastupurushamandala* can be used to plan convincing buildings in a modern style, for example at Mahatma Gandhi's Sabarmati *ashram* (Hindu religious community, 1963) in Ahmedabad. In a sense,

Hindu architecture stands at a crossroads, its mainstream unchanged for centuries, with its options for future development ranging from the kitsch Hindu-European Renaissance fusion of the Temple of the Vedic Planetarium, being built by the International Society for Krishna Consciousness in West Bengal, to the bare elegance of Sameep Padora's Shiva temple (2010) at Wadeshwar in Maharashtra, which is a plain *sikhara* with a porch, built from local stone but infused with contemporary aesthetics. All these buildings conform with the rules laid out in the *shastra*s, suggesting that the tradition could be susceptible to considerable innovation.

SPIRIT & SOCIETY

THE EAST ASIAN SEARCH FOR HARMONY

───────────────○───────────────

Traditional East Asian architecture is an elegant, modular approach to building, applicable irrespective of function. As a result, in China, Korea and Japan, religious buildings tend to be effectively indistinguishable from other structures in the time-honoured style. In these societies many faiths existed side by side – whether of foreign origin, such as Buddhism and Islam; or with indigenous roots, such as Confucianism, Taoism and Shinto – and their places of worship could be almost identical. The resultant religious complexes, built largely of wood, feature carefully ordered sequences of spaces, reflecting the mutually dependent hierarchies of traditional East Asian culture. In this sense the buildings embody underlying spiritual themes which are common throughout East Asian society and – like the architecture – largely have their origins in China. One or two specific types of building are unique to East Asia's most ancient faiths and through them can be glimpsed religious beliefs of considerable antiquity. This heritage suggests that the region's architecture has been suffused with spirituality from the earliest times.

◀ **THE GEOMANTIC GRID**

1747, FORBIDDEN CITY, BEIJING, CHINA

A Scene Described in the Qianlong Emperor's Poem "Bird's Eye View of the Capital", by artist Xu Yang, shows China's fifteenth-century imperial palace complex, or Forbidden City, laid out like a temple: mountains to the north, a north–south axis and nested enclosing walls.

EAST ASIAN ARCHITECTURE

China is the birthplace of East Asian architecture. Both Korea and Japan adopted it with little alteration, alongside profound influences from Chinese religion and civilization in general. It is thus possible to outline the story of religious architecture in East Asia largely in terms of that of China. The major exceptions relate to Buddhism (see pages 175–183) and Shinto (see pages 214–215).

Chinese religious architecture

In China, buildings of all kinds follow the same rules: they are propitiously set in the landscape (ideally south-facing, with a hill behind them, overlooking water); and they are contained within a high-walled, north–south axial enclosure, entered from the south, within which hall-like buildings surround a series of courtyards. The most important of these structures run east–west across the axis, resulting in a ladder-like plan and a sequenced hierarchy of spaces. They have roofs with prominent eaves, supported on timber columns arranged to a prescribed proportional pattern, and they sit on rectilinear platforms of ramped earth. Stone and other permanent materials are used for supporting and enclosing walls.

This flexible, modular, elegant architecture proved sufficient for almost all architectural needs throughout East Asia for two or three millennia. Uniquely among major world cultures, then, the region never adopted the principle that religious buildings should be made out of permanent materials, or have a specific architectural form of their own.

There are a few important exceptions to this rule. The pagoda (see pages 164, 175–181) is the most widespread: it is a Sinicized *stupa*, unique to Buddhist temples, and often made of stone or brick. Much rarer, but arguably more significant, are the open-air altars for imperial sacrifice, such as the Temple of Heaven in Beijing (see pages 212–213). These have roots deep in the past, and represent the sole building form that is both religious and uniquely Chinese. They can also claim a wider significance: open-air sacred complexes, from Brahmin altars to European stone circles, were commonplace in the ancient world but China was the only country to develop them into a mature architectural form, rather than subsume them into, or replace them by, roofed temples. Although they are less distinctive in form, the Shinto shrines of Japan also have unique architectural features with ancient indigenous origins.

◀ RITUAL BRONZE

*c.*1200BCE, HUNAN, SOUTHERN CHINA

During the Shang dynasty (1500–1046BCE), types of bronze container were used to offer food and drink to ancestors in rituals, possibly held in palace-temples, the ceremonial details of which are unknown. This is a *zun*, a vessel used for wine. The rams – probably the sacrificial animal for the ritual – are realistically rendered. Most bronzes only had stylized *taotie* designs (also visible here, below the *zun*'s lip).

▶ GOLDEN MIREUK

1939–2005, BEOPJU TEMPLE, CHUNGBUK-DO, SOUTH KOREA

East Asian religious architecture has, historically, been characterized by its distinctive Chinese influences. Beopju was founded in 553 at sacred Mount Songni but was rebuilt from 1624 onwards, when the five-storey wooden pagoda was erected. The monks cultivated a belief in Maitreya (Mireuk in South Korea), the *buddha* of the future. The giant (33m/108ft) statue of Mireuk was gilded in 2002–2005. Its platform base is derived from those of Chinese imperial open-air altars.

There have also been moments in history when religious buildings of stone made a brief appearance in China. For example, many early Chinese mosques (see page 152) had stone prayer-halls; and from the seventeenth century, Western influence led to the creation of stone churches. Stone *stupas*, and even one or two temples, imitating those of Tibet and elsewhere, were sometimes built in China proper.

Hallowed palaces, sacred spaces

Rammed-earth altars of geometrical form are known to have been in use in China up to 3,000 years ago. Imperial sacrifices on tiered open-air altars are documented from the Western Zhou dynasty (1046–770BCE). All the main traits of East Asian architecture were already present in the known structures of this era.

A building excavated at Fengchu, Shaanxi, seems to have been both a palace and a temple to the spirits of deceased ancestors. Rites conducted there may have included human sacrifice. It had a south-facing rectilinear enclosure, 43.5m (143ft) long and 32.5m (107ft) broad, raised on a rammed-earth platform 1.6m (5ft) high. The enclosure was divided into courtyards by structures running east–west. The largest hall would have contained tablets, inscribed with the names of the ancestors, and elaborate ritual vessels made of bronze.

Fengchu suggests that Chinese temple and palace architecture alike have a common root, bound up with ancient ideas about ancestor worship and imperial power. This relationship might explain some of the words for Chinese religious buildings. Ordinary Taoist and Confucian temples are *miao*, which originally meant "ancestral temple". Any building founded by an emperor, whether a temple or a palace, is a *gong*. The original word for a government office may have been *si*, which is the word used today for a Buddhist monastery. Perhaps all Chinese architecture originated with ideas about religion and can be seen as imbued with spirituality.

Moral philosophies

In the sixth century BCE, China was developing a civilization of global significance and sages such as Confucius and Laozi had begun to form sophisticated moral philosophies. Taoism at that stage would have had few implications for places of worship; its most logical home was in wildernesses, caves and mountaintops. Taoism advocated a harmony with the underlying forces of the natural world, which is suffused with the life-force, or *qi*, that underlies all creation. In Chinese architecture, the siting of a building, or indeed a settlement, must respond to the local flow of *qi*, and structures therefore tend to complement, rather than dominate, their natural surroundings.

Confucius, in turn, promoted the performance of ancient rituals, which helped to maintain the correct relationships between people, and therefore social harmony. The

◑ AT ONE WITH NATURE

*c.*600, MOUNT HENG, SHANXI, CHINA

The Xuan Kong Si, or Hanging Temple as it is widely known, today dates mostly from the sixteenth century, although a temple has been here for 1,500 years. It began life as a Buddhist institution before Taoist shrines and imagery became ever more evident. Built on beams which project horizontally from the cliff-face of the sacred mountain, the temple conforms with traditional plans but in compact form. The vertical poles play no real structural role but do provide visual reassurance. As well as being a fine piece of engineering, the temple embodies the East Asian ideal of harmony between man and nature.

hierarchical, interdependent sequences of space that characterize Chinese architecture express such principles vividly.

From Qin to Tang – an age of hope and faith

The Qin and Han dynasties (221–206BCE and 206BCE–220CE, respectively) were China's first era of national unity. Palaces and temples had by now become separate buildings. Capital cities such as Luoyang were built around a great north–south axis, in which the largest complex, sitting astride the axis, was that of the imperial palace. The fifteenth-century Forbidden City in Beijing is a famous survivor. Such palaces dwarf any known Chinese temple, reflecting religious thinking in which emperors were the essential players in a metaphysical compact between heaven (*tian*) and humanity. The most important religious buildings in the capital were a temple to the emperor's ancestors and a number of altars for imperial sacrifices.

Under the Han, ambitious tomb complexes developed, with a burial mound, an ancestral temple and an underground palace for the spirit of the person buried, often constructed out of cut stone. The 76m-high (249ft) pyramid of earth built by the "First Emperor of Qin", Shi Huangdi (who died in 210BCE), famously guarded by its buried army of terracotta soldiers, is one of the earliest and most ambitious. Open-air "spirit roads" of paired beasts, along which the spirit of the deceased could move from tomb-mound to temple, also developed. Such features would remain standard for imperial burials – and, to an extent, those of other high-status deceased – until the imperial era came to an end in 1912.

Towards the end of the Han dynasty, Buddhism arrived from India (see page 176). From this period until the Tang dynasty (618–907), Chinese religion experienced its most rapid period of development: Buddhism put down strong roots; Taoism embraced a vast pantheon of existing local deities; and Confucianism suffused the education system and family and imperial ritual. The landscape of China filled with countless monasteries and temples. Chinese civilization also began to transform the existing cultures and religious practices of Korea and Japan, as well as parts of Southeast Asia.

By the end of the Tang era, Chinese architecture had acquired its distinctive canon of details. To aid the choosing

⊙ *SHEN DAO* OF THE THIRTEEN TOMBS
1368–1644, CHANGPING, NEAR BEIJING, CHINA

Thirteen of the Ming emperors are buried in a tomb complex near Beijing, the entrance to which is approached along a south–north *shen dao* ("spirit way") – this is curved, to confuse spirits. The long (7km/4 miles) approach is lined with large statues of guardian animals and some humans, including administrators such as this one, reflecting China's Confucian sense of hierarchical order.

of sites, the system of geomancy known as *feng-shui* ("wind–water") developed, though it may only have been widely applied much later, in the Ming dynasty. Wide eaves of individual buildings began to acquire their distinctive upward curve. The *dougong*, or bracket set, which rises from the tops of columns and supports the eaves, was an important focal point. The proportions of the entire building are derived from the size of the individual brackets, divided in turn into fifteen subsections in a system known as *cai-fen*.

Very few buildings of any kind survive from this era, but hundreds of structures, almost all of them temples, survive from the Liao (907–1119) to the Jin (1115–1234) dynasties, when new sects and schools developed in all three Chinese religions. Mosques and Nestorian Christian churches existed too, although only the mosques survive.

By now Confucianism, Taoism and Buddhism had become the pillars of orthodox, officially sponsored religion. The imperial policy of *Sanjiao* (the "three teachings") held that good religious practice depended equally on all three faiths. Distinctions between the faiths often blurred: Confucius was honoured as a deity, just like a Taoist sage; and the Taoists portrayed heaven as a place that was organized into a complex, hierarchical bureaucracy, which reflected Confucian thinking. Few people had ever seen themselves as following one religion to the exclusion of others.

In 1103 and 1145 the emperor approved a detailed prescription, the *Yingzao Fashi* (*Building Method*), covering every aspect of architecture. This classifies buildings by status rather than function: for example, the highest number of brackets in a *dougong* – the auspicious eight – was permitted only to structures sponsored by emperors, whether temples or palaces.

Traditional religious buildings survive in relatively large numbers only from the Ming (1368–1644) and Qing (1644–1911) dynasties. Many older structures were badly damaged or demolished during the Taiping rebellion of 1850–1864 and the peak of the secularized Cultural Revolution in 1968–1970. Today, Taoist temples are again being constructed, superficially entirely traditional in style, if often built of painted concrete rather than timber.

Because of China's historic loyalty to timber, rather than stone, its buildings are comparatively easily replaced, but much of the detail of its architectural history has been lost. Buildings of real antiquity are comparatively rare. Yet, as its surviving temples and open-air altars show, China maintains one of the world's oldest architectural traditions, reflecting a culture that is precociously humanistic and rich in spiritual traditions at one and the same time.

⊙ PRIMAL PRINCESS OF THE AZURE CLOUDS

*c.*1770, AZURE CLOUD TEMPLE, MOUNT TAI, SHANDONG, CHINA

Mount Tai is the most important of China's sacred mountains – the focus of major imperial sacrificial rituals. A Taoist temple has stood here since at least 1008. After a major restoration in 1770 this became the Bixia (Azure Cloud) temple. The complex is arranged symmetrically on an axis and enshrined in one of the halls is a large bronze statue of Bixia Yuanjun, the goddess of the mountain.

TAOISM

Taoism originated as a philosophy in a short and enigmatic book called the *Dao De Jing*, or *Tao Te Ching* (the *Classic of the Way and Virtue*). This poetic text is attributed to Laozi, who probably lived in the sixth century BCE. Unlike the Confucian texts (see pages 210–211), this book has almost nothing to say about ritual, let alone about other aspects of religion such as deities or the afterlife. It simply encourages people to live in harmony with *dao* ("the way"), a flowing, holistic state of being which is the essence of the natural world.

At first, Taoists had little need for religious buildings. Their natural home was outdoors in places close to the spirit world. When Taoist temples appeared they reflected this, being known as *dong* (meaning "grottoes"), or *guan*, which might have referred to mountaintop platforms or observatories. Taoism's development of a complex network of holy places was underpinned by an interest in the underlying energies that coursed through all things, such as *qi* and its opposing but complementary principles *yin* and *yang*. Perhaps the best-known places are its five sacred peaks.

Mount Tai in Shandong province, in the east, was arguably China's most sacred place, but there were also mounts Hua in Shaanxi, in the west; Heng in Hunan, in the south; Heng in Shanxi, in the north; and Song in Henan, in the centre.

Taoism also came to embrace a vast pantheon of local practices and deities, organized to reflect the earthly hierarchy, with divine city officials senior to local village earth gods. Taoist iconography became rich and complex, and prominent images in temples included figures such as the Eight Immortals or Xiwangmu (the Queen Mother of the West), as well as deities associated with specific places. The resulting religion embraced a complex range of traditions, and the Taoist canon of writings contains more than 1,000 works. A distinction is often made between "philosophical Taoism", the tradition closest to the teaching of Laozi and other sages, such as Zhuangzi (fourth century BCE); and "religious Taoism", the great complex of ritual, magical and alchemical practices, especially the pursuit of immortality, which dominated temple life from the late Han dynasty onwards.

During this era, characterized by messianic movements, Taoism became an organized religion. Zhang Daoling, who had a vision of a deified Laozi in 142CE, founded the Zhengyi sect that is known today by several names, including Orthodox Unity (see page 17). Most of Taoism's hereditary priesthood belongs to this sect, which has its headquarters at Mount Longhu (Dragon and Tiger Mountain), Jiangxi province. At about the same time, Emperor Wudi (reigned 141–87BCE) ordered temples to Laozi to be built throughout his empire. Several later emperors followed suit.

Archaeological traces of one of the four Taoist temples in the imperial palaces at Daxing, dating from the Sui dynasty (581–618CE), have been found: with its 14m-high (46ft) raised platform, 73m (239ft) long and 47m (154ft) wide, it must have been an impressive sight. During the Tang dynasty (618–907), the faith even began to influence the traditional shamanic practices of Korea and Shinto in Japan.

Song-dynasty (960–1279) rulers such as Zhenzong (reigned 997–1022) developed an official temple network, in partnership with existing local lay religious associations, which meant that Taoism reached into many communities.

In the twelfth century, Wang Chongyang founded the major monastic order of Chinese Taoism, known as Quanzhen (Perfect Truth). The order's headquarters, the Bai Yun Guan (White Cloud Temple) in Beijing, is today the base of the Chinese Taoist Association.

The Yuan dynasty's (1271–1368) Yongle Gong (Temple of Eternal Joy) in Ruicheng, Shanxi, is one of the great Taoist buildings of China. It was rebuilt from 1243 with patronage from the rising Mongol khans, and retains three halls, the largest 28m (92ft) wide and 15m (49ft) deep, its interior covered in fourteenth-century paintings of Taoist deities. At the other end of the hierarchy, a little hall to the deity Tangdi, in Henan's Bo'ai prefecture, is a reminder of the kind of structure that probably once stood in every village. The only qualities that mark such buildings out as Taoist architecturally are their tendency to stand on exceptionally high platforms, and to be located in mountainous regions.

Despite destruction, closure and conversion to secular use from the 1960s onwards, Taoist temples and monasteries are being restored, extended and reopened in China today, and new ones are being built.

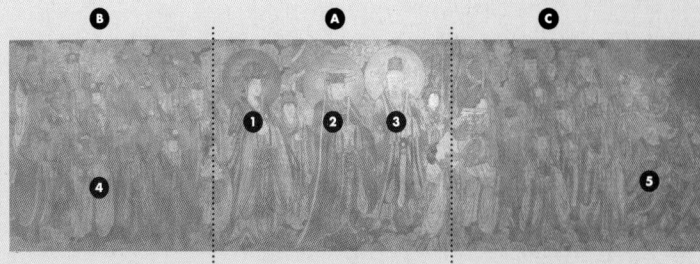

◀ A PROCESSION TO HEAVEN

*c.*1300, UNKNOWN TAOIST TEMPLE, SHANXI, CHINA

This mural is the west-wall half of a pair from a temple hall, depicting a procession of deities moving towards real statues at one end of the hall. Led by attendants carrying a portable altar, the central area **A** is dominated by three large deities: probably, from left to right, the Queen Mother of the West **1**, the King Father of the East **2**, and a Taoist priest **3** (probably the founder of a lineage, but also embodying the Taoist Heavenly Sovereign). To the left **B**, other beings include personifications of the Chinese zodiacal signs **4**. To the right **C**, at the front of the stately procession, are various saints, led by the perfected Tianyou **5**, bearing a sword. Most are dressed as officials, reflecting the bureaucratic nature of the Taoist heaven. The scene may have been a backdrop for a mortuary ritual known as the Rite of Sublimation, in which priests aimed to assist a dead soul in its path to heaven.

CONFUCIANISM

Confucius (the Latinized form of Kong Qiu or Kongzi, "Master Kong") was a teacher and minor official from Qufu who lived from 551 to 479BCE. The core Confucian texts are known as the Five Classics and the Four Books, though Confucianism has been refined by generations of sages. Confucius's thinking, laid out in the collection of his sayings known as the *Lunyu* (*Analects*), portrays a world in which correct relationships are the key to maintaining social harmony. This is a world of hierarchy, but also mutual dependency, in which children respect their parents, and parents respect rulers; but those in authority need to exercise power wisely or they will lose their right to rule.

The focus of this teaching is on human social conduct and the responsibilities of the living, rather than the supernatural or the afterlife. But Confucianism is interested in correct ritual behaviour (*li*), and in man's relationship to heaven (*tian*) and to his ancestors. *Li*, one of the five virtues at the heart of the Confucian way, covers behavioural propriety in general, but includes a wide range of traditional rites, encoded in the *Zhouli* (*The Rites of the Kingdom of Zhou*). These serve to maintain an individual's relationship to his ancestors and an emperor's relationship with heaven; neglect of the last in particular would lead to social chaos. Confucian scholars became experts in the proper performance of such rituals.

It was during the Han dynasty that Confucianism rose from being one of several competing moral and political

⚆ TEMPLE OF CONFUCIUS

1302–*c*.1644, DACHENG HALL, BEIJING, CHINA

Beijing's Temple of Confucius is second only to that at Qufu, Shandong. Built under the Yuan (1271–1368), it was expanded by successive dynasties and has three main courtyards aligned on a central axis. Dacheng Hall, or Hall of Great Accomplishment, is the main building. The marble staircase has a central ramp carved with dragons, over which the imperial palanquin would be carried.

philosophies to being the defining ideology of the state. Figures such as Emperor Wudi (reigned 141–87BCE) helped to change China into a society in which power was in the hands of a highly educated administrative élite, the members of which had to pass examinations in which they were tested on their knowledge of Confucian texts. Study of the Confucian classics soon spread to every school. The offering of sacrifices to Confucius himself became compulsory, and by the Tang dynasty these had come to join imperial sacrifices to heaven and to the royal ancestors as central rituals of the state cult.

The influence of Confucianism spread beyond China. A Confucian academy was established in Korea in 372CE, and to this day the faith remains an important feature of Korean culture. In Japan, where it was known from about 405, Confucianism influenced the sixth-century creation of the (primarily Buddhist) state, and helped to shape modern Shinto and Zen Buddhism.

In 630, it was ordered that every district and county in China build a temple to Confucius. No school or examination hall, for example, was without one. Many of these were converted into teaching rooms by modernizing reformers in the nineteenth century, and by the Communist authorities from the 1950s onwards. Some buildings survive, often incorporated into schools that are otherwise entirely modern. Such complexes sometimes had semi-circular pools in front of the entrance, said to imitate a feature of the colleges of the ancient Zhou dynasty, or large numbers of flat sculpted stones or stelae, inscribed with the names of those who had successfully passed imperial examinations.

Ancestral temples, such as the large Chen Family Temple in Guangzhou (1890–1894), are classified as Confucian. Influential historical figures and heroes may be honoured in a similar way, such as Zhang Fei, a soldier of the Han dynasty, who has a temple dedicated to him in Yunyang, Sichuan, which dates from the Ming and Qing dynasties. Less exalted individuals – for example, exceptionally competent administrators or incorruptible magistrates – were memorialized in distinctive stone gateways known as *peifang*.

However, the most important building associated with Confucius is the palatial temple complex built on the site

◐ THE ROYAL ANCESTRAL RITE

JONGMYO SHRINE, SEOUL, SOUTH KOREA

The Jongmyo is the ancestral shrine of the Joseon dynasty (1392–1897), and the Grand Ancestral Rite used to be conducted there five times a year. Today, the rite is held there once a year, each May. Unlike in China, where it no longer dominates public life, Confucianism continues to play an important role in Korean religious life.

of the Kong family residence near Qufu, Shandong. In 8BCE Confucius's descendants were given lands by the emperors from which to fund elaborate sacrifices to their forefather. By the seventh century the rituals performed there were matched in significance only by those performed by the emperor on China's holiest mountain, Taishan or Mount Tai (see page 206), and in the capital city. Today, Confucius's birthday is still commemorated at Confucian temples each September and in Taiwan it is celebrated as Teacher's Day.

Confucianism plays a role in modern China comparable to that of Christianity in parts of the West: it is less common than it was as a self-conscious religious affiliation, but as an influence on the development of cultural practices and attitudes it underpins many aspects of East Asian society.

RITUALS FOR A PROSPEROUS YEAR

1420 AND LATER, TEMPLE OF HEAVEN, BEIJING, CHINA

The Tiantan ("Altar of Heaven"), usually known as the Temple of Heaven, in Beijing, is the most important survivor of the ancient Chinese tradition of imperial sacrificial altars. Such structures had been a central requirement of ritual life in China since the Western Zhou dynasty (1046–770BCE).

Today's temple, founded in the Ming era, is the result of major alterations and rebuildings in c.1542, 1749–1751 and 1890. It comprises two altars, the most important of which is the open-air Circular Mound Altar, or Altar of Heaven. However, the roofed Hall of Prayer for Good Harvests (Qi Nian Dan, which is more accurately translated as the Hall of Prayer for a Prosperous Year), a three-tiered circular structure with a spectacular timber interior (right), is now more famous. Ultimately, the hall is derived from a roofed *mingtang* ("hall of light"), an ancient ritual structure the form of which was suffused with cosmological symbolism. The decorative imagery emphasizes auspicious and imperial themes, especially as they relate to the heavens. The most important rituals carried out at the Temple of Heaven were the emperor's midwinter and midsummer sacrifices to heaven.

▶ TEMPLE OF HEAVEN

1420 AND LATER, BEIJING, CHINA

Located within a nested sequence of walled enclosures **A**, the Circular Mound Altar **B** and the Hall of Prayer for Good Harvests **C** are both three-tiered circular altar platforms, the latter topped by a roofed temple. They are linked by a marble processional way **D**, the *danbiqiao*, 360m (1,181ft) long and 28m (92ft) wide, along which is located the small, circular Imperial Vault of Heaven **E**, which housed the tablets of the main deity, Haotian Shangdi ("Emperor Above in High Heaven"), and those of the imperial ancestors. Many details of the design have sacred significance: for example, circular elements symbolize heaven and square ones symbolize Earth.

❶ Four 19m-high (62ft) columns hold up the hall's rising sequence of roofs. They symbolize the four seasons. The columns and the crossbeams together form a shape reminiscent of the Chinese character *jing* ("well"): thus the columns are known as *longjing zhu* ("dragon well pillars"). The circular form of the building combines with the four crossbeams to embody heaven (the circle) and Earth (the square).

❷ Eight smaller columns, covered in depictions of clouds (indicative of heaven), support the upper roof. Two outer rows of twelve columns, not seen here, symbolize the months of the year and the two-hour segments into which the twenty-four hours of the day are divided. The building thus embodies the turning of the year. The stones used to construct the nearby Circular Mound Altar have comparable meaning.

❸ The dragons (*lung*) depicted are the five-clawed emblems of imperial power. Only buildings, clothing and objects closely associated with the emperor himself could bear this sign of authority. In Chinese culture the dragon is powerful and to be feared in a respectful way; it is just, benevolent and the bringer of good fortune.

4 The plumage of the phoenix (*fenghuang*) has five mystical colours (black, white, red, green, yellow). This sacred bird, born in the sun, is associated with the female *yin* aspect of being, and often with the empress; when paired with the dragon, it symbolizes the harmony of *yin* and *yang* (represented by the dragon).

5 Red, the colour of the element fire, was highly auspicious and was particularly associated with summer and the south, both themes relevant to the Hall of Prayer for Good Harvests. The colour was the dominant one in important buildings of all kinds, from timber in temples to the sheer sides of city walls.

6 The colour scheme of the building depends on red, green, white, yellow/gold and black, the five colours that represented the five elements, plus blue for the heavens. The five elements were forms of energy in a constant state of flux, and every aspect of life came to be categorized under them, from the planets and cardinal directions to emotions and tastes.

7 At the centre of the circular roof, representing heaven, is a gilded roundel carved with an image of an intertwined dragon and phoenix. This simultaneously embodies the harmony inherent in cosmic energy and evokes imperial authority. In the space beneath, the emperor maintained this harmony by performing ancestral rites using the tablets of the heavenly god, Haotian Shangdi.

SHINTO

Shinto is Japan's indigenous religion. Its most ancient belief is that the world is charged with sacredness – understood as a range of divine forces, but especially the ubiquitous and powerful spirit-beings known as *kami*, which can be beneficent if favourably disposed, or vindictive if upset. Offerings are made to them, oracles consulted and prayers made. They exist in objects, topographical features and even people.

Shinto also displays a deep concern with purity, which means it is standard to find places for ritual ablutions near the entrances to *jinja*, or shrines. Because Shinto is largely focused on matters relating to this world, it has little to say about salvation and the afterlife, which may be one of the reasons for Buddhism's success in Japan (see pages 180–183).

There were various kinds of religious architecture in ancient Japan, from massive royal keyhole-shaped tumuli, or *kofun*, such as that of the fourth-century CE emperor Nintoku in Naniwa (modern Osaka), to timber grain-stores which were raised on stilts and placed in the compounds of chieftains – in addition to their practical function, these storehouses were the focus of fertility-related rites and seem to have been the model for the first Shinto shrines, about which little is known. Among the grave goods of the rice-cultivating Yayoi culture (*c.*300BCE–*c.*300CE) are small ceramic images of grain storehouses that bear a remarkable similarity to the architecture of the great Shinto shrine at Ise.

Following contact between Japan and Korea in the early sixth century, Buddhism appeared, bringing Chinese influences with it. In general, the Shinto cults coexisted with the new faith, but one cult in particular was brought to the fore under Emperor Temmu. His family claimed descent from Amaterasu, the sun goddess, and he invoked her on the way to the battle in which he came to power in 672. Her shrine at Ise, southeast of Nara, became a state-sponsored imperial complex. In 685 he decreed that the two main shrines at Ise – to Amaterasu and Toyouke, the harvest goddess – be rebuilt every twenty years. In 712, the orientation of the shrines was shifted from east–west – as befitted a sun shrine – to north–south, and a strict regularity and symmetry were imposed on the buildings. Although these developments reflect the influence of Chinese architecture, the Ise site, which remains Shinto's most prestigious sacred space, preserves intact an indigenous form of timber architecture – carefully renewed, refined and curated for some 1,500 years – which has its roots in the storehouses and chieftain's halls of prehistoric Japan.

In addition to the two major shrines, Ise contains almost 120 minor ones, set in a forested sacred landscape around the Isuzu River. The Naiku, or Inner Shrine, compound is the most important space. This sits on a platform 105m (344ft) long and 45m (148ft) wide, which raises the shrine about 4–5m (13–16ft) above ground level. Around the edge

◗ INSIDE THE SACRED ENCLOSURE
SEVENTH CENTURY ONWARDS, ISE NAIKU, MIE, JAPAN

This view north along the main axis of Ise's Naiku, or Inner Shrine, is from within the second of the four exclusive enclosures. The *torii* gate was added after a period of neglect in the fifteenth and sixteenth centuries. On either side are trenches, *ishi-tsubo*, used by priests during ceremonies. Beyond, the gateway to the third enclosure is topped by *katsuogi* – roof-ridge logs, unique to Shinto architecture. During Japan's Heian era, shrines were ranked and categorized into three groups, all of which received offerings from the imperial court. Ise was ranked first.

of this platform stands a close-set series of four high fences, one inside the other. The shrine contains various buildings, of which the most sacred is the inner sanctuary, or *honden*, formed by a thatched wooden hall. The *honden* is 15m (45ft) long, 10m (33ft) wide and less than 10m (33ft) high. Its thatched roof is made distinctive by the X-shaped *chigi* at the end of each gable and the bundle-shaped weights called *katsuogi*, which lie along its ridge. A single column supports the middle of each gable, its base set deep in the ground. Only Shinto shrines are permitted these features. Shinto shrines are also instantly recognizable by the *torii* gateways, often festooned with strips of paper, known as *gohei*. The form of these gateways may have its origins in the *peifang* gates of Confucian China, which in turn were probably based on the *stupa* gates of early Buddhist India (see pages 168–169).

There are a great many – one estimate suggests 100,000 – Shinto *jinja* but not all are as archaic in style, or rebuilt as frequently and systematically, as those of Ise. Six variant styles are recognized and in some the shrine building is almost indistinguishable from a smaller Buddhist temple. In Shinto, only priests and priestesses, or members of the imperial family, may enter the *honden*, where the *kami* is believed to reside. The *kami* may take various forms: for example, an unadorned rock, or at Ise an ancient mirror. Many have never been seen by outsiders.

◭ *IWAKURA* "ROCK ABODE" SHRINE

WEDDED ROCKS, FUTAMIGAURA, ISE BAY, JAPAN

Trees and rocks have long been holy in Shinto. The Meoto Iwa, or Wedded Rocks, are said to have given shelter to Japan's first couple, Izanagi and Izanami. The rice straw rope, or *shimenawa*, binds the divine partners and signifies a boundary to the sacred. An entrance to a shrine usually has a *torii* gate, such as that atop the "male" rock.

Buddhist and Shinto sites alike are visited by a steady flow of people, and host especially large gatherings at great festivals, such as the spring rice-planting festival. Shinto celebrations also include dramatic open-air processions in which portable shrines (*mikoshi*) are carried through the streets.

Between the eighth and the thirteenth centuries, the distinctions between Shinto and Buddhism blurred significantly. Each *kami* was believed to be an incarnation of a specific *buddha* or *bodhisattva* and images of them proliferated. For example, there are scenes of the *bodhisattva* Kannon (see page 182) standing with the *kami* of the 133m-high (436ft) Nachi waterfall. Devotional "shrine *mandala*" paintings depicted schematized versions of specific Shinto shrines and the spirit-infused landscapes in which they stand.

In 1871, the Meiji dynasty raised Shinto to a state religion and turned Ise into a place of enormous sacral power. Defeat in 1945 led to the disestablishment of Shintoism in 1946, and the shrines today are run by private groups of citizens.

CHRONOLOGY

c.9000BCE
World's oldest known temple-like structure at Gobekli Tepe, Turkey.

c.4000BCE
Temple at Eridu, Iraq, is one of the earliest known Mesopotamian temples.

c.3500 onwards
Watson Brake earth mound, Louisiana, USA: one of the first large-scale ritual structures in North America.

c.3200BCE
Platform-mounds and sunken courts of the Supe Valley civilization, Peru: the first large-scale ritual architecture in South America.

c.2630–c.2611BCE
Tomb-temple and pyramid of Djoser at Saqarra, Egypt: first major complex made of cut stone and the first Egyptian pyramid.

c.2500BCE onwards
Avebury and Stonehenge complexes, Britain: monumental, open-air sacred landscapes.

c.2549–c.2460BCE
Pyramid of Cheops, Giza, Egypt (146m/479ft): for several thousand years, the tallest attested building in the world.

c.2112–c.2095BCE
Ziggurat at Ur, Iraq: a major example of the Mesopotamian ritual "manmade mountain".

c.1960BCE
Earliest surviving parts of the Great Temple, Karnak – the greatest of ancient Egyptian temples.

c.967–c.960BCE
Solomon's Temple, Jerusalem: the most sacred building in Judaism (influential in Christianity and Islam).

c.595BCE
Enlightenment of Shakyamuni Buddha at Bodh Gaya, a key event in the birth of Buddhism. He dies in *c.485*BCE and his burial mound is the first *stupa*, a building type still in use.

586BCE
Babylonian destruction of the Temple in Jerusalem and Jewish exile; one conjectured result is the synagogue.

551–479BCE
Confucius (Kongzi) transmits his ideas, later collected in the *Analects* (*Lunyu*).

516BCE
Jewish Temple rebuilt following the end of the Babylonian exile in 539BCE.

6th century BCE
Laozi's *Dao De Jing* written, the founding text of Taoism (Daoism).

5th century BCE–5th century CE
Bhakti theism transforms Vedic faith into Hinduism.

447–c.406BCE
Rebuilding of the temples on the Acropolis, Athens – high point of ancient Greek temple architecture.

3rd century BCE
Origin of a permanent religious architecture in India (mainly Buddhist) with widespread *stupas*, *chaitya* halls and monasteries.

By c.200BCE
Date by which the synagogue is known to exist, the first building type designed for weekly congregation – a defining idea for churches and mosques.

8BCE
Temple of Confucius, Qufu, China, attested (legendarily founded 478BCE): greatest temple in Confucianism, and one of the largest in East Asia.

33CE
Death and resurrection of Jesus Christ at Jerusalem, key event in the founding of Christianity.

70
Destruction of the Temple of Jerusalem; synagogues survive as Jewish places of worship.

c.118–c.128
Pantheon, Rome: domed temple to all the gods.

c.150
Pyramids of the Sun and Moon, Teotihuacán, Mexico – one of the greatest sacred complexes in Mesoamerica.

4th–6th centuries
*Stupa*s (90m/295ft) of Kanishka, Shaji Ki Dheri, Pakistan, and pagoda (161m/528ft) of Yongningsi, Chang'an, China, may have been among the tallest buildings in the world.

312 onwards
Constantinian churches – such as old St. Peter's, Rome, and Church of the Holy Sepulchre, Jerusalem – constitute the first true church architecture; modelled on the Roman basilica, this form is often used in churches to the present.

5th century
Origin of the cut-stone Hindu temple, already with the defining elements which would remain standard to the present.

Late 5th century
Peak of Buddhist cave temples at Ajanta, India, the finest in the subcontinent.

523
Songyue pagoda, Henan, China, the earliest dated surviving pagoda (the East Asian form of *stupa*).

532–537
Hagia Sophia, Constantinople (Istanbul): great domed central church for Eastern Orthodox Christianity.

6th–7th century
Likely last rebuilding of the Mahabodhi, Bodh Gaya, India: central place of pilgrimage for Buddhists.

7th century
Bamiyan *buddha*s, Afghanistan: greatest cliff-cut, open-air sculptures of Buddhism. Destroyed 2001.

622
Hijra of the Prophet Muhammad from Mecca to Medina, key event in the birth of Islam.

By 632
The Prophet's house at Medina, Arabia: the first mosque was a template specified by the Prophet himself, the form of which is seen in mosques to the present day.

684
Last rebuilding of the ancient Ka'ba at Mecca, Arabia, the focal point of prayer in Islam.

684–691
Islamic Dome of the Rock, Jerusalem: unique, shrine-like building, embodying the victory of a new faith.

685 onwards
Rebuilding ordered of the Shinto shrines at Ise, Japan, which has continued every twenty years (with some exceptions) to the present.

7th–9th century
Maya pyramid-temples, plazas and ballcourts: high point of religious architecture in the Americas.

c.706–715
Umayyad Mosque, Damascus, Syria: defining the palatial Friday mosque.

745–749
Buddhist Todaiji, Nara, Japan: greatest surviving early East Asian Buddhist monastery.

c.756–c.773
Hindu Kailasa temple, Ellora, India: greatest cliff-cut Hindu temple.

c.780–c.850
Buddhist Borobudur *stupa*, Java, Indonesia: great open-air *mandala*-cum-*stupa* and high point of Buddhist architecture in Southeast Asia.

848–852
Great Mosque, Samarra, Iraq: one of Islam's largest, and influential in the development of Islamic style.

1009/10
Hindu Rajarajeshvara temple, Thanjavur, India: one of the great southern Indian temples, influential for its size and prominent *gopura* tower-porches.

c.1032
Jain temples at Mount Abu, India: high point of Jain temple architecture.

1088 onwards
Friday mosque, Isfahan, Iran: addition of *iwan*s and domes – a new and influential format for the mosque courtyard and *qibla* bay.

11th century
Romanesque cathedrals and abbeys: the emergence of a European Christian architecture of vast interiors, ambitious vaults and lighting effects, and stylistic restlessness. Peak of Hindu temple-building at Khajuraho, India – the most exquisite of northern Hindu temples.

c.1105 and c.1155
Buddhist Ananda and Thatbinnyu temples, Pagan, Burma (Myanmar): great *stupa*s-cum-temples.

After 1113
Angkor Wat, Cambodia – greatest of Southeast Asian Hindu temples.

From 1140
St. Denis abbey, Paris, France: the emergence of Gothic, a ravishing architecture unique to European Christianity.

From 1194
Chartres cathedral, France: great early Gothic cathedral, its stained glass intact.

From 1243
Taoist Yongle Gong, Ruicheng, China: exquisite major Taoist complex, its wall paintings intact.

13th/14th century
Process begins of the transformation of the southern Hindu temple into the *gopura*-dominated temple-city – for example, Srirangam, Madurai.

Perhaps from 1311
Spire of Lincoln cathedral, England (160m/525ft), the highest building in the world (fell in 1549).

1356–1362
Mosque-mausoleum of Sultan Hassan, Cairo, Egypt: one of the great works of Mamluk architecture.

1420 and after
Temple of Heaven, Beijing, China: open-air complex of sacrificial altars, the holiest place in a sacred city.

1420–1467
Brunelleschi's dome at Santa Maria del Fiore, Florence: the Renaissance rebirth of the dome in European Christian architecture.

By *c.*1490
Latest phase of the Temple of Coatepetl, Tenochtitlán, Mexico, the last great Aztec temple. Destroyed *c.*1521.

By 1493
The Coricancha, Cuzco, Peru, the last great Inca temple. Destroyed *c.*1534.

1506–1667
St. Peter's, Rome, rebuilt: with its great dome, the highest achievement of High Renaissance/Baroque architecture. Central church of Roman Catholic Christianity.

1550–1557
Sultan Suleymaniye mosque and others, Istanbul, Turkey: the high point of Ottoman mosques, with prayer halls covered by a single dome – influential in Islamic architecture to the present.

1555 and later
Cathedral of the Intercession on the Moat (St. Basil's), Moscow – one of the great Russian Orthodox churches.

Around 1563
Metropolitan cathedral, Mexico City: in this period Christian Baroque style becomes the first architecture of faith to be present on every continent.

After 1581
Sikh Golden Temple, Amritsar, India: the most sacred Sikh place.

1611/1612–1637/1638 Masjid-i Shah/Imam, Isfahan, Iran: one of the great works of Safavid architecture.

1631–1647 Taj Mahal, Agra, India: the greatest Islamic mausoleum and high point of Mughal architecture.

1730 onwards Temples at the Summer Palace at Chengde (Jehol), Hebei, China, represent high points of Qing dynasty temple architecture, including the Tibetan-styled Putuozongchangmiao.

1743
Neumann's Basilica of the Fourteen Holy Helpers, Germany – a defining work of Rococo architecture.

1784/1785
Wat Phra Keo, Bangkok – a royal Buddhist temple.

*c.*1795
Sabbathday Lake Meeting House, Maine, USA – the plain architecture of Nonconformist Christianity.

1841–1846
Church of St. Giles, Cheadle, England, a representative of Gothic revival architecture in Europe and its colonies.

1859 and 1927
New Synagogue, Berlin, and Temple Emanu-El, New York (1927), built in an era of "cathedral" synagogues.

1871
Kuthodaw Buddhist monastery in Mandalay, Burma (Myanmar), marking the Fifth Buddhist Council.

1882
Work begins on Sagrada Familia, Barcelona, Spain, an early attempt to create a modern Christian architecture.

1948
Following the Holocaust, the modern State of Israel is founded and many new synagogues are built.

1950
Notre Dame du Haut, Ronchamp, France – a great achievement of Modernist Christian architecture.

1955–2008
Extension and rebuilding of the Great Mosque, Mecca, Saudi Arabia, to better accommodate pilgrims from across the globe.

1961
Sacré-Coeur Cathedral, Algiers, Algeria – a concrete, centralized building for a reformed Catholic Church.

1963
Sabarmati *ashram*, Ahmedabad, India – an example of modern architecture for Hinduism.

1976–1986
Faisal mosque, Islamabad, Pakistan – a "national mosque" for a newly created nation.

1980
Thorncrown chapel, Arkansas, USA – modern architecture for evangelical Nonconformist Christianity.

1984–1995 Mosque and Islamic Cultural Centre, Rome – modern architecture for Islam.

1992–1995 Shri Swaminarayan Mandir, London – the Hindu diaspora creates an ambitious global architecture.

2000 White Temple, Zuisenji, near Kyoto, Japan – an example of modern architecture for Buddhism.

FURTHER READING

*In a vast field, the following books (with a few websites)
are particularly engaging or authoritative starting points.*

General Reading/The Themes of the Sacred

Coogan, Michael D. (ed.) *World Religions: The Illustrated Guide.*
Duncan Baird Publishers (DBP): London, 2003.

Eliade, Mircea. *The Sacred and the Profane: The Nature of Religion.*
Harvest (Harcourt, Inc.): New York, 1959.

Heilbrunn Timeline of Art History: www.metmuseum.org/toah/

Holm, Jean with Bowker, John. (eds.) *Sacred Place.* Continuum:
London, 1994.

Mirsky, Jeannette. *Houses of God.* Constable: London, 1966.

Musgrove, John. (ed.) *Sir Banister Fletcher's A History of
Architecture.* (19th edition.) Butterworths: London, 1987.

Foundations: The Ancient World

Beard, Mary; North, John; and Price, Simon. *Religions of Rome.
Volume I: A History.* Cambridge University Press (CUP):
Cambridge, 1998.

Burkert, Walter. *Greek Religion: Archaic and Classical.* (Translated
by John Raffan.) Blackwell Publishing: Oxford, 1985.

Coe, Michael D. *Mexico: From the Olmecs to the Aztecs.* (4th edition.)
Thames and Hudson: London, 2008.

Cunliffe, Barry. (ed.) *Prehistoric Europe: An Illustrated History.* Oxford
University Press (OUP): Oxford, 1998.

Frankfort, Henri. *The Art and Architecture of the Ancient Orient.*
Penguin: Harmondsworth, 1954. (1970, revised edition.)

Malek, Jaromir. *Egyptian Art.* Phaidon Press: London, 1999.

Osborne, Robin. *Archaic and Classical Greek Art.* OUP:
Oxford, 1998.

Pemberton, Delia. *Treasures of the Pharoahs: The Glories of Ancient
Egypt.* DBP: London, 2004.

Saunders, Nicholas J. *Ancient Americas: Maya, Aztec, Inka
and Beyond.* Sutton Publishing: Stroud, 2004.

Spivey, Nigel. *Greek Art.* Phaidon Press: London, 1997.

Wilkinson, Richard H. *The Complete Temples of Ancient Egypt.*
Thames and Hudson: London, 2000.

Peoples of the Book: One God & One Sacred Word

ArchNet: https://archnet.org/lobby/

Armstrong, Karen. *Islam: A Short History.* Phoenix: London, 2000.

Bloom, Jonathon and Blair, Sheila. *Islamic Arts.* Phaidon Press:
London, 1997.

Cohn-Sherbok, Dan. *Judaism: History, Belief and Practice.*
Routledge: Abingdon, 2003.

Craft Brumfield, William. *A History of Russian Architecture.*
CUP: Cambridge, 1993.

Ettinghausen, Richard; Grabar, Oleg; and Jenkins-Madina, Marilyn.
The Art and Architecture of Islam, 650–1250. Yale University Press
(YUP): New Haven and London, 1987. (2003, revised edition.)

Frishman, Martin and Khan, Hassan-Uddin. *The Mosque: History,
Architectural Development and Regional Diversity.* Thames and
Hudson: London, 1994.

Hillenbrand, Robert. *Islamic Architecture: Form, Function and
Meaning.* Edinburgh University Press: Edinburgh, 1994. (2000,
revised edition.)

Krautheimer, Richard. *Early Christian and Byzantine Architecture.*
YUP: New Haven and London, 1965. (1986, revised edition.)

Krinsky, Carol Herselle. *Synagogues of Europe: Architecture, History,
Meaning.* MIT Press: Cambridge, Massachusetts, 1985.

Koch, Ebba. *Mughal Architecture: An Outline of its History and
Development, 1526–1858.* OUP: Oxford, 2002.

Levine, Lee I. *The Ancient Synagogue: The First Thousand Years.*
YUP: New Haven and London, 2005.

MacCulloch, Diarmaid. *A History of Christianity: The First Three
Thousand Years.* Allen Lane: London, 2009.

O'Kane, Bernard. *Treasures of Islam: Artistic Glories of the Muslim
World.* DBP: London, 2007.

Stemp, Richard. *The Secret Language of Churches and Cathedrals:
Decoding the Sacred Symbolism of Christianity's Holy Buildings.*
DBP: London, 2010.

Wilson, Christopher. *The Gothic Cathedral.* Thames and Hudson:
London, 1990.

Man & Cosmic Order: South Asian Cycles of Rebirth

Beguin, Gilles. *Buddhist Art: An Historical and Cultural Journey.*
River Books: Bangkok, 2009.

Dehejia, Vidya. *Indian Art.* Phaidon Press: London, 1997.

Flood, Gavin. *An Introduction to Hinduism.* CUP: Cambridge, 1996.

Guy, John. *Indian Temple Sculpture.* Victoria & Albert Museum:
London, 2007.

Himalayan Art Resources: www.himalayanart.org/

Kramrisch, Stella. *The Hindu Temple.* University of Calcutta:
Calcutta, 1946.

Mitter, Partha. *Indian Art.* OUP: Oxford, 2001.

Patry Leidy, Denise and Thurman, Robert A. F. *Mandala: Architecture
of Enlightenment.* Thames and Hudson: London, 1997.

Skilton, Andrew. *A Concise History of Buddhism.* Windhorse:
Birmingham, 1994. (1997, revised edition.)

Spirit & Society: The East Asian Search for Harmony

Chinnery, John. *Treasures of China: The Glories of the Kingdom of
the Dragon.* DBP: London, 2008.

Little, Stephen with Eichman, Shawn. *Taoism and the Arts of China.*
Art Institute of Chicago: Chicago, 2001.

Steinhardt, Nancy S. (ed.) *Chinese Architecture.* YUP: New Haven and
London, 2002.

Watanabe, Yasutada. *Shinto Art: Ise and Izumo Shrines.* Weatherhill:
New York, 1974.

Watson, William. *The Arts of China to A.D. 900*; (with Ho, Chuimei)
The Arts of China 1600–1900. YUP: New Haven and London, 2000.

INDEX

ACKNOWLEDGMENTS

To Liu Hong, Lily, May and Ann, for everything and more, and for reminding me what's *really* sacred.

With thanks to a team who went the extra global mile several times over, with patience, acuity, diligence, excellence and creative flair: Julia Brown, Emma Copestake, Allan Sommerville, Susannah Stone and Christopher Westhorp.

Acknowledgments also to Hazim Abbas, the Very Rev. Dr. David Hoyle, Sharman Kadish and Lydia Morey.

PICTURE CREDITS

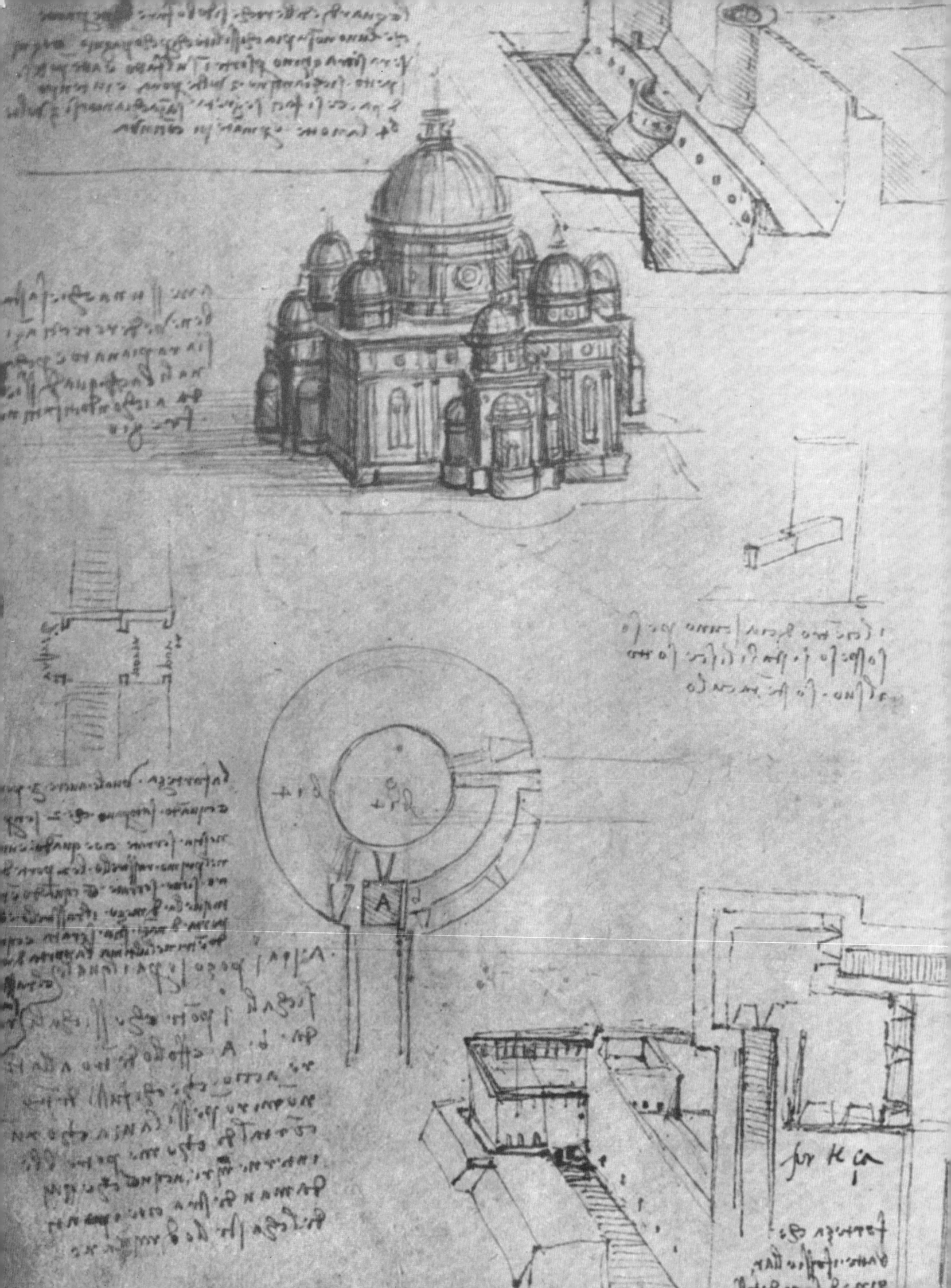